Additional praise for *Culture and Authenticity*

"This book is a timely as well as systematic discussion of one of the crucial issues of our time. It should be required reading for researchers and students alike."

Jonathan Friedman, Lund University

"In this beautifully written and accessible book, Charles Lindholm, a renowned anthropologist, dares to bring us back to the days of a broad comparative study of culture. Lindholm provides an insightful, sweeping account of authenticity across time and space, in chapters that cover a wide range of topics, such as art, cuisine, ethnicity, citizenship, and religious fundamentalism."

Roy Richard Grinker, George Washington University

"Lindholm brings a sharp sense of history, the full range of the best contemporary anthropology, and a quick wit to the topic of culture and authenticity, in this very readable and thoughtful book."

Richard Wilk, Indiana University

Culture and Authenticity

Charles Lindholm

Blackwell
Publishing

BLACKWELL PUBLISHING

350 Main Street, Malden, MA 02148-5020, USA
9600 Garsington Road, Oxford OX4 2DQ, UK
550 Swanston Street, Carlton, Victoria 3053, Australia

First published 2008 by Blackwell Publishing Ltd

1   2008

Library of Congress Cataloging-in-Publication Data

Lindholm, Charles, 1946–
Culture and authenticity / Charles Lindholm.
    p. cm.
  Includes bibliographical references and index.
  ISBN 978-1-4051-2442-3 (hardcover : alk. paper) – ISBN 978-1-4051-2443-0 (pbk. : alk. paper)
    1. Culture. 2. Cultural awareness. 3. Cultural property. 4. Authenticity (Philosophy)–Social aspects.
5. Group identity. I. Title.

HM621.L56 2008
306.01–dc22

                                              2007011996

A catalogue record for this title is available from the British Library.

Set in 10/12.5pt Minion
by SPi Publisher Services, Pondicherry, India
Printed and bound in Singapore
by Utopia Press Pte Ltd

The publisher's policy is to use permanent paper from mills that operate a sustainable forestry policy, and which has been manufactured from pulp processed using acid-free and elementary chlorine-free practices. Furthermore, the publisher ensures that the text paper and cover board used have met acceptable environmental accreditation standards.

For further information on
Blackwell Publishing, visit our website at
www.blackwellpublishing.com

Contents

Acknowledgments   vii

Introduction   1
     Defining Authenticity   1
     Why Authenticity Emerged   3
     The Inventor of Authenticity   8

Part 1: Personal Authenticity   11

1   Authenticity and Art   13
     Totems, Relics, and the Origins of Art   13
     The Cult of the Artist and the Romance of the Primitive   16
     Parody, Appropriation, and Desacralization   21

2   Authenticity and Music   25
     History Versus Heart in Classical Music   25
     Real Music about Real Life for Real People   29
     Marketing Authentic Performance   35

3   Seeking Authenticity in Travel and Adventure   39
     Real Life is Elsewhere   39
     Staging Authenticity   43
     The Whole Adrenaline Thing   47

4   The Commodification of Authenticity   52
     Get the Genuine!   52
     The Dialectic of Authenticity and Imitation   56
     Who Buys What in the Marketplace of the Soul?   59

Contents

5   Authenticity and the Self   65
    Marketing Feeling   65
    Ecstatic Religion and Improvised Style   67
    Saving the World for Pleasure   71

Part II: Collective Authenticity   75

6   Authentic Cuisine and National Identity   77
    Inventing Real Belizean Food   77
    If Real Italians Eat Pasta, Do Real Indians Eat Curry?   80
    Terroir, Power, and French Cuisine   83

7   Authentic Dance and National Identity   88
    Collective Identity and the Speech That Cannot Lie   88
    Without Rumba There Is No Cuba   91
    Tango: The Dance of the Scream   94

8   Modes of Authenticity in the Nation-State   98
    Primordial Nationalism   98
    Who Belongs?   103
    Missionary Politics   108

9   Israel and Authentic Jewish Identity   112
    Defining Jews, Founding Israel   112
    Jews on Horseback   115
    The Poly-Ethnic Theme Park   118

10 Authenticity On the Margins   125
    Genes Make the Tribe   125
    First Nations: Identity and Identification   128
    The Empty Center and the Tears That Bind   133

Conclusion   139

An Anthropology of Authenticity   141

Notes   146
Bibliography   160
Index   169

Acknowledgments

More people helped me with this book than I can count. Here I can only thank a few, whom I have arranged alphabetically: Paul Brodwin, Andrew Buckser, Alanna Cooper, Claire Creffield, Kathryn Dahm, Lisa Eaton, Augusto Ferriauolo, Katherine Frank, Nicole Hayes, Jane Huber, Deirdre Ilkson, Martin Jay, Stephen Kalberg, Riva Kastoryano, Nadav Kenan, Siv Lie, Richard Loren, Keith McNeil, Harry Norris, Steve Parish, Victoria Phaneuf, Rosalie Robertson, Amalia Sa'ar, James Schmidt, Elaine Sturtevant, Jeff Weintraub, Robert Weller, Corky White, Lew Wurgaft, and José Pedro Zúquete. I am grateful to Steve Young for the work he did checking quotes and the accuracy of the bibliography. I would also like to thank the anonymous reviewers whose comments helped me in my rethinking of the book, the students who have taken my class on this topic, and the Anthropology Department and the University Professors Program at Boston University for supporting my research. I am deeply grateful to Cherry Lindholm for her expert editorial work, her encouragement, and everything else. This book is dedicated to her, with love.

Introduction

Defining Authenticity

The quest for authenticity touches and transforms a vast range of human experience today – we speak of authentic art, authentic music, authentic food, authentic dance, authentic people, authentic roots, authentic meanings, authentic nations, authentic products. A desire for authenticity can lead people to extremes of self-sacrifice and risk; the loss of authenticity can be a source of grief and despair. Authenticity gathers people together in collectives that are felt to be real, essential, and vital, providing participants with meaning, unity, and a surpassing sense of belonging. Authenticity can also be sought internally, through transformative ecstatic experiences, or externally, in the consumption of goods that symbolize the really real. If a Rembrandt can be called authentic, so can Coca Cola. Authenticity can describe tourist sites, the scent of floor polish, and the president of the United States. It can be found in moments of extreme danger, in the pleasures of carnival, in the taste of champagne. Authenticity can be ratified by experts who prove provenance and origin, or by the evocation of feelings that are immediate and irrefutable. The hope for an authentic experience draws us to charismatic leaders, expressive artists, and social movements; it makes us into trendy consumers, creative performers, and fanatical collectors. Authenticity, in its multiple variations, exalted and ordinary, is taken for granted as an absolute value in contemporary life.

Given all these varied usages, how can authenticity be defined? At minimum, it is the leading member of a set of values that includes sincere, essential, natural, original, and real. Most of these terms can also serve as intensifying adverbs: 'I'm really telling the truth', 'essentially, the argument is'. But it is impossible to put 'authentically' into any of these constructions. Unlike its cousins, authenticity stands alone; it has higher, more spiritual claims to make. In legal jargon authenticity means that signatures, documents, and paintings were actually authored by the person whose name is on them. In computer language authenticity indicates that a message received is indeed the same as the message sent, and that the sender is indeed the person who signed the message. For connoisseurs and collectors, a piece of period furniture is authentic if its source can be traced, and if its characteristics mark it as fitting properly into a recognized category: Camembert is authentic if it comes from the right region of France, is made in the correct manner, and looks and tastes like Camembert is supposed to look and taste. By extension, the same is true for individuals. Persons are authentic if they are true to their roots or if their lives are a direct and immediate expression of their essence. Similarly, collectives are authentic if their biological heritage can be traced and if the members act in the proper, culturally valued manner.

From this evidence, there are two overlapping modes for characterizing any entity as authentic: genealogical or historical (*origin*) and identity or correspondence (*content*). Authentic objects, persons, and collectives are original, real, and pure; they are what they purport to be, their roots are known and verified, their essence and appearance are one. As we shall see, these two forms of authenticity are not always compatible nor are both invoked equally in every context, but both stand in contrast to whatever is fake, unreal, or false, and both are in great demand.

How has the global quest for the certainty of authenticity been realized in practice? What are its different forms, when and why do they occur? What consequences follow from pursuing various modes of authenticity? What are the sources of the modern thirst for the genuine? Any answers to these questions must be provisional and incomplete. As the old story goes, blind men describing the elephant do so according to their own experience: the one who grabs its tail says the elephant is like a rope, the one who touches its legs says it is like a tree trunk, the one who strokes its ears says it is like a huge leaf. Yet these differences can be resolved by comparison. As Nietzsche puts it: "The *more* affects we allow to speak about one thing, the *more* eyes, different eyes, we can use to observe one thing, the more complete will our 'concept' of this thing, our 'objectivity' be."[1]

Therefore, this journey to a more complete and objective concept of authenticity is made up of a series of comparative case studies that will show how people from different cultures and periods have sought refuge and inspiration in their own pursuits of authentic being. The text traces this process from two perspectives, beginning with chapters on various modes of seeking personal authenticity (through art, musical performance, travel and excitement, consumption, and self-exploration or expression) and then turning to analysis of more collective forms (the construction of group identity through food and dance, forms of nationalism in Germany and France, the definition of Judaism in Israel, and the identities of minorities). Of course, this division is hardly absolute, and in fact both individual and group continuously intertwine and influence one another.

But before beginning the exploration of the manifestations of authenticity, let me set the stage with a short history of its emergence, and with a portrait of one of its most influential proponents, whose life and thoughts provide a template for later seekers after the really real: Jean Jacques Rousseau.

Why Authenticity Emerged

Where did authenticity come from? According to Lionel Trilling,[2] it grew out of the simpler, more modest virtue of sincerity, which itself arose during the sixteenth century as a result of the gradual breakup of face-to-face feudal relationships in European society. Like other traditional cultures around the world, the highly personalized universe of medieval Europe was held together by a taken-for-granted social order that provided its members with secure positions in a divinely sanctioned hierarchy. Local authorities served church and state, and were served in turn by their vassals. The family replicated this order, with the father exercising a sacralized authority. This stratified and sanctified worldview ordered the daily lives of the faithful. For most of those living in this cosmically ordained system, there was little or no travel away from their locality, and little or no social mobility within it. What mattered was whether persons were able to live up to their obligations to the neighbors and kinsmen they had known and who had known them all their lives.

This stable world was transformed utterly by the breakup of the feudal system and the massive movement of individuals out of the countryside and into mixed urban environments. Henceforth, people were no longer quite sure where they belonged, what their futures held for them, or who their neighbors were. They had begun the irreversible plunge into modernity, which can be succinctly defined as the condition of living among strangers. In this desacralized, and unpredictable environment it became possible to break out of prescribed roles and pursue secular dreams of wealth, power, and fame. But the pleasures and possibilities of social mobility coincided with feelings of alienation and meaninglessness, as well as a greater potential for guile and deceit. Former inferiors could now pretend to be better than they actually were; origins could be hidden and high-status positions falsely claimed; neighbors could cheat and betray one another and vanish into the anonymous urban wilderness. In this ambiguous milieu it is also not surprising that sincerity, doing what one says one will do, became a desired trait. The erosion of a sacred hierarchy, the fragmentation of roles, and the sense of a loss of significance were offset by the sincere person's reliable integrity. As Polonius advises his son: "To thine own self be true and it doth follow, as the night the day, that thou canst not then be false to any man."

This shift was supported by the newly rising Protestant bourgeoisie whose values had begun to transform the moral climate of Europe. The Protestants asserted that all persons are ultimately responsible for their own salvation. This could only be accomplished by scrutinizing one's soul to uncover and root out any evil impulses. For them, it was not enough to act morally; they now had to be certain that the intent behind the act was also wholesome. As a result, sincerity became their defining virtue. The rise of sincerity also correlated with the radical egalitarianism that was preached and often actually practiced by Protestants, who defined themselves not only in opposition to the hierarchies of the Catholic church, but also against the formalities of a remote and increasingly illegitimate courtly society. Instead of an ostentatious display of silks and jewels, they deliberately wore plain clothing and appeared without adornment, revealing themselves in public 'as they really were'. Similarly, they spoke simply, eschewing the flattery and rhetorical flourishes of the gentry.

But self-interrogation and egalitarian modesty had two paradoxical consequences that led away from sincerity and toward authenticity. The first was the ambiguity of representation. How could persons thrown back on their own interpretations of themselves and their duties be certain that the appearance of sincerity was not actually the result of self-delusion and pride? Couldn't the unpretentious man actually be sinfully proud of his modesty, couldn't the believer persuaded of his sincerity actually be the worst of hypocrites, capable of lying even to himself? The second was the relation between the perception of inner truth and the demands of the social order. Wasn't being true to one's own intuition of right and wrong more important than conforming to social rules? The shift is from being as one appears, to discovering what one truly is.

Support for this transformation came from another direction: the rise of scientific reason. From the time of Galileo, scientists relied on their own critical examination of the material at hand, carefully weighing and measuring claims against consequences. They took all the relevant data into account and allowed no emotional bias, prior authority, or false reasoning to contaminate the conclusions. The exemplar for skeptical practice was René Descartes (1596–1650), who believed that underlying reality could only be discovered by eliminating all social and personal preconceptions.

I will now shut my eyes, stop my ears, and withdraw all my senses. I will eliminate from my thoughts all images of bodily things. . .I will regard all such images as vacuous, false and worthless. I will converse with myself and scrutinize myself more deeply; and in this way I will attempt to achieve, little by little, a more intimate knowledge of myself.[3]

Detached from the rules and standards of the world, Descartes looked within in order to find the ultimate and undeniable laws of nature, which he believed would put human beings in concordance with the mind of God. His quest was, in its essence, a transcendental one. By favoring introspection, discounting civilizational influences, and in its indifference to moral constraints, the Cartesian pursuit of a valid science supported an increased focus on discovery of one's own authentic, therefore divine, being.

Coincident with the scientific revolution were the voyages of trade and exploration that began in the fifteenth century and expanded exponentially afterwards. The West, it became clear, was part of a larger world, in which there were other advanced civilizations that could rival or even surpass European accomplishments. The unconscious acceptance of the customs and habits of ordinary life was no longer possible when the new plural environment offered both the attractions and threats of exotic otherness. Anxiety about the stability of the taken-for-granted resulted in intensified efforts to ratify the Western experience as somehow absolute and true. The result was a heightened concern with cultural and personal authenticity.

Meanwhile, travelers' accounts of primitive indigenes were interpreted by some intellectuals and artists as commentaries on corrupt Western values. Tribes living in isolation (or even peasants living in the countryside) were imagined and portrayed as representative of coherent and pristine rural cultural traditions, integrated with nature, unashamed, communal, loving, and close to the paradisiacal Garden of Eden. They were authentic in the double sense of being pure and original and of being without falsity. At the same time, they were regarded as being in contact with mysterious and primordial spiritual forces no longer perceptible to modern humanity. This imagery of the primitive was to have a great effect on later romantic notions of authenticity.

The gradual triumph of capitalism and wage labor provided yet another impetus for developing the modern ideal of authenticity. In the old system, a worker's inner feelings and sense of self were irrelevant, since each person was locked into an occupation that would last a lifetime. It was enough that the role was properly filled. But when work in the open market was no longer hereditary or connected to any larger meaning system, labor began to lose its capacity to define identity. Instead there was increasing alienation from occupations that seemed meaningless and, worse, destructive of the worker's eternal soul. The obligation to act in a servile manner toward superiors was a special source of revulsion. Where subservience had been part of a larger cosmic order of deference, now it stood against the new ideal of spiritual equality. Work ceased to be a calling demanded by God, and became the enforced imposition of unwanted inferiority by an increasingly alien and antagonistic superior power. As a result, the early Protestant distaste for aristocratic artifice was extended to become a generalized contempt for role-playing in general. The workplace came to be pictured as battleground, where combatants must put on carapaces and conceal their true feeling selves behind standardized roles, which may only be shed at home, among family or friends. The association of authenticity with familial intimacy, spontaneous emotional expressivity, and the overturning of all forms of pretense reflected the psychological consequences of the European transformation to modernity. As Judith Shklar informs us:

> Romantic morality may reflect much of the anguish of people who leave the social world of their childhood behind them and adopt new manners and roles. The true inner self is identified with one's childhood and family, and regret as well as guilt for having left them behind may render new ways artificial, false, and in some way a betrayal of that original self. This personal self is seen as having a primacy that no later social role can claim; and indeed the latter may be despised as demeaning, 'stereotyped,' or simply 'fake' – in any case less genuine than the primordial self.[4]

The refutation of public roles and the new interest in personal authenticity also correlated with the gradual democratization of European political systems. Judith Shklar's remarks are again relevant: "If men accept themselves as the sum of their roles, it is said, then they are doomed to inequality. Only if we assume that there is a self, apart from all social definition, which is capable of morality and therefore deserves respect, can we justify the claims of equality on which not only social justice but liberty itself depends."[5] This notion of fundamental human equality, essential to the Enlightenment, implies and even requires belief in a sacred and universal moral self, existing beneath the social framework. This premise not only supports the political right of each person to life, liberty, and the pursuit of happiness, it also can motivate a search for a transcendental spiritual essence that is assumed to lie beneath the surface of roles and convention. When individuals try to commune with and express this hypothetical inner source, sincerity has evolved into authenticity.

The social consequences of this new vision were profound. Protestants throughout Europe began to declare that they were not obliged to follow whatever rules were handed down from above; instead, one's duty was to make a personal judgment as to whether those rules were moral and equitable. These judgments could be made by referring to one's inner light and not by mere obedience to social roles and official powers. Soon enough, this critical attitude spread beyond the church and became gradually engrained in ordinary life not only among the vanguard of true believers, but also among Catholics and lukewarm Protestants. Just as a dissatisfied congregant had a duty to find (or even found) another church more in tune with his or her values, individuals also began to make personal decisions about whether the state deserved their loyalty. If not, the citizen had an obligation to stand up in opposition and seek, or establish, an alternative collective that would offer a more genuinely authentic reality.

This new, spiritually tinged attitude toward the state has been well captured by the historian Lynn Hunt, who shows that in revolutionary France the rebels were motivated by their strong "belief in the possibility and desirability of 'transparency' between citizen and citizen, between the citizen and their government, between the individual and the general will." Accordingly, there should be no artificial manners or conventions separating men from each other and no institutions blocking the sharing of "authentic emotion" between citizens and their delegates.[6] According to this revolutionary ideal, the nation was not based on roles and duties, but on the passionate sensation of merger in the embrace of the collective.

To understand the emotional power of this experience, it is worth quoting the great French historian Jules Michelet. In the new revolutionary order,

> there are no longer any mountains, rivers, or barriers between men. Their language is still dissimilar, but their words agree so well that they all seem to spring from the same place, from the same bosom. Everything has gravitated towards one point, and that point now speaks forth; it is a unanimous prayer from the heart of France. Such is the power of love . . . Henceforth, unity, more pure, and free from this material condition, will consist in the union of hearts, the community of the mind, the profound union of sentiments and ideas arising from identity of opinions.[7]

Ever since, collectives have sought to tie their members together in deeply felt "unions of hearts." Unfortunately, as Freud wrote: "it is always possible to bind together a considerable number of people in love, so long as there are other people left over to receive the manifestations of their aggressiveness."[8] As we shall see, accusations of inauthenticity can easily provide the rationale for these manifestations.

The Inventor of Authenticity

If one man could be regarded as the inventor of modern authenticity in both its personal and collective guises, it would be Jean Jacques Rousseau (1712–1778) whose writings explored and promoted all the routes that seekers have since taken in quest of the elusive ideal. Rousseau earnestly believed it was necessary to demand absolute honesty from the world and from himself, and he was the first writer to present the reading public with a completely positive picture of someone who lives an authentic life by indulging his own inner emotional demands regardless of the opinions of others. This exemplary figure was Rousseau himself. In his celebrated autobiographical *Confessions* (published posthumously in 1781) he shamelessly revealed himself as self-serving, cowardly, obsequious, masochistic, sexually deviant (he was aroused by being spanked), and paranoid. As he proudly proclaims "let the numberless legion of my fellow men gather round me and hear my confessions. Let them groan at my depravities and blush for my misdeeds. But let each one of them reveal his heart at the foot of Thy throne with equal sincerity, and may any man who dares, say, 'I was a better man than he.'"[9]

Rousseau's confessions were the harbinger of a new ideal in which exploring and revealing one's essential nature was taken as an absolute good, even if this meant flying in the face of the moral standards of society. For Rousseau, the judgments of others counted for nothing, so long as one was directly experiencing authentic feeling. Only then could a person be said to have a real existence. He declared: "To live is to make use of our organs, our selves, our faculties, every part of ourselves which gives us the feeling of our own existence. The man who has lived the longest is not he who has passed the greatest number of years, but he who has *felt* life."[10] Yet the social world does not promote the pressing necessity to feel life; instead, it thwarts that desire. In this aspect of his philosophy, Rousseau was the earliest and most potent spokesman for the predominant modern belief that the cultural/social surface represses the expression of the authentic natural self.

Rousseau also had ambitions for social reforms that would reconcile the tension between 'the sentiment of being' – that is, authentic feeling – and the rules of civilization. Rousseau began his project with the famous insight that "Man was born free, and everywhere he is in chains."[11] Influenced by travelers' accounts of simple native cultures, he argued that human evolution went from primitive purity to modern corruption, much as innocent children become degenerate adults. Degradation occurred because the growth of civilization destroyed the original nature of placid noble savages, who were motivated solely by *amour de soi* (self-love), and so were without greed or ambition. Only with the appearance of the division of labor and the resulting differences in wealth and property did humans learn to covet their neighbor's possessions and to puff themselves up in hopes of exciting envy. Motivated by *amour propre* (vanity), human beings then violently sought prestige and status at the expense of others and became slaves of culture and tradition.[12] As a result, individuals now only see themselves in the eyes of others. If admired, they are proud; if held in contempt, they despise themselves. Civilization has robbed the human race of independence and deformed its true nature; it has made us slaves of power and imitators of fashion. Not only are we enchained; we have even grown to love our chains, and to embrace the invidious social world that has destroyed our genuine being.

To remedy this dire situation, Rousseau imagined an egalitarian society where all citizens would be merged into the encompassing general will of the community. Personal preferences and distinctions would vanish in the homogenizing unity of the collective, as realized in great symbolic festivals where participation in the milling crowd would work its solidifying magic. It was this aspect of Rousseau's philosophy that made him a hero of the French Revolution and of radical political movements ever since.

Other aspects of Rousseau's philosophy also had a huge impact on the modern value of authenticity. He was one of the first to argue that some remnants of the original authentic character of humanity could still be found in simpler cultures, which he believed to be closer to the state of nature. His nostalgia for the primitive 'noble savage' was manifested in later theories of tribal purity, nationalism, and ethnic pride. Equally influential was Rousseau's firm belief that children were repositories of humanity's fundamental innocence, which has found its modern expression in therapeutic injunctions to achieve authenticity by 'getting in touch with the inner child' and in the American child-centered educational system. Finally, Rousseau also believed that certain receptive souls, such as his own, were more attuned to the authentic promptings of the heart. They could shut out daily reality and discover fulfillment through cultivation of reverie and other trance-like states of consciousness. "As long as this state lasts, we can call ourselves happy, not with a poor, incomplete and relative happiness such as we find in the pleasures of life, but with a sufficient, complete and perfect happiness which leaves no emptiness to be filled in the soul."[13] In this, Rousseau presaged the present-day search for the really real within.

Thus Rousseau, the most poetic, the most expansive, the most paradoxical, and the most exasperating of all philosophers, expressed and reflected the trajectory of authenticity in his writing. He preached the truth of self-loss in the equalizing public collective of citizens while simultaneously he idealized communion with the unique inner self resistant to all social pressure. At the same time he praised purity of origin and the primordial integrity of the noble savage or innocent child. The rest of this book will follow some of the pathways that Rousseau first blazed, beginning with a history of the notion of art as the authentic expression of an artist's inner genius. How did art gain this exalted position, and how can the viewer be sure an artwork really is what it purports to be? What happens when the notion of artistic authenticity is challenged?

Part 1

Personal Authenticity

Chapter 1

Authenticity and Art

Totems, Relics, and the Origins of Art

Certification of the authenticity of paintings and sculptures is absolutely crucial for maintaining their worth. This is because of the danger of forgery. Anxiety about counterfeiting is a result of a belief that a charismatic radiance – an 'aura' – emanates from the singularity of the work of art itself.[1] Because each artwork is thought to have its own unique aura, copies cannot, by definition, project the necessary ineffable radiance. The reasoning is circular (only authentic art objects have a charismatic aura, art objects emitting that aura are authentic), and theological in origin, so that counterfeiting becomes a kind of sacrilege. This notion of authenticity, Walter Benjamin says, is a diluted residue of the halo surrounding cultic objects that 'primitive'[2] peoples believed represented or embodied the sacred, and which were the foci of collective worship. As he writes: "The unique value of the 'authentic' work of art has its basis in ritual. . . . Secularization affords authenticity the place previously held by cult value."[3]

Benjamin's analysis echoes Émile Durkheim, who, in *The Elementary Forms of Religious Life*,[4] argued that the prototypical cultic objects were the totems worshipped in the religions of Australian aborigines and other indigenous peoples. The totem was, Durkheim says, the "emblem" or "flag" of the clan; representations of it were tattooed or painted on the bodies of the people, worn as amulets around their necks, shaven into their hair. Most importantly, the totem was represented in an object that served as the center for collective rituals. These objects were not necessarily beautiful or unusual in themselves; usually they were simple images of totem plants and animals. They were revealed during the climactic moments of ritual, where they served as manifestations of impersonal supernatural powers (called *mana*, *orenda*, or *wakan* by American Indians) that could be summoned to rejuvenate the community during its rites.[5] Durkheim argued that these revitalizing powers, thought by the aboriginals to inhere in the totem, actually emanated from the group itself, arising during the ritualized state of ecstatic communion he called collective effervescence. In a real sense, the group *is* God – an insight to which I will return in later chapters.

These cultic items were treated with veneration and awe only because they functioned both as symbolic representations of the clan totem and as inspirations for the clan's ritual performances. This was why they were decorated, beautified, placed in special containers, and otherwise marked off from the mundane. The same principles operated during the medieval period in the West when the relics of saints were treated much like the sacred totems of the aborigines. Although they were often worn bits of wood or cloth, or grisly bits of flesh and bone, as holy relics they were encrusted with gold and jewels, wrapped in fine linen, and displayed in ornate showcases where they could be venerated by the faithful.

While there are fundamental similarities, there are also crucial distinctions to be made between totems and relics. Totems were endowed with the collective and depersonalized spiritual energy of the entire tribe; they displayed their power only when awakened in ritual. In contrast, medieval relics were particularized and humanized, each one permanently imbued with the redemptive powers of a named saint or martyr. In the medieval relic individual charisma had begun to replace the abstract force of the primitive cultic object. The saintly relics are the forerunners of the later Western conceptualization of artworks as the products of an individual artist's unique visionary genius. Relics are transitional between totem and artwork: personal, yet not created; they gain their spiritual authority solely by virtue of their degree of closeness to the saint or martyr, with the holiest being the actual body parts.

According to medieval historians, there was intense competition for possession of saintly bones, skulls, and other holy remnants, since the sanctity (and popularity) of churches rested in large measure on the number and quality of the relics displayed within them. A devout pilgrim might travel many miles to gain the spiritual blessing of gazing on and perhaps even touching a cloth that had once been worn by a great saint – perhaps even by Jesus himself. So, when Bishop Hugh of Lincoln (later canonized) was allowed to handle the arm of Mary Magdalene at a rival shrine, he surreptitiously bit off a finger and took it back to his parish, where it remains today.[6] To meet this kind of voracious demand, relics became profitable items of exchange. Professional traffickers in holiness traveled around medieval Europe, buying and selling splinters of the cross and bits and pieces of various saints and their wardrobes to those with funds to buy.

Demand led inevitably to a proliferation of sacred objects and to questions about their authenticity. Although Mary Magdalene seems to have had as many arms as Kali, and although only a sequoia tree could have produced all the existent fragments of the true cross, the Holy See could check records of the history of the object and the miracles associated with it and provide incontrovertible official validation of sacred status. Warring claims could be settled by papal intervention. For example, the body of the Irish St Abbanus was deemed to exist miraculously both in the monastery where he began preaching and in the one where he died. Vendors selling suspect objects and body parts could be obliged to undergo official ordeals, such as submersion in boiling water, to test whether their goods were genuine or not. But the final proof was the capacity of the relics to work certifiable miracles. If they did, they were genuine, if not, they were false, no matter what external evidence was marshaled to support their authenticity.[7]

The collection and verification of relics and the miracles associated with them has obvious parallels with the work of modern museum curators, who also seek out and acquire artworks that, like the bones of saints, provide a channel to the sacred. Curators too must demonstrate that the objects they have accumulated are not forgeries, and therefore are worthy of contemplation and devotion. No doubt modern museum curators envy their medieval counterparts their methods for certification, since their own attempts to authenticate the authorship of artistic productions are far more open to controversy.

Procedures required to verify the authenticity of any artwork are complex. The first of these is a technical matter of tracing genealogy. A painting may be considered an original if historical records prove its authenticity. Who were the previous owners? Can its paper trail of ownership be plotted from the day it was originally sold, and are there contracts, letters, and other texts documenting these transactions? Is the painting mentioned in the artist's letters or the letters of his contemporaries? Other questions of genealogy then may be asked and answered by mechanical means. Is the canvas of the proper age? Is the wood of the frame from the same period? Can the chemical composition of the paint be determined and compared with paint from the artist's other works? Is there insect damage matching what might be expected? Like the investigators of a crime scene, art historians must become forensic scientists in order to verify the attribution of a work of art.

The technical expertise used to determine a painting's history stands very much at odds with the second process of authenticating art: establishing correspondence. For this type of accreditation, a painting may be considered an original if it is certified as such by experts who are believed able to recognize the artist's paintings without the aid of the technical means outlined above. These aesthetically sensitive authorities use their experience, taste, and intuition to determine if the artwork in question follows the style and pattern of other paintings that are already recognized as legitimate. Does the brushwork, the design, the color; the indefinable 'feel' of the painting recall other authenticated works? Where does the painting fit within the canon of the artist's known compositions? But the most important thing is whether the work glows with the indescribable radiance of other works painted by the artist. If experts agree that the painting in question has that aura, then it is authentic. Authentic art objects are original, real, and pure; they are what they purport to be, their provenance and authorship are known and verified, their essence and appearance are one.[8]

When an artwork is authenticated it takes its place in the modern temple of the cult of the aesthetic and of the artist/genius: the museum. In these magnificent buildings paintings are placed behind ornate frames, surrounded by uniformed guards, and viewed with awe by devoted pilgrims. The high priests of the faith are the curators who instruct the public on the significance of their experience and champion the religion of art and genius. The artists – especially those long dead and assured a place in the pantheon – are the reigning gods of the art museum, their sanctity proven by the miraculous impact of their remaining creations. For believers, contemplating these sacred relics can heal the wounded soul and redeem the debased modern world. As Lionel Trilling put it, today art is "expected to provide the spiritual substance of life."[9]

The Cult of the Artist and the Romance of the Primitive

The belief in the godlike artist/genius has deep roots in human history. Max Weber argued that the aesthetic impulse was originally linked to the ecstatic trances of shamans, who incarnated the spirits and acted as magical healers of their people. The human vessel of the gods and the carver who created cultic images of those spirits were one and the same person. The creations that resulted from their communion were not seen as the products of individual imagination, since the shaman's personality was erased during trances. Though individual ability in the physical realization of the vision was recognized, prime credit was given to the inspiring deity. Remnants of this way of thinking may be seen in present-day Australian aboriginal art, which originates in dreams or represents traditional stories and motifs. For Australian aboriginals, these objects are not art but paraphernalia required for ritual performance. So, while

Western collectors of aboriginal works are likely to be interested in ascertaining their authenticity, the fame of the maker, and the aesthetic quality of the piece, aboriginals look for aspects that fit them for ceremonial use.

With the evolution of more complex and hierarchical social formations, the roles of priest and artisan separated, as craftsmen became independent manufacturers of cultic objects, masks, and other sacred artifacts as well as makers of purely secular items. With this shift there was increased recognition that some artisans were more technically capable than others. These experts were in greater demand than their less able colleagues, but in religion the main thing remained the ritual, not the beauty or complexity of props or surroundings. The skilled workers who built the Gothic cathedrals and manufactured the sacred receptacles for the holy relics of medieval Europe were doing God's work, but they were not conduits of God's power, as the shamanic maker of cultic objects had been in simpler societies.

This attitude began to change during the Renaissance when a newly emerging class of thinkers and visionaries took a more activist stance toward their lives. Reflecting the gradual fragmentation of the medieval cosmic order and their own increased social mobility and lofty ambitions, they reversed the valence of the aboriginal universe. Where the shaman/artist was an empty vessel inhabited and controlled by external supernatural forces, members of this new class put themselves at the center of the cosmic picture as the active embodiments of God, capable of transforming the world through their personal creativity.[10] The heroes of this human-centered and individualistic ideology were the great artists, who achieved immortality because, like divine beings, they could fabricate singular new realities out of their own imaginations.[11]

The high evaluation of the artist/creator evolved until, as Charles Taylor writes, by 1800 "the artist becomes in some way the paradigm case of the human being, as agent of original self-definition." For the artist, as for the modern individual, "self-truth and self-wholeness are seen more and more not as means to be moral, as independently defined, but as something valuable for their own sake. Self-wholeness and the aesthetic are ready to be brought together."[12] To accomplish this goal, artists looked for inspiration in their own personal passion and sensibility, and their work had value insofar as it was an authentic expression of that inner reality – just as relics were the unique remnants of a particular holy saint.

It is precisely because an art object has transcendent value as the personal creation of a particular artist/genius that a forgery must be removed from the museum wall, even though its aesthetic quality has not changed. Clearly, what has been lost is the sense of direct connection with the painter. As a result, the painting is designated *inauthentic*. From this perspective, any copy or imitation, or work of art that is 'in the manner of' or even 'from the school of' can never emit the ineffable halo of genius. It is to validate authorship that the art historical modes of authentication (by genealogy or by correspondence) developed.

But there are problems with each of these. On the one hand, genealogical accreditation by means of technical research on provenance and forensic proof rationalizes the value of the work and therefore undermines the charismatic aura that is at the heart of its attraction. It becomes simply a thing, like any other, to be studied with technical instruments and analyzed with scientific detachment. On the other hand, accreditation by correspondence relies wholly on a subjective sense of emotional communion with the artwork that is akin to a believer's faith in prophecy. This preserves aura, but, because there is no absolute guarantee that the work is the sacred object that it purports to be, it also means there can be apostates and heretics who do not recognize its charisma. It is no surprise then that highly respected authorities can and do disagree over the authenticity of very well-known paintings, so that even works by the great master, Rembrandt, are under dispute. In contrast, tribal members were not likely to deny the spiritual power of the cultic object, nor did the medieval faithful look askance at the relics enshrined in their cathedrals.

The sacred aura of art has also been inevitably diminished by commodification, which reduces art objects to items of exchange. Museums try to obscure the polluting influence of commerce on their art objects by concealing the buying and selling aspects of their operations. The spectator pays an entrance fee and there are marked-off places for shopping and eating, but the main spaces of artistic display are "exchange-free zones, for the re-presentation of the authentic and pure."[13] In the museum, art is referred to as priceless – outside the grasp of capital. Nonetheless, donating artwork to a museum is a tax write-off that elevates the donor's status while also markedly raising the monetary value of other works by the same artist. In a real sense, the museum curator is a banker in disguise, overseeing specialist assaying departments. And so the priceless artwork is desacralized in spite of the mystifying labors of the museum.

The attenuation of art's aura has also been accelerated by the rapid development of mechanical imitation, so that even the most sacred idols can now be photographed, filmed, replicated in miniature, and otherwise turned into multiple images that allow consumers to satisfy their ravenous desire "to get hold of an object at very close range by way of its likeness, its reproduction."[14] Under the influence of this new democratic spirit of inquisition, distinctions collapse and secrets are exposed. As images of the sacred are marketed to a public seeking to penetrate every mystery, the original object is diminished by a proliferation of copies and by constant public exhibition. It loses its sacred halo and becomes a pallid ghost of its former self. As a result, the image of the genius also becomes problematic, and the transcendent quality of art is less and less plausible. The curator and the art historian are high priests of a religion on the wane.

One predictable reaction to the desacralization of art was the attempt to recapture lost authenticity through a retreat to origins, finding a truer reality in primitive cultic artifacts that presumably had their auras intact. Modernist artists, eager to become more authentic themselves, identified with the artist/savage. When Pablo Picasso first saw African masks he felt he had met kindred spirits: "They were against everything – against unknown threatening spirits...I, too, I am against everything. I, too, believe that everything is unknown, that every-thing is an enemy!...All fetishes...were weapons. To help people avoid coming under the influence of spirits again, to help them become independent. Spirits, the unconscious...they are all the same thing."[15] For Picasso, the masks were not cultural objects, to be explained, catalogued, and hung in display cases. They were expressions of pure id. Inspired by his vision, Picasso's created his seminal modernist painting *Le Demoiselles d'Avignon* as new sort of art. It was not meant to be beautiful. It was an exorcism.

From within this mindset, primitive artifacts that had been seen as repellant at worst, childish or crude at best, were now reinterpreted as suitable for display in museums and private collections. In particular, cultic objects once held in contempt as the unsavory symbols of vulgar, bloodthirsty paganism were viewed as powerfully expressive representations of a pure primitive soul untainted by civilization. In response, a trade in 'authentic primitive art' became fashionable, championed most formidably by Nelson Rockefeller whose philanthropy led to the opening of the Rockefeller wing of primitive art at the Metropolitan Museum in 1984.

In this spectacular exhibit, masks, totems, and other anthropomorphic sculptural items are removed from their ceremonial and ethnographic contexts and placed within a generic category of primitive art: non-Western, preliterate, crude yet strikingly attractive objects that had once had a function in mysteri-ous primordial rites. Simple utilitarian ordinary items were of no interest; nor were cultic objects that did not have the craftwork and elegance Western con-noisseurs deemed beautiful. A spoon had to be aesthetically designed, deco-rated and carved, and defined as a ceremonial spoon, to be put on display. Objects had to have been made for ritual purposes by tribal people untouched by civilization, preferably using traditional tools (no steel adzes or commercial dyes). Once categorized as art, these oracular objects were valued not for what they could tell us about their sources, but for their supposed intrinsic aesthetic worth and their enigmatic but potent expressive capacity. They were presented as primal cultic/aesthetic creations from the dawn of time, emanating a strange power to awaken us moderns to our hidden and truer selves, long suppressed beneath the constraints of civilized life. To the Western art collector this art was "pristine, primeval and, as such, liberating."[16]

There was, however, a murderous paradox involved in the collection and display of primitive art. If the polluting touch of civilization kills primitive authenticity, then authentic cultic objects, it was assumed, could no longer be produced because the authors no longer lived in their pristine worlds; they had been corrupted by colonialism, tainted by capitalism. All these fallen people could produce were mere commodities, devoid of spiritual power. As Shelly Errington writes: "The message was that once upon a time Africans were great artists, now they are commercial hacks; once they lived in harmony, now they live in decadence; once their work was pure, now it is polluted."[17] Furthermore, as primitive objects and their makers became more recognizable to a Western audience they lost their aura of mystery. Disenchantment increased when makers of primitive art began to use familiar Western materials and technologies that were more durable and efficient, but no longer exotic.

Faced with problems of commodification and the loss of mystery, collectors searching for authentic items ventured to more and more exotic and difficult to reach backwaters, where they ransacked whatever remained of the culture that they wished to immortalize. The excuse for the desecration was that the local people had no respect for their own heritage; it was up to Western art dealers to preserve the authentic artifacts of the primitive in all their primal power. Local entrepreneurs soon became aware of the strange compulsion of Westerners to find and collect old and worn artifacts, and became experts at manufacturing them, aging them, and hiding them away in remote locations where they could be eagerly discovered and purchased. The more avidly the primitive versions of the authentic sacred are sought, the more counterfeit they are likely to be.

The disappearance of authentic primitive art led to a marked shift away from the collection of anonymously produced sacred objects and toward the purchase of items made specifically for the market in tribal art by named individuals. In other words, the market for primitive art became much more like the market in Western art, foregrounding the genius of the creator and his or her aesthetic intentions. There remained significant differences, however. Tribal or ethnic objects still had to have 'cultural markers' to validate their authentic character. For example, a real American Indian object ought to incorporate traditional designs and themes; people who are actually Indians must manufacture it in a traditional manner using traditional materials.

These requirements may seem self-evident enough, but they are often imposed by outsiders seeking authenticity, as they understand it. For example, the production of contemporary southwestern American Indian art was cultivated in the 1920s and 1930s by interested eastern patrons, including the

Rockefellers and the Dodges. Local Indian craftsmen and women were trained and encouraged to emulate traditional designs and patterns, and their work was judged by elite white collectors who believed their innate good taste could discriminate between the falsity of tourist trinkets and the truth of genuine Indian art, unaffected by the baneful influence of tourism. Anything "garish and restless" was disparaged as an alien intrusion, as were innovations or designs borrowed from other pueblos. A Zuni piece had to be recognizably Zuni to be collectible.[18] The desires or aesthetic inclinations of the indigenous artisans were not taken seriously – it was assumed they needed to be taught to retain what was best of their culture and to resist the corruption and kitsch of mass society.

Another reaction to the problem of assigning authenticity to ethnic or tribal art has been the increased importance placed on blood. Marginalized groups seeking to control valuable artistic production now often claim that only those people proven to be genealogical members of the group (defined variously as a tribe, nation, race, or ethnicity) have the right and the innate capacity to produce its characteristic art forms. The major issue for determining the authenticity of an art object then becomes the legal and moral question of whether the maker can prove his or her kinship with the group: authenticity equals ancestry. As we shall see, genealogical essentialism has been widely applied to collectives the modern world, and not always so harmlessly.

Parody, Appropriation, and Desacralization

Issues of authentication and the rise of highly professionalized indigenous artists left a vacuum in the market for primitive art that was soon filled by what was formerly called tourist art, which had previously been disdained by collectors as fraudulent, imitative, and corrupt; in other words, as wholly inauthentic.[19] This remarkable revaluation can be explained partly by rubbish theory: i.e., that durable goods falling outside accepted categories of value eventually re-emerge as collectibles.[20] But there is more to it. These new art objects are a characteristic aesthetic expression of the worldwide confrontation between local and colonial cultures. As old certainties declined, the members of the colonizing first world became fascinated with this moment of conjunction, when the 'other' reflected 'us' not only by producing pseudo-authentic items they thought would be valued by Western connoisseurs, but also by manufacturing for themselves copies, parodies, and pastiches of the new world that was entering into and rapidly disintegrating their own.

These artworks are part of a larger postmodern aesthetic that has arisen out of the collapse of old values of authenticity and artistic genius – whether of

21

cultures or individuals; circumstances which led Marcel Duchamp to redefine art as anything that is made by man and to convert a urinal into his iconic masterpiece. As the boundaries of art and culture have eroded, for many avant-garde artists human history has become "a department store in which one can shop for usable pasts, with full credit at one's disposal... it is not authenticity that is sought, but just the opposite – an exaltation in artifice and allusive irony."[21] For these vanguard artists, there is no longer any notion of authenticity, only multiplying simulacra reflecting one another.

The crisis of authenticity in the visual arts has mainly affected artists of the international art market in New York, Paris, Munich, and other urban art centers who exhibit in galleries catering to wealthy buyers who wish to be members of an aesthetic elite. Marketing cultural capital in the realm of aesthetics requires an appearance of innovation among avant-garde artists and their clients, who need to differentiate themselves from the masses by their advanced and unconventional taste. In the postmodern era, the requirements for high-status marketing occur within the context of the larger philosophical loss of faith in the old verities, as outlined above, which then becomes the primary source for innovation. This has led to the evolution of a highly intellectualized international artists' community reliant on an amalgam of appropriation, copy, simulacra, replication, pastiche, and popular reference to challenge the conventions of authenticity; their work often meditates on the sinister intrusion of economic interests into the art world and reflects personal concerns about the psyche of the artist in an era when art itself has lost its accepted boundaries and significance. In general, the artistic vanguard seeks to overturn the authority of the gallery and the museum and to subvert traditional concepts of art.

Yet, as George Marcus has written, postmodern parodies and burlesques "are still all too easily appropriated in different ways – as entertainment, as light but tolerable critique, even as celebrating power elites or certain media and culture industries – by those who are the very subjects, by implication, of the critiques of power relations this art develops."[22] The fact that the avant-garde parodic appropriation of earlier sacralized art is then re-appropriated by the rich and powerful for the purpose of legitimizing their elite status is paradoxical, to say the least. This paradox corresponds with an art market where cultural (and economic) capital depends on the artist's creative capacity to make a product that is acknowledged to be unique and therefore collectible by critics, dealers, curators, and buyers. However, it is not enough for an artist to have a signature item or novel conceptual approach that is readily available for purchase. International artists also must sell their works by appearing at openings, having dinners with prospective buyers and influential dealers, critics and curators, teaching seminars at prestigious institutions, and establishing personal ties with cosmopolitan circles of the wealthy and powerful who wish to have their status and taste ratified by their public consumption of art objects that can only be appreciated by taste-makers who are ahead of the curve. In other words, the market value of contemporary art is linked in very direct ways to the ability of the artist to project a personal charisma and attract a following. So, although genius may be out of fashion in the discourse of art criticism, in practice the artist/genius lives on, seeking headlines and nurtured by the buyers' need to believe that the works they have purchased will, in time, be enshrined in museums alongside Rembrandts and Goyas.

Obviously, a buyer's assurance about the genius of an artist becomes more and more problematic when there are no accepted standards for excellence or even for decent workmanship, and when beauty and tradition have been discarded except as objects of burlesque and transgression. Considerable intellectual labor and ingenuity is required for a dealer to teach a wealthy client to appreciate the counter-hegemonic intent of any particular postmodern piece while simultaneously pointing out that this same piece is bound to be 'important' in the future history of art. It is at this juncture that an appeal to 'taste' returns, and with a vengeance. Lacking objective aesthetic standards, collectors ratify their identities by surrounding themselves with art that they believe reflects and expresses what they wish to appear to be – that is, highly cultivated persons who appreciate and understand avant-garde art that seems meaningless, silly, outrageous, or ugly to the uninitiated. Collecting such art is risky business, since the identity actually conveyed could well be unintended: dupe or fool or, even worse, a vulgarian. So, instead of favoring adventurous purchasing, the absence of standards stimulates potential buyers to pay close attention to market values and to follow the advice of experts who guarantee good taste as well as good investment. So it is that despite (and also because of) the contemporary debunking of aura, beauty, and genius, the price of safe old masters, like blue-chip stocks, has soared into the stratosphere, while today's postmodern art heroes are over-promoted and then abandoned by fashion-conscious curators and gallery owners – perhaps to be rediscovered at a later date when time has put a valuable patina of nostalgia on their work.

The response of avant-garde international art to the crisis of authenticity is inescapably full of tensions and contradictions. Postmodern strategies of parody, appropriation, subversion, pastiche, autobiography, and deconstruction have a very real and powerful intellectual rationale, since these modes reflect the situation of high art in the contemporary era, when taken-for-granted notions of the ultimate value of beauty, the aura of originality, and the concept of genius have been undermined by a capitalist art market which turns cultic objects into commodities, and by the effects of mechanical reproduction, which fatally erodes the experience of awe. But the cost of the turn to parody and psychobiography is increased obscurity and subjectivity both in high art and in the critical apparatus surrounding it, increasing the rift between the public who retain a naïve confidence in the transcendental content of art and the elite international artist who has no such faith left.

But despite the elite artist's loss of belief in the artistic myth, the conventions of authenticity have not been dispensed with. The international avant-garde still subscribe to romantic notions of themselves as countercultural radicals, despite their unavoidable enmeshment in the marketplace. Pressed to assert proprietary rights and establish recognizable brand names, postmodern artists also continue to proclaim originality for themselves and their work. In fact, the cult of personality is more rampant than ever, since without aesthetic or professional artisanal standards artists are obliged to project personal charisma to retain clients. In consequence, avant-garde art also has become more and more self-reflective and solipsistic, as the artist often relies on the only thing known to be true: his or her own fragmented identity. The claim to genius resurfaces, but instead of being a creator of transfiguring beauty, the artist now expresses personal disintegration. Or there may be a fascination with the irrefutable products of the body, with self-mutilation and performance, a return to ritual and relic in hopes of resacralization. Meanwhile, buyers who have the courage to purchase avant-garde art often do so because they are convinced these subversive works will someday be displayed in the very temples of art whose existence the artists have called into question, and that the artists themselves are the new gods of personal authenticity: free, untrammeled individual geniuses, expressing themselves outside of and against the constraining boundaries of history and convention.

Chapter 2

Authenticity and Music

History Versus Heart in Classical Music

There are significant differences in the ways authenticity is understood in the visual and the musical arts. A painting that is verified to be the work of the person whose signature is at the bottom is authentic; one that is an imitation or facsimile is a forgery. It is inauthentic. That is simple enough, though the implications can be complex, as the present concern with parody and appropriation attest. But in art forms like music there is no concrete object to worship or copy, only the act of performance.[1] How is authenticity measured then? Is it even relevant? The answer to the second question is an emphatic yes. For listeners and performers alike the question of authenticity in musical presentation is endlessly engrossing and controversial. The debate always revolves around two different approaches: historical/genealogical or romantic/expressive. Is the performance true to the original score of the music; or does the performance convey the emotional core of the music? Ideally, both should be true, but in actuality different aspects of authenticity are stressed in different musical genres and at different periods.

Until recently, in classical music the dominant mode was romantic and expressive. Nineteenth-century interpreters of the canon felt few qualms at changing compositions and techniques to make them more appealing to their own ears. The notion of historical accuracy was not part of their vocabulary, since they believed that the classical tradition was a living one and that they were its rightful inheritors; as a result, singers sang unselfconsciously, with little or no awareness of different historical complexes of style; conductors sped up or slowed down tempi as they pleased, and instrumentalists played blithely according to the conventions of their era. For example, when he conducted

Beethoven's *Eroica* Gustav Mahler accelerated the pizzicatos of the finale to represent a child's stumbling steps. He had no worries about the historical veracity of his adaptations; nor did Arturo Toscanini, Leopold Stokowski, and other lesser luminaries who imposed their own visions on period music.[2] Their assumption was that the skills, intuition, and genius of the interpreter were all that was necessary to present a piece with authenticity and conviction. As the great harpsichordist Wanda Landowska wrote in her memoirs:

> At no time in the course of my work have I ever tried to reproduce exactly what the old masters did. Instead, I study, I scrutinize, I love, and I recreate . . . I am sure that what I am doing in regard to sonority, registration, etc., is very far from the historical truth . . . Little do I care if, to attain the proper effect, I use means that were not exactly those available to Bach.[3]

Landowska thought she was revitalizing Bach's music by her empathy for his compositions and by her own creative ability.

But this sort of certainty has become much rarer today, having been undermined by the quickening pace of change and the disillusionment so characteristic of the last hundred years. In this context, romantic freedom began to seem self-indulgent. In response, the musician and composer Arnold Dolmetsch (1858–1940) built replicas of archaic lutes, crumhorns, rebecs, and harpsichords, which he then taught himself to play. He also resurrected and performed early and previously unknown musical scores. His ultimate dream was to recapture the simple sacred songs of his illiterate peasant ancestors. This music, he thought, was a reflection of a *Gemeinschaft* deeply tied to the soil, respectful of tradition, and happily integrated into village communities – a quest for a musical Eden that was part of a larger folkloric search for genuine traditions. Over time, many artists and listeners were influenced by Dolmetsch's vision, and have turned toward what is called the historical performance movement, in which a piece is played as closely as possible to the way it was played when the score was composed. In the mid-1980s record companies transferring classical music from LP to CD were choosing 'original instrument' performances by a ratio of two to one.[4]

The difference between the romantic and historicist perspectives can be concretely illustrated in their views concerning instrumentation. If we assume, as historicists do, that authenticity means replicating the sound of the original as closely as possible, then guitars can never be used in a Baroque piece, since today's guitar is a relatively recent invention with a different sound quality than the obsolete lute. Similarly, only Baroque violins can play a Baroque concerto; nor can Bach be played on the piano, since the piano was invented long after his death. For historical purists, Bach's keyboard compositions must be played on the harpsichord for which they were composed. In contrast, the major Bach biographer of the nineteenth century wrote that the pianoforte "floated in the mind of Bach" as the potential ideal in clavier compositions.[5] He believed Bach would be thrilled to hear his pieces played on the piano, which has far greater range and dynamics than the primitive harpsichord. From this perspective, modern pianists are simply realizing Bach's dreams when they interpret his music on a much-improved instrument.

What is most crucial according to expressive romantics is not the authenticity of the instrument, but the degree to which the performer is able to convey the emotional essence of the music. In contrast, historical purists believe that authenticity requires a set of technical rules and norms to regulate the performance of early music, precisely so that the ego of the performer can be subdued and unwarranted innovation kept at a minimum. Only by exercising such discipline, they argue, can the original inspiration of the composer shine through the obscuring fog of time and fashion. Both parties assume that performance authenticity is the ultimate goal to be sought, but their methods for achieving that goal are completely at odds. The romantics aim at spiritual union and give preference to the interpreter; the historicists aim at transmission of the original and focus on mechanics. The romantics are passionate and inspired; they are the prophets of music who claim to embody its elusive spirit; the historicists are precise and studious; they are musical priests, repeating its sacred texts. To hark back to the model of authenticity I outlined earlier, the interpreter follows a method of content or correspondence, subjectively intuiting and becoming at one with the inner truth of genius, ignoring form for expression; the historicist practices empirical genealogical methods, using the technical means of forensics and textual analysis to remove the accretions of time and reveal the original in its pristine state. This is the version of authenticity that an enterprising record company was invoking when it put a sticker on its version of the famous Pachelbel Canon proclaiming it was the "authentic edition. The famous Kanon as Pachelbel heard it."

This turns out to be more difficult task than it seems, since no one has the least idea what Pachelbel looked like, let alone how he heard his music. Even to begin to make a claim for historical authenticity, a musician must study the notation of the past and discern its meaning, both of which are very hard jobs. We do not know what ornamentation Baroque musicians used; notations from the Renaissance are almost totally opaque; we are not even sure how fast allegro was to Beethoven. Without accepted agreement on these fundamental matters, it is impossible to replicate earlier music with certainty. Therefore it is not uncommon for different performers, each equally aiming at historical authenticity, to produce quite different versions of the same piece.[6]

As mentioned, historically authentic performance also requires playing period instruments in the same manner as they were played in the past. Ideally, these instruments would be as old as the music they are used to interpret, but old musical instruments have usually lost their tone and their quality has altered greatly. The solution is to manufacture 'imitation originals' that can reproduce the sound heard in earlier times. This leads to other problems. Must these instruments be built according to the exact techniques of Bach's era (if those techniques can be recaptured and replicated), or are technical shortcuts allowed? Can substitutes be made for materials that are no longer available – such as the quills from now-extinct species of ravens? What happens when an instrument is radically different from those played today? For example, a Baroque violin is structurally quite removed from our contemporary instrument, has a different sonority, and requires different playing techniques. Given these variations, how can we be sure that the sound coming from a modern imitation is actually the same as the sound that was produced by the originals? How much should we care?

There are even more vexing questions about what an historically authentic performance might be. Should the orchestra change its shape and the seating arrangements of the players to conform to what is known of earlier orchestras, which were much smaller and differently organized than today's? Should an authentic recital of Bach recapture the first time the piece was ever presented, or ought an authentic performance consist of an approximate amalgam of what is known about the presentation of early music in general? For example, we know that the concert format is a relatively recent invention, as is the convention of silence between the segments of an orchestral piece. Would a truly authentic rendition encourage the audience to applaud and walk around to greet friends in the middle of the performance, as used to be the case?

In spite of these issues, the historicist approach has succeeded because it meets the yearnings of the shrinking classical music audience, which maintains a defensive moral posture of unswerving loyalty to the standards of the past, and determinedly resists both the arrogance and flourishes of the romantics and the postmodern artistic milieu of transgression, parody, and personality. Instead, classical music is seen by the faithful as "a celebration of the 'sacred history' of the Western middle classes, and an affirmation of faith in their values as the abiding stuff of life. As these values...come more and more under attack... so the concert becomes more vital as a ritual of stability in an unstable world."[7] Nonetheless, even though the members of the classical music audience may cling to the old familiar compositions as the identifying markers of a besieged identity, they also have a modern hunger for novelty, which can, however, be satisfied only so long as the new is couched in the comforting language of the tried and true.

Therefore, since the late twentieth century there has been a voracious market for classical music that can claim to recapture the original sound of familiar masterpieces, albeit played on unfamiliar instruments in unusual settings. In the production of historical authenticity, novelty is twinned with the recognizable and traditional, so that audiences can hear something new while convincing themselves that they are listening to something old. This characteristic doubleness – returning to the past without foregoing the pleasures of the present – is the source of the success of contemporary classical music that seeks authentic historical reproduction at the cost of romantic interpretation – though this ascendancy has been and will be challenged by musicians who want to assert their own genius, and believe they know the music in their hearts, not in their heads.

Real Music about Real Life for Real People

It would seem that classical music and country music have little in common, aside from the fact that both are performative. Certainly, their audiences hardly overlap. Classical music is played for a small, self-consciously elite group; its audience is formal, its presentation stylized, its atmosphere rarified. In contrast, country (or country and western as it is sometimes called) is the descendent of rural old-time or hillbilly music and favors the casual, raucous, and rude; it is the music of boots and cowboy hats, heard on radios and jukeboxes by workingmen and women (or those who want to identify themselves with workingmen and women) across the United States and throughout the world. If classical fans define themselves against county music, country music aficionados return the favor, with interest. One perceptive critic outlines the typical country fan's polarized worldview as follows:

> We are hardworking, honest, far from home, patriotic, vulnerable. They are slick, dishonest, untrustworthy, powerful, cruel. They own the factories, have more education, think they are better than we are. They do not respect other people or what makes this country great. They use big words, hold all the cards, and will stab you in the back. But we are better than they are because we work hard, care for our families, stick together, and keep faith with each other. We made this county. We hold the key to true happiness because we know that happiness is home and family and doing right by each other. We have good friends who go way back with us, and we do the best we can.[8]

29

In sum, high-class people – who are 'uptown', who wear suits and go to concerts – are affected and fake, just as their music is pretentious and phony. Both are completely inauthentic. In contrast, the working classes – who are 'down-home', wear jeans, and go to honky-tonk bars – are honest and genuine. They listen to "real music about real life for real people."[9]

Nonetheless, like their counterparts in the classical world and despite their antipathies, country music fans and performers are engaged in passionate debates about the authenticity of their music. A major question for them has been whether real country music requires the legitimating twang of the pedal steel guitar that was played in the smoke-filled honky-tonk bars where the music is thought to have originated. For many country music lovers, only the whining, poignant sound of the pedal steel can express the deep pain that is the emotional signature of their music. And only the honky-tonk provides the proper beer-soaked ambiance for experiencing that pain.

This nostalgia ignores the fact that what is now known as country music did not actually originate in bars, nor was it first played on the pedal steel guitar. It actually began in fiddling contests that were much like modern-day wrestling matches, pitting good guys against bad guys. Arguably the first country (then known as hillbilly) music star was fiddlin' John Carson, who was recorded in Atlanta in 1923. The pedal steel guitar was an innovation, one of many that occurred during the heyday of the Grand Old Opry, the national performance center for country music, which began its live radio broadcasts from Nashville in 1926.[10] For generations of country musicians, the Opry served as the ultimate arbiter of taste and style. It was on the Opry that Roy Acuff, one of the first great individual stars of the genre, made his debut in 1938. Today that era is looked upon as the model for authentic performance, and Acuff's group is seen as the archetypical traditional country string band. Yet Acuff introduced the droning sound of the Dobro into country, favoring it because of its emotional quality and disguising its novelty by dressing the Dobro player in the most rustic costume of all the band members. Other new instruments, such as the snare drum and the electric guitar, were also introduced into the sound, and it was in this era that the pedal steel guitar became increasingly popular.

This was also the era when the image of the music was redefined. Acuff's own singing style radically broke with tradition: he clowned shamelessly and sometimes burst into tears on stage, in stark contrast to the stoicism of earlier performers. Along with a new emphasis on the artist's expressivity, tobacco-chewing old geezers playing fiddles and wearing suspenders began to be replaced by cowboys decked out in sequins and fancy boots. For an increasingly sophisticated audience, the cowboys' aura of freedom and association with the opportunity and risk of the frontier provided a more appealing image than the backward hillbilly chewing tobacco and guarding his moonshine.

This was especially the case after the great labor migrations of the thirties and forties when the audience for country music moved into the city to find work. Starting in the southwest and then spreading to the rest of the country, exiles from the farms and ranches congregated in rundown bars to lament their vanished rural past while staking a claim for a new identity in the present. No longer rustics, but not yet integrated into the city, the music they identified with evoked loss, nostalgia, resentment, manly honor, and self-pity. In the honky-tonks country music was becoming the music of the new rootless American working class. It articulated the lament of the betrayed wanderer, searching for love and settling for lust, far from home, working hard, drinking hard and fighting hard, wishing for salvation, but without much hope of ever reaching it.

The exemplar of this new style was Hank Williams, the tragic angel of country, who never worked as a cowboy, but always wore a cowboy outfit. Williams spoke directly to the experiences and emotions of his audience. "His heroes are undone by their own desires, tempted by illicit sex, plied with alcohol, rejected by a cooled lover, and left alone bathed in guilt and remorse, groping for eventual reunion with wife, home, and God."[11] Williams died at age 29 in the back of a Cadillac, the victim of his excesses, and thereby became the martyred saint of honky-tonk, a style that reigned supreme until it was threatened by the dominance of rock music in the fifties.

Faced with extinction, country music entrepreneurs responded by softening the harsh sounds of honky-tonk and inaugurating the Nashville sound, with its smoother arrangements, sweeter voices, and extensive use of orchestral arrangements. Lovers of the rough down-home authenticity of honky-tonk derided the new music as a sellout to uptown commercialism, and Nashville practitioners had to work hard to reconcile their new jazz- and pop-influenced style with the demands of hard-core fans. Yet today the Nashville sound is remembered with nostalgia, as new country singers stage glittery extravaganzas that seem, to modern purists, closer to Las Vegas nightclub entertainment than to its down-home roots.

This pattern is an old one. Country music has always been divided between more 'traditional' music and more 'popular' styles, which Richard Peterson calls hard-core and soft-shell. In Peterson's typology, hard-core performers have local accents and sing in nasal tones, often out of meter. They write their own songs about their own lives; their lyrics are concrete, simple, personal; they show a wide range of emotions and involvement when they sing; their music is rough and energetic; their origins are southern; they tend to come from humble families; the men wear working clothes, the women are dowdy, gaudy, or broadly sexual. Their stage presence is informal, friendly, and modest, they tell anecdotes about themselves and connect directly with the audience as if they were their co-workers, family members, or neighbors. Soft-shell music contrasts on every point. The singers' voices are trained, smooth, and synchronized, and they sing with an even beat; the songs are more general in topic and are often sung in the third person; they are written by hired songwriters and fit the media-constructed persona of the singer; soft-shell music is easy-listening; soft-shell performers don't stress their origins, but most have come far from their roots and are nostalgic about them; they remain distant from the crowd and keep their lives private. Above all, they are clearly professional entertainers.

It is usually assumed by dedicated country fans that the hard-core style is the purer, original, and therefore more authentic form, which has been supplanted and corrupted by the commercialized sounds of soft-shell. In this myth, valiant hard-core practitioners struggle to maintain their integrity against mass marketing and commodification. A narrative of original purity and untrammeled expressivity polluted by the marketplace is characteristic of the discourse on authenticity in all popular arts, but history shows a reality that is quite different, and much more complex. The fact is that hard-core sells, no less than soft-shell, and the history of country music reveals that neither is prior, but that there has always been an oscillation between the two, often in the career of a single individual (the archetypical case is Patsy Cline). It also has to be kept in mind that by the 1920s, when country music was first being recorded, even the most rural musicians had listened to popular music on the radio and wanted to emulate what they heard. The Skillet Lickers, who were a very early traditional hillbilly band, hoped to play hot jazz, and were disappointed when they were relegated to the country niche. Other performers of the era had similar ambitions and experiences. Popular genres were never so clear in the past as they now appear to have been in retrospect, and the lines between them were largely a result of marketing decisions by record companies.

But capitalism and niche marketing cannot take all the blame (or praise) for the divisions that exist in country music. Even before the advent of radio and records there were two popular folk genres opposed in a manner roughly equivalent to today's soft/hard distinction. Parlor or domestic music was sung (mostly by women) and consisted of ballads, lullabies, and popular songs. Assembly or frolic music was instrumental; it was performed by men at dances and in public contests. Frolic was the first to be commercially accepted in the mid-1920s; it gave rise to fiddlin' John Carson's recording debut. But the radio formats of the 1930s favored family entertainment and brought back the domestic tradition. The widely held belief that rough, 'male' music is a more authentic country sound is historically incorrect: hard only exists in relation to soft.

All this goes to show that country music, like any commercial product, has adapted to the market. Nashville eventually displaced honky-tonk and barn dances not only because of the threat of rock music, but also because a more urban and sophisticated listening audience was no longer interested in the music that appealed to their ancestors. Raised on the complex arrangements and the sweet voices of popular tunes, fans demanded that their own music keep up with the times. Like every commodity, country music has always had to respond to the changing tastes of its audience and to shifts in production, distribution, and consumption. In modern times, this has meant quite a radical movement away from its original style(s).

Yet if the music is always changing, and if its genealogy is vague and hard to substantiate, and if it has grown ever more distant from its rural roots, how can any country performance today be defined as authentic? The short answer is that all of these questions become immaterial when the focus is on the character of the artist, not on the history of the genre. That is, if *real* country musicians perform the music, then it *is* country music, whatever the instrumentation, orchestration, or venue. Instead of concentrating on history and technique – that is, on a contested genealogical mode of authentication – country music critics and fans have been obsessed with the depth of feeling and spontaneous truth of the performance – the correspondence between outer appearance and inner reality in the creative act of the artist. This was so especially after the onslaught of rock and roll and the rise of the 'countrypolitan' Nashville sound. Within this new smoother genre, "country music is no longer defined by the presence or absence of certain instruments, or by certain performance styles, but instead by a 'feel'. The sum of this 'feeling' allows the performer to claim country roots, sincerity, and loyalty without necessarily having rural origins or a traditional sound."[12]

The romantic emphasis on immediacy, involvement, and personality coincides with a belief among the audience that the true practitioners of hard-core country music are indeed what they portray themselves to be – men and women who could just as well be farmers, truck drivers, construction workers, housewives, or hairdressers. It is their very ordinariness that gives them the capacity to sing heartfelt songs about real life. As Hank Williams put it: "You have to plow a lot of ground and look at the backside of a mule for a lot of years to sing a country song."[13] Romantic identification with the performers also corresponds with a pervasive fear that successful musicians will abandon their roots, fake their feelings, and betray their loyal fans in pursuit of money and mainstream acceptance.

This is the reason why soft-shell country artists (Kenny Rogers for example) are so regularly disparaged by country music enthusiasts as less genuine than hard-core singers (such as Johnny Cash). Soft-shell music is professional, detached, and commercial. Its performers are musicians first, and give no impression that they have ever seen the backside of a mule – or even the handle of a shovel, for that matter. So, although soft-shell country music can make the same claim to *genealogical* authenticity as hard-core, it does not appear to be as intensely lived or personal in its expression, and so is perceived as less genuine in its realization. Rough and ready hard-core performers get credit for expressive authenticity; in compensation, smooth soft-shell performers more easily cross over into easy-listening pop music, and are more likely to succeed there than their hard-core cousins. This means that country performers feel a constant pull toward smoother, more commercially viable styles, as well as the opposite impulse to maintain credibility and retain their audience base by reaffirming hard-core attitudes and values. This tension is intrinsic not only to the country music industry but also, I suggest, to all popular performative subgenres appealing to an audience that is, or thinks it is, oppressed or marginalized. In other words, almost everyone.

An instructive comparison can be made with the blues, which grew from the same roots as country. In both genres songs allude to poverty, hard work, lost love, male freedom, female duplicity, sexual desire, the basic injustice of the world, the inevitability of drinking, suffering, and sin, while offering a faint hope of redemption. Both genres share a similar self-mocking humor, a braggadocio, and a barroom milieu. The archetypical blues club is very much like a honky-tonk bar. It is dingy, dimly lit, smoky, and funky. The drinks on offer are cheap beer and raw whisky. It is in a dangerous neighborhood or on the outskirts of town. The audience is working class and unaware of its own authenticity. Most importantly, like country, authentic blues must be played and sung with full emotional commitment. Neither technical skill nor mechanical adherence to tradition makes for real blues: only the performer's heart and soul matter. The blues is a feeling. You either have it, or you don't. The major difference between country and blues is that only African-Americans can have the real blues feeling, or so it is believed by audiences and, sometimes, by performers.

Because they serve as the location for the music of a marginalized group, blues clubs have much in common with honky-tonks or, for that matter, with any other venue based around an alternative musical genre. Heavy-metal bars, folkie coffee houses, Goth nights, hip-hop performances, raves, all array true believers against the Philistines; all provide the inspiring feeling of belonging to a spiritual elite who worship the same countercultural musical gods and oppose the bourgeois norms. In these liminal 'third spaces' disorder, drunkenness, casual intimacy, unpredictable encounters, and loss of control are permitted and valued as expressions of what the sociologist David Grazian calls a 'nocturnal self' – that is, a more authentic and spontaneous state of being that can bloom when audiences are free from the constraints of the job and the responsibilities of home and family.[14] Thus liberated, spectators can finally 'be themselves'. However, the listener is only expressively 'real' while in the club.

Through their familiar furnishings and the behaviors they elicit, these countercultural third spaces give regular patrons a comforting feeling of belonging to a subculture with more genuine values than the mainstream; a community where people really care about one another, where the authentic expressive self is welcomed, and where everyone is united by a common enthusiasm for music that is believed to be especially deep, heartfelt, and real. Hard-core blues fans and hard-core country fans (and Goth or hip-hop or jazz fans) ignore the souvenirs and monogrammed tee shirts that are sold to transient tourists, and cultivate a sense of collective authenticity based on shared knowledge about what their music *really* is. And, when a club becomes too popular among dilettantes and sightseers, the hard-core fan will move on, looking for a more remote locale and another band that is still real, and known only to the initiates. As Yogi Berra is supposed to have said: "No one goes there anymore. It's too crowded."

Marketing Authentic Performance

The fan's imagination obscures the reality that hard-core music, of whatever genre, is a commercial enterprise. Country music impresarios have always sought out performers who could fit audience stereotypes of what an authentic performer ought to be: southern, working-class, rural, and unschooled. The same is true in the blues genre, where rural, illiterate blacks, preferably blind, have automatic credibility other performers – especially whites – could never hope to match, Within the polarized uptown/down-home, soft-shell/hard-core worldview of the audience, these aspects of biography indicated immediacy and genuineness. For this reason, early Opry performers were presented as rustics with hay in their hair, symbolizing their freedom from the contamination of the city. The pretense was that they just happened to show up on stage, when in fact almost all of them were polished professional musicians living in Nashville – hardly a farm village. How much the audience was taken in by this ploy is hard to say, but any large deviation from the standard was not permitted.

In the 1950s and 1960s the backsides of mules were no longer part of the daily life of either performers or their audiences. This led to a greater emphasis on expressivity, since the historical roots of the music had almost vanished. But feeling does not exist in a vacuum; like rusticity or the cowboy ethos, feeling has to be marked out in a standardized manner to be recognized and accepted as authentic. The sacred everywhere requires its rituals. For example, successful country artists cannot be wholly manufactured in the recording studio; they must play live music and entertain their audiences in person. They have to go on tours, give revealing and intimate interviews to fan magazines, and make themselves readily available to their fans. Ideally, to show they are not snobs, they should speak with rural accents, keep their vocabulary and grammar simple, and talk openly about their personal tribulations. Out of respect for the audience, they must start their performances on time and greet the crowd warmly. The authentic country band dresses in casual clothes or western gear and performs without choreography, giving the necessary appearance of modesty and spontaneity. The atmosphere of an authentic country performance is informal and celebratory; fans call out to the musicians, who answer back. The hometowns of band members are mentioned, and jokes are made about any Yankees in the group. There is talk about the band's latest record releases and upcoming show dates. After the act, artists spend a great deal of time signing autographs and talking to their fans.

When 'countrypolitan' Nashville music arrived, with its smooth, jazzy arrangements and its emphasis on studio recording for a popular audience, it had to fit within the pre-existing symbolic framework of expressive revelation and connection with the core audience, or else lose its authenticity credentials. This meant that highly urban and sophisticated Nashville performers went on tour as much as possible, joked with audience members, and stressed their down-home qualities. But because the Nashville sound was primarily driven by recordings, some adaptations had to be made to accommodate the more impersonal environment of the studio. Publicists emphasized that Nashville recordings were made in a relaxed, collaborative backstage-type atmosphere that is real, like the Opry, not phony and slick, like a synthetic pop record, nor formal and rehearsed, like classical music. The obvious professionalism of the musicians was offset by the assumption that high skill levels are not the result of training, but of natural abilities, which are turned to the service of the spontaneous expression of feelings in music. According to an archetypical story (heard in jazz and blues circles as well) when a Nashville studio musician was asked if he could read music, his reply was "not enough to hurt my picking." The image is of neighborhood musicians who are just ordinary folks, gathered together on the back porch for an evening of unrehearsed fun.

Regardless of variations in musical form or political differences, country and blues audiences, hip-hop enthusiasts, Goths, and all the other hard-core devotees want their idols spontaneously to convey strong and true feelings through their playing, drawing listeners from the mundane into the ecstatic.[15] The artist's performance is expected to be instinctive and unstudied, coming directly from the heart and soul. The audience's belief in the authenticity of the performance is a particularly clear expression of what Erving Goffman has called the modern quest for backstage reality; that is, a reality free of artifice.[16] Like all others searching for the really real, the hard-core fan of any subcultural genre is looking for immersion in a more authentic truth in the hopes of breaking the chains of restricting roles, at least momentarily. This hope motivates the search for the ultimate funky and hidden club, where only the true cognoscenti gather. For the seeker after primal emotional authenticity (Grazian's nocturnal self), the musicians and their retinue who permanently inhabit these sites are believed to have special capacities for immediacy and feeling. They are the gods of the night who destroy the deadening influences of daytime bureaucratic and technical rationalization.

The flattering image of performers as deities of spontaneity and authenticity is not merely a fantasy of fans; it is very likely to be internalized by artists and their entourages as well, who want to be in reality as the fans imagine them. That is, they want to really *live* the music. So performers and those close to them are prone to behave in ways that symbolize their nocturnal anti-establishment character; they may wear unconventional clothing styles, have special ways of speaking, and hold eccentric beliefs. Performers who see themselves at odds with convention and who live lives that embody that self-image are also susceptible to heavy drinking and drug addiction, rejection of stable jobs and relationships, the frantic pursuit of excess, an irregular lifestyle, and the other clichés of rebellion. These are all self-authenticating strategies of individuals who, not content with stimulating others to momentary ecstasy, try to live out in their daily lives the fantasies of their audience.

This tendency of countercultural performers to play out a countercultural identity through self-destructive behavior is increased by a central tension in the romantic image of performative authenticity – namely, that what seems spontaneous to the audience is in fact a standardized act that requires considerable forethought, expertise, and practice on the part of the artist. Furthermore, someone has to lug equipment and set up the stage; management is required to organize trips, rehearsals, and payments. The most spontaneous-seeming performer is locked into at least some degree of bureaucracy: daily drudgery always shadows nocturnal ecstasy. Caught on the horns of this dilemma, artists who have romantic notions about authenticity and performance may be especially inclined to impulse and excess in their daily lives. By yielding to anti-establishment desires and refusing to conform, they demonstrate to others, and, more importantly, to *themselves*, that they are indeed the spontaneous, expressive, emotional individualists they portray themselves to be on stage, despite the technical and commercial requirements of providing the audience with the performance they expect. For idols of authenticity, being really, really real can mean being really, really self-destructive.

Chapter 3

Seeking Authenticity in Travel and Adventure

Real Life is Elsewhere

Musicians aren't the only ones driven to excess in order to prove their authenticity to themselves and others, nor are collectors of primitive art the only ones who trek to remote regions in search of "things that are elemental and ancestral; forces of the landscape and nature rather than artifices of the city and the self."[1] Adventurous, spiritually motivated tourists also want to get off the beaten track and venture deep into dangerous territory where they can test their physical and psychological limits and gain a heightened sense of who they really are. Tourism that promises to take the traveler 'back in time' to places 'untouched by the outside world' caters to the modern desire for self-realization.

A fine example of the tensions and implications of these forms of tourism is provided in a recent account written by the journalist Lawrence Osborne of his trip to the reclusive Kombai people of Papua New Guinea. The tour leader, who resembles "an American backwoodsman of centuries past," promises to take his clients to visit people living "in the last wild place left" who know "little or nothing of modern civilization."[2] To reach their goal the travelers must penetrate an inaccessible and pestilent jungle with few comforts or guarantees of safety. They also have to spend a large amount of money. These sacrifices mentally prepare the travelers for a profound experience. With scary stories of spirit possession and cannibalism in their minds, the tourists venture into the primeval forest accompanied by a train of porters wearing nothing but penis sheaths. After many bug bites and other tribulations, the travelers arrive at the fortified tree-houses of isolated clans who are said never to have seen a white man before.

The locals appear terrified when first approached, but are gradually mollified. The tourists are excited by the emotional intensity of the encounter. As one says: "the look in his eye – it was incredible. I've never seen a look like that." They are also impressed and awed by the apparent naturalness of Kombai who glide soundlessly through the jungle and look at the tourists "with the pity that the naked feel for the clothed." Despite their bad teeth and constant coughing, the Kombai happily laugh and sing with "a ripple of vowels and tones that must have been thousands of years old." Interacting with the friendly but incomprehensible natives while slogging doggedly through the deep jungle, the travelers experience "a shimmering animal joy – not pleasure or excitement – that deepened each day."[3]

Worried about the impact their visit is making on the timeless Kombai, the tourists lament, "nothing remains unknown forever." But the tour leader reassures his charges that the trip will disconcert them more than it will transform the Kombai. "Wasn't that why we had come – not to study an alien culture but to be changed ourselves? Wasn't that what travel used to be all about?" In defense of the notion that travel is all about changing ourselves, the author cites a passage from the 1961 journal of Carleton Gajdusek, who spent considerable time in New Guinea researching tropical diseases and who wrote rhapsodically about the sensuality of the people he was studying. "It is strange," Gajdusek mused, "how mediocre all in civilization seems – art, journalism, philosophy, motion pictures, and even music, whenever I leave or 'come out from' the New Guinea bush. . . . Perhaps it is their great remoteness from the real nature of man and his natural world environment that makes them appear flat and unreal." Like Gajdusek, when the tourists return to civilization they also feel disconnected. "We suddenly realize how weird and noisy our culture is." They consider getting together again and returning to the Kombai, who "will probably be the same. But maybe not."[4]

Osborne's account is more nuanced than many in the genre, and includes postmodernist ruminations about the author's own self-consciousness, references to prior travelers and writers, and reflexive doubts about the purity of the Kombai. But it is stereotypical in the way it portrays local culture as a collection of oddities. The Kombai serve as generic archetypes of primitive otherness – guileless humans at ease in the jungle, with almost no possessions, absolutely different and unreadable. Precisely because they are so opaque, civilized fantasies can be projected on them, such as a belief in their self-sufficient happiness, their naturalness, and their charitable pity for the clumsy tourist. The main point of the story is that the tourists are spiritually both destabilized and revived by their trip to a primeval world where the noise of modern life is absent. Through overcoming the difficulties of travel the tourists overcome their own personal fears and weakness; by experiencing the pristine immediacy of the jungle and its people they experience their own true inner essence.

The narrative of escape and subsequent reintegration at a higher level of awareness and authenticity is darkened with regret over the disappearance of wild places where the disenchanted modern visitor can be revitalized by contact with pristine native people. At the same time, the travelers are stricken by an insidious fear of mistaking a manufactured act for a real interaction. Were the natives really afraid of them at first, and did their later friendly overtures come from the heart, or was it all fake, put on in collusion with the tour guide for the sake of money? Evidently, the search for the pure primitive culture is as quixotic as the search for pure primitive art. The pristine object of desire begins to lose its appeal as soon as it is seen; the savage innocent is polluted by the arrival of the traveler paying to find savage innocence.

Tourists who trek through steaming jungles in New Guinea in search of the last wild people in the last wild place are at the cusp of a much larger phenomenon. By the reckoning of the World Travel and Tourism Council 174 countries consume or invest more than six trillion dollars every year on tourism; in 2005 travel and tourism accounted for approximately 221 million jobs. According to these statistics, tourism is now the largest industry in the world. And, although tourism remains mainly located in the developed Western nations, it is significant that exotic locations like Cambodia and Albania are among the fastest growing destinations, while the 'top 10 travel economies to watch' (Montenegro, China, India, Réunion, Croatia, Sudan, Vietnam, Laos, Czech Republic, and Guadeloupe) are mostly remote and exotic. Furthermore, unlikely countries such as Iran and Sudan are now investing heavily in tourism.[5] All this indicates that the days are rapidly disappearing when a sedate trip to the seaside or a cozy cottage at the lake was sufficient for a vacation. Middle-class people now want much more out of their holidays; and while most do not journey to the remotest jungle in search of the savage, they desire at minimum a taste of something foreign and exciting; if not the primitive, then at least the exotic,[6] if not heroism, at least adventure.

Dean MacCannell, who was the first to turn the study of sightseeing into a respectable scholarly enterprise, persuasively argued that all of the enormous and constantly expanding enterprise of worldwide tourism is a spiritual response to modern fragmentation, instability, and feelings of inauthenticity. As he writes: "Modern man is losing his attachments to the work bench, the neighborhood, the town, the family, which he once called 'his own' but, at the same time, he is developing an interest in the 'real life' of others."[7] From this point of view, every tourist, even the most prosaic, is trying to construct a meaningful cosmos through the accumulation of a multiplicity of authenticated sights (and sounds and tastes) that can then be ordered like postcards in an album. By experiencing, collecting, and collating alternative realities, the tourist personally remakes coherence and mends the world, at least symbolically.

MacCannell probably overstates his case. Certainly, there are different types of touristic experiences, some intense and transformative, but others that are much less so. It is hard to see how leaf-peepers busing through the New England autumn or kids riding a rollercoaster at an amusement park are embarked on a world-mending venture. Nonetheless, most modern students of tourism agree that the "quest for authenticity is essential, if not to all tourism, at least to its more prestigious forms."[8] For instance, the explorer tourists, slogging through the leech-filled jungle to discover (and eventually destroy) the elusive innocence of the savage, would not feel satisfied without experiencing "a close relationship with the necessary and the accidental (which) endows the most routine activity with authentic edge."[9] They expect, and find, rejuvenation when they reach a world as far as possible away from their own, which changes them not only because of its purported primal spiritual power, but also because of the dangers and discomfort they have gone through to reach it. Tourists of this type resemble pilgrims to a holy site, practicing austerities along the way to ensure the validity of their religious experience.

At the opposite end of the spectrum are the vacationers who lounge by the pool with a drink in hand while being waited on by attentive servants. In luxury tourism, guests escape the demands of jobs and relationships by sinking into opulence and excess, drinking too much, eating too much, partying too much. Their experience is expressly marketed as one of infantile regression, often with reference to 'home' and to the caring and nurturing attentiveness of the staff that serve as permissive parents.[10] Meanwhile, the really real 'inner child' is allowed to take over. One step beyond this is the sexual tourist seeking out forbidden pleasures in foreign locales. These predators are the bourgeois descendents of the slumming aristocrats and flâneurs of the turn of the twentieth century who sought out 'real life' in brothels, opium dens, bars, and taverns, mingling with marginalized people who were fantasized to have no pretenses of respectability, no roles to live up to, no honor to maintain, no constraints on their behavior. In these settings, transgressive experiences could easily be purchased.

Though staggering from the bar in order to have paid sex with a compliant child is far from slashing a pathway through a remote jungle to reach untrammeled natives, there are some telling parallels. The explorer communes with the savage tribesman in order to discover his or her own natural uncivilized being; the hedonist is also hoping to free the savage within, but does so by casting off all restrictions on appetite, allowing the impulses to be in command, and so unleashing the authentic 'nocturnal self'. Explorer and hedonist both separate from the mundane in order to find a world that seems more real and spontaneous than their weary and constrained ordinary existences. However, hedonists are quite disinterested in the real lives of the anonymous servants, minions, and sex workers who allow them to indulge their fantasies, while tourist explorers want to penetrate behind the front stage, where behavior is controlled and aimed at impression management, and go backstage, where behavior is relaxed, intimate, and spontaneous. For them, the assumption is that the more informal the setting, the more removed from buying and selling, the more real it is, and the more valuable it is.

Staging Authenticity

Naturally, the tourist industry strives to capitalize on the desire for backstage experience. For instance, the Scottish tourist board recently recognized that tourists were looking for 'real traditional music' performed in informal 'sessions' held in the backrooms of pubs where audience and performers mingle. Ideally, in such a session, playing is impromptu and spontaneous (therefore authentic), and anyone can take part. There is no set schedule of songs, nor any fixed beginning or ending point. Accordingly, the Traditional Music and Tourism Initiative (TMTI) was initiated to sponsor, schedule, and monitor sessions, making an express effort to 'recreate' the experience of stumbling across an informal gathering of musicians. The effort was successful in attracting sightseers, but the nature of the session changed, as the musicians are now paid, a schedule is set, and a certain level of expertise demanded. Like the savage who loses authenticity when he becomes a tourist attraction, musical sessions now have become suspect.[11] We can reliably predict that savvy tourists, aware that the sponsored sessions are scripted, will search for even more obscure sites where musicians meet and play solely for each other, without remuneration. Yet, as soon as tourists arrive, the situation changes, so that even if they do discover a spontaneous music session in Scotland today, they are likely to suspect staging.

Is this really a problem? Some theorists have argued that tourists today do not really want to penetrate appearances to find the spontaneous, unrehearsed truth backstage; instead, they are quite pleased to experience the manufactured world they have seen on television and imagined in their dreams. They don't care if it's all a fake; they expect fakery and appreciate it when it is well done. So long as it's amusing! The impromptu backstage session, just like the generic tropical island complete with sailing boat, rum and coke, hula girls, and palm trees on the beach, is a synthetic media version of paradise, constructed and promoted by advertising; colorful, safe, and pleasurable. This perspective is drawn mainly from the influential work of Jean Baudrillard, who believes that real experience (which tends to be time consuming and boring) has become less engaging than intensified, scripted, exciting representations of reality.[12] As Umberto Eco puts it: "the American imagination demands the real thing and, to attain it, must fabricate the absolute fake."[13]

And yet, this argument is not wholly convincing. Commodification and stereotypical media presentations of a fantasy hyperreal world does not necessarily loosen the hold the ideal of authenticity has on the imagination, or its power to motivate. The island paradise, like the impromptu music session, may be a cliché, but naïve tourists who take the image to be reality are then inspired to seek it out. This entails taking at least some minimal risks, breaking the bonds of the ordinary, and undertaking a genuine journey outward, *elsewhere*. The manipulation of tourists' hopes and dreams by publicists and promoters simply makes their struggle to find authenticity more arduous, more ambivalent, and the results more unsatisfactory. Their hope of discovering something real is not non-existent, it is just doomed.

But perhaps some sophisticated travelers do view commodification and simulation as a game and simply enjoy the play, without any desire for or even any concept of the genuine. This would seem to be the attitude of the cosmopolitan travelers who go to the Out of Africa Sundowner at the Kichwa Tembo Tented Camp in Africa's Serengeti. This event offers well-to-do tourists a fantasy experience based on a Hollywood movie that romanticized the Africa of the twenties. While drinking at a black-tie outdoor bar set up on the spectacular escarpment, the holiday-makers are entertained by attractive Maasai performers who give the spectators free souvenirs and then dance and socialize with them. The songs performed have African origins, but are sung in greatly altered American popular movie versions, while the rhythm is taken from the now-tamed universal rebel music of reggae. According to ethnographer Edward Bruner, the dancers are "the human equivalent of the Lion King.... It is a Disney construction, to make the world safe for Mickey Mouse."[14]

By engaging in this joke-like performance, the tourists are not only provided with a pastiche of black Africa derived from Hollywood movies, they are also encouraged to see through the show and to mingle with the actors. Strangeness is minimized in a comfortable, safe, and familiar cabaret presented in a controlled and friendly environment of ironic self-mockery. This seems a perfect example of Baudrillard's theory of the ubiquity of simulacra. The tourists are quite happy to engage in a parodic constructed reality, transparently manufactured to conform to their most superficial fantasies. But it is noteworthy that the Maasai who dance, laugh, and socialize with the customers do not reveal that the gifts they offer are actually provided by the managing company, it is not mentioned that the servile waiters avoiding eye contact are also 'warrior' Maasai, nor is it made clear that the performers are in fact employees of white tour agencies. The tourists are led to believe that the Maasai are acting on their own behalf, and that their friendliness, humor, and generosity are truly spontaneous. The point is that even if the Maasai dance performance may be enjoyed as a postmodern joke, some deep-rooted desires for a real, felt experience remain.

A different kind of authenticity is sought by tourists interested in history. As the modern consciousness of fragmentation and subsequent nostalgia for the integrity of the past has spread, so has the interest in retracing origins. Tourist attractions have quickly been constructed to gratify this fascination with beginnings. For example, the burgeoning Chinese tourist industry has recently opened up the remote mountainous region of the southwestern province of Guizhou to tourism. The Han Chinese use the term *Miao* (meaning 'sprouts' or 'weeds') to refer to a variety of indigenous groups who live in the mountains inland from the river system. Most of the tourists who have ventured to this faraway place have been from Japan. This is because some Japanese ethnographers have reported that the Miao customs and material culture resemble those of ancient Japan. Guizhou has been publicized as a living museum where Japanese tourists can experience their ancestral heritage.[15] The truth of this claim does not matter. What does matter is that vacationers believe it to be true. As Edward Bruner writes, "to develop a new site for ethnic tourism, it is not necessary to study the ethnic group or to gather local data, but only to do market research on tourist perceptions."[16]

The rapid worldwide growth of historical and cultural theme parks also is another response to the desire for an ethnic/racial/religious/national mooring in a floating world. The first such national park, Skansen, was built in Sweden in the1890s, juxtaposing buildings from different eras and providing Swedes with a living history lesson. Later other European nation-states also began to "materialize the nation" in large-scale theme parks.[17] Now China too has witnessed the building of an enormous Splendid China tourist park in Shenzhen, which, significantly, is the most modern city in China, and the one most transformed by the onslaught of free market capitalism. As one commentator argues, in recreating the glories of the imperial past, the Splendid China Park offers "the calming certainty of a timeless identity" to Chinese disoriented by the rapid changes occurring in their society.[18] It is also significant that abutting Splendid Park is the new China Folk Culture Villages, which contain 'authentic replicas' of the standardized dwellings of 21 of China's 56 officially recognized *minzu* (ethnic) groups, who are portrayed in the brochure as happy participants in the colorful mosaic that is China.

Historical and cultural theme parks, like the collectives they symbolize, require authentication to be convincing. This can be accomplished in several ways. One is popularity. When places and objects are recognized, surrounded, viewed, and revered en masse, the object of veneration is legitimized by the collective act of worship, just as an aboriginal Australian totem is made holy by the communal ritual surrounding it. For cultural and nationalistic theme parks or heritage tourism that aims to rediscover ancestry, authenticity is also ratified by expert testimony, which indicates the significance of otherwise nondescript sites or objects. "This stone marks the exact spot where the general fell." "This is the actual house where the treaty was signed." "This is the spot where your ancestors were born."

Yet there is still room for doubt even when the site would seem to have objective textual and material validation. Edward Bruner shows how complex the problems of verisimilitude can become, particularly in instances of 'authentic reproduction' where it is not the thing itself, but a facsimile, that is on offer, when he charts the development of Abraham Lincoln's childhood home, New Salem Village in rural Illinois. Because the original settlement no longer existed, a simulacrum was built according to the best historical records. Pragmatic and scholarly questions immediately arose as to whether this meant constructing a site that would look credible to modern visitors, or a site that would actually appear as it did in 1830. Pursuing what Bruner calls immaculate authenticity would mean no modern plumbing, no paved roads, and no security system. In the name of comfort and safety (and to attract more tourists) these novelties were permitted. In 1830, the houses were new. When reconstructed, they were artificially aged. In 1830 the site had no trees. Now trees are preserved. These novelties were meant to satisfy tourist expectations of what a traditional rural settlement *should* look like.

Other problems quickly arose, such as how the actors playing the parts of Lincoln's contemporaries ought to dress. In 1936, when the village was still young, the performers wore blue jeans, wool shirts, and leather boots, which clearly marked them off from the guests. Nowadays, many of the visitors wear exactly the same garb, so new items of period clothing have had to be 'discovered' in order to differentiate the actors from the paying customers. Moral issues intruded as well. In the modern family park, some elements of the original village, such as gangs of thugs, and the existence of gamblers and prostitutes, have not been represented. Similarly, in the reconstruction of colonial Williamsburg, slaves were at first not included, then, when political attitudes toward the past changed, they were.[19]

To keep their 'credibility armor' intact in spite of these problems of representation, the managers of reconstructed historical sites try their best to demonstrate that they are not in the business of creating artificial fantasies, but that they are doing their best to stage a genuine version of the real past, as documented and authenticated by experts.[20] There are heated academic disputes about the validity and even the morality of making such claims for places like Williamsburg or New Salem, which must necessarily reach compromises in order to market comfortable, politically correct, touristically appealing, hygienic reproductions of yesteryear. Are these presentations liberating because they permit visitors to supply their own meanings or are they "preparing the way for the new world order of Disney Enterprises" by replacing reality with "a sanitized and selective version of the past?"[21]

Both of these perspectives are correct and both are inevitable. The representation of historical reality is always controlled, to a degree, by those in power who manipulate what is shown, more or less consciously, for their own ends; at the same time, elite control is never total, and onlookers are always active agents who construct their own narratives to make what they see conform to what they think they know about the past and the present. We can usefully ask what these narratives are, how they are disseminated, who holds them, and why. But for the purposes of this book, the basic question is whether the tourists visiting these contested historical sites are looking for authenticity at all, or are they content just to have fun and be fooled.

The answer seems to be that the vast majority of tourists clearly differentiate such sites from playful Disneyesque amusement parks or other tourist sites where authenticity is neither demanded nor expected – except by children who really hope to see Mickey Mouse or Cinderella. In historical theme parks visitors wish to believe that what they are seeing is as genuine as it can be, taking account of modern needs for comfort and safety. In fact, the credibility armor donned by the museum establishment is a direct response to the inquiries and critiques of the customers who keep a sharp lookout for any evident flaws in presentation. It is precisely *because* the staff makes every effort to meet these critiques that the public retains a high degree of faith in the authentic reality of these reconstructed historical and cultural sites. This reflects a shared belief (or hope) that the past provides a solid and reliable base upon which a solid and reliable present can be built. Tourists are not paying to be reminded that history is unstable and contingent.

The Whole Adrenaline Thing

Tourism is an immensely popular way for ordinary people to escape from the everyday, manufacture meaning in their lives, and pursue a more intense reality 'elsewhere'. The alternative reality may consist of trekking to a primitive tribe deep in the jungle, involve a fantasy of reliving the past, or simply mean seeking out a clichéd image of paradise in a luxury hotel. In all cases, what is sought is something not found in daily life, though less adventurous tourists do not want to leave the comfort and security of the mundane behind them. Nonetheless, what is paid for is not the everyday, but a contrast to the everyday, providing a bright moment of difference that casts a glow on the rest of the year. The glow is shadowed, however, because tourists are always worried about the reliability of the stories they are told, anxious about the honesty of their guides, suspicious of the natives' friendship, afraid that seemingly spontaneous actions are actually staged performances, concerned that the servants will cheat them and laugh at them. Pervasive apprehension and cynicism arise because commodification and mediated reality corrode certainty about the spiritual, moral, and even the practical reality of all touristic encounters. As MacCannell writes: "The dividing line between structure genuine and spurious is the *realm of the commercial.*"[22] A fundamental question for the modern tourist is how to keep the exchange of money from tainting efforts to escape from the constraints of daily life.

A characteristic way for modern tourists and seekers to escape from uncertainty about the authenticity of their experiences has been through the stimulation of powerful bodily sensations. Because of their overwhelming and undeniable felt physical reality, such sensations are experienced as existing beyond the corrosion of commercialism. Sexuality, indulgence, or arduous struggle in the jungle, all serve this purpose. For the same reason, many young, educated middle-class Americans are now increasingly finding ways to press themselves to and even beyond their physical and mental limits, intensifying sensations to the maximum. Almost inevitably, their activities are extremely dangerous. The sociologist Stephen Lyng has termed this sort of voluntary high-risk activity 'edgework', and he comments that "the modern consumer confronts a plethora of possibilities for placing himself in harm's way" as indicated in a tremendous surge in the popularity of white-water rafting and kayaking, skydiving, surfing, hang gliding, bungee jumping, mountain climbing, off-road motorcycling, and other extreme avocations.[23] Some edgeworkers have even made the search for risky action into a permanent lifestyle, living like ascetics on the margins of society, sleeping in flophouses, eating cereal for months on end, and working at low-paying jobs in order to have the opportunity to continue testing themselves on untouched ski slopes or riding the big surf. "In such circumstances, in the most majestically indifferent settings on earth, accident and necessity unite under the sign of mortal danger to yield the purest possible encounter with the real."[24]

Nicole Hayes has documented an alternative community of adventurers in Whistler, a chic skiing and mountain biking center in the Coast Mountains of

Canada, north of Vancouver, which simulates the appearance a European alpine village, but with all modern conveniences and without the snooty Europeans. Most of the people who come to Whistler are middle-aged tourists who happily relax in the mass-produced luxury of the resort's ersatz chalets where they are cosseted by a swarm of servants. An entirely different vision of the ideal holiday is held by the self-styled adventure travelers, edgeworkers in training, mostly under 30, who hold most of the menial jobs in Whistler.

These young people, who usually come from the same background as the paying tourists, nonetheless hold them in contempt for their crass materialism, security consciousness, and bourgeois moderation. In contrast, they identify themselves as a special breed, living life to the fullest by practicing both extreme hedonism (excessive consumption of drugs and alcohol, sexual promiscuity, partying for days on end) and the reverse but parallel virtue of extreme asceticism (eating poorly, living communally without heat or hot water, sleeping little). Mostly, they differentiate themselves by their spiritual desire for "a *real* experience" which involves hiking, biking, and skiing in "the pristine, the primitive, the natural, and – the untouched." Above all, they seek "the whole adrenaline thing." This means taking extreme risks; having an 'out-of-body' experience while jumping off an 85-degree hill; risking life and limb fording an icy raging river; mountain biking down a slippery slope where a fall could mean death. The underlying philosophy is to "push the envelope...get out of your comfort zone."[25] For established adventure tourists at Whistler, the value of being extreme is going to the verge of death, and yet surviving because of an ability to focus and keep control under the most frightening conditions. Goading each other into more and more extreme behavior, the young travelers achieve communion with nature, with each other, and with what they believe to be their own authentic inner selves, as well as gaining feelings of power and control over their fates. Experientially, it does not matter that these feelings are illusory (survival in risky sports depends much more on luck than adventurers like to admit, and even the most skilled edgeworkers have a high fatality rate).

Studies have shown that voluntary risk-takers in the United States seek out situations where "the immediate demands of the situation filter out much of the reflexive, social aspect of the self" leaving only the immediate, reactive, and intuitive.[26] The climber working her way up a steep and slippery rock must be completely focused on the moment, paying close attention to the texture of the stone, the shifting of her weight, the sights and smells and sounds of the mountain. The worrisome everyday recedes; she does not think about her job or relationships or other ordinary matters, nor does she worry about how she looks to others, or if she is who she appears to be. All that matters is using all her skills and training to move upward in a situation where death is literally at her fingertips. As she moves, adrenaline rushes stimulate strong physical sensations; her strength increases as her heart beats faster, preparing her for fight or flight. Yet she must maintain command and not allow her emotions to push her toward the bad decision that would plunge her to her death. With every physical and mental capacity strained to the utmost, the moment is painted in lurid colors, like a supersaturated photograph. As one free jumper says, when he leaves the plane "suddenly everything seems so real. Free fall is much more real than everyday life."[27] Or, as the skydiver mantra succinctly puts it: "Eat, fuck, skydive!"[28]

Lyng concludes that in extreme situations edgeworkers "experience a sense of cognitive control over essential objects and a feeling of identity or sense of 'oneness' with these objects." The ineffable feeling of communion and their sense of 'hyperreality' leaves them with deep feelings of personal authenticity, communion, and faith that their 'true' selves control their actions in extreme situations. He outlines the scholarly debate as to whether the edgeworker is (1) escaping alienation through the magical re-enchantment offered by risk (a diagnosis based on the work of Max Weber), (2) embracing a new postmodern mode of disintegrated being in which time and space are imploded in moments of extreme experience (following Baudrillard), or (3) resisting domination by transgressing limits of the body (referring to the later Foucault). Lyng comes down on the side of Foucault, remarking that in the modern world "the need for dramatic action to liberate the self becomes ever more urgent. Playing with boundaries in acts of transgression and transcendence, exploiting limits, and crowding edges may be the sole remaining form of resistance and one of the few possibilities for human agency that can be found in the disciplinary society."[29]

There is something in this, but the Weberian perspective is closer to the truth: edgeworkers are more like religious mystics hoping to achieve ecstasy than they are like political radicals who want to overthrow (or even alter) the system. And, like other religious virtuosos, edgeworkers generally feel something like contempt for lesser mortals who cannot live up to their high standards, that is, those who are overweight, soft, inept, and, worst of all, concerned about their safety and comfort. Furthermore, despite their personal asceticism, edgeworkers are paragons of consumption when it comes to their equipment. Capitalism, as it turns out, is excellent at manufacturing and marketing high-quality skis, mountain bikes, hang gliders, and the other hi-tech equipment the edgeworkers prize. From a Marxist point of view, the antics of edgeworkers simply divert attention away from the more urgent business of analysis and meaningful political action. If the edgeworker has any political affinity at all it is with the simplest forms of anarchism, in which radical individualists desire nothing more than igniting, as one of Lyng's contributors exults, "one free explosion after another, for a new order that's no order at all."[30]

Unfortunately, the same can be said of violent criminals, who are also edge-workers and anarchists in a very real sense, since they too seek the intoxicating sensation of exercising control in chaotic and dangerous situations, as well as the pleasure of igniting "one free explosion after another." Like edgeworkers, violent criminals want to experience the rush of adrenaline and the feeling of being immersed in something far 'more real' than daily life. Like edgeworkers, they can become addicted to these heightened moments and commit brutal crimes for the sake of experiencing intense sensations of hyperreality.[31] There is no doubt about the power of danger and risk to give a vivid sense of signifi-cance to life, but as a way of being it is at best asocial, at worst purely destruc-tive. The superfluous risks taken by edgeworkers (and criminals) indicate the pathos of modern life; they are not a means for its transformation.

Yet it is precisely because edgeworkers are such narcissists that they are the heroes of today, much admired by the press and the public. A successful risk-taker is engaged in a high-wire performance in which actor and act must be totally in synchronization, providing the public with an example of a genuine correspondence between outer and inner, appearance and reality. The perfor-mance of authentic correspondence may be one reason why sports figures are also admired: like edgeworkers, they too appear all of a piece, wholly engaged in the moment due to their physicality and professional responsiveness to the immediacy of an unfolding situation. Because it is a game, sport cannot be faked; a real skill must be actually demonstrated in front of a live audience. Similarly, workers who must cope with violence and the risk of death as a matter of course – policemen, firemen, emergency-room doctors – are media darlings not primarily because of the social good they accomplish, but because of the way their surface and inner being are forced to coincide due to the pres-sure of danger and the requirements of the job. Safecrackers, wise guys, and other criminals are Hollywood heroes for the same reason. While engaged, there is no backstage or front stage; they *are* what they do, demonstrating real skill and taking real risks. There is also a parallel with countercultural musicians who appear to be wholly in the moment while performing, and whose intensity inspires fans to ecstasy and adulation. Edgeworkers, extreme tourists, and other postmodern seekers also want that really real feeling. They are the most enthusi-astic acolytes of the church of authenticity, exemplars of real life inspiring the pale souls stuck in a world saturated with the fake and the simulated.

Chapter 4

The Commodification of Authenticity

Get the Genuine!

When I did a web search for "authenticity" I discovered "Authenticity Consulting" which promises to meet the goals of every employee through stimulating the "authentic participation" of the workers. The brochure of Patrick Henry College in Purcellville, Virginia, proudly proclaims that the school provides an "authentic Christian environment" for devout students. There is an "Authenticity Resort" located 80 kilometers south of Adelaide in Australia. In almost every issue of *The New Yorker*, the Champagne consortium buys full-page ads to remind readers that authentic champagne can only be produced in the Champagne region in France. Similarly, Johnnie Walker announces "In a Crass and Insincere world, Something That Isn't." And who can forget that Coke is "the real thing"?

These claims are a twentieth-century phenomenon. According to Miles Orvell, in the Victorian era, authenticity was not part of the vocabulary of American merchandisers and their clients. Instead, ordinary Americans were mesmerized by the apparently infinite capacity of newly invented machines to make realistic facsimiles of objects that had previously been available only to the very wealthy. The Chromolithograph, for example, produced passable copies of fine artworks that could be easily purchased by anyone. Due to such advances, plebeians could now begin to imitate the upper crust, and they did so with gusto. Manufacturers openly promoted fake goods of every sort as substitutes for expensive originals and consumers proudly piled up these proliferating imitations in a tumult of fabrics, shapes, textures, gee-gaws, and bric-a-brac. In this exuberant aesthetic "imitation became a central category, not merely endured, but exulted in."[1]

The explosion of shameless copying occurred just as the highly efficient American factory system began to churn out an overwhelming surplus of manufactured goods. To absorb this flood, the populace had to be convinced "that, first of all, there was *enough* for everyone, that in fact there was *more than* enough, that indeed there was *so much* that it must be very natural, very easy, and almost a God-given right, to own things."[2] Despite Puritanical inhibitions, this did not prove to be very difficult. In fact, conspicuous consumption has always been insidiously appealing to Americans. This is because, in this egalitarian, individualistic, and fervently capitalistic society, there are no ascribed hierarchies of authority, no aristocracy, no ancient origins to point to. The main way for people in the United States to distinguish themselves has always been through the purchase, accumulation, and display of possessions. All this stuff furnishes what has been called an 'identity space', that is, "a sum of products configured into an arrangement that expresses what I am."[3] (Daniel Miller calls this process 'objectification'.[4]) The paradox of objectification is that the individual's *inner being* is both experienced and revealed by means of the *external objects* it chooses (or disdains) to surround itself with. As this occurs, reality becomes self-consciously *mediated* and no longer *immediate*.

This process, which has existed ever since human beings began to manufacture their own cultural reality – that is, ever since human beings could be defined as human – has been transformed and accelerated under present conditions, particularly in the United States, where the fantastic quantity of things made possible by capitalism has stimulated an equally fantastic proliferation of optional identities. At the same time, individuals have become more and more anonymous and isolated and therefore more anxious about who they are – an anxiety heightened by the multiple possibilities available to choose from. These circumstances, according to Jean Baudrillard, have led to "a proliferation of myths of origin and signs of reality; of second-hand truth, objectivity and authenticity. There is an escalation of the true, of the lived experience."[5] To feed the hunger for the really real, the media fabricates 'absolute fakes' that appear more brightly colored, vivacious, and compelling than the factual world itself. This transposition is obvious when people talk about their experiences of an earthquake or love affair or bank robbery and say it was so vivid that it was "like a movie." Evidently, the most powerful references available today are images from the cinema. When the external world has been so invaded and colonized by the media, the question of 'what is really real' can no longer be answered with any confidence by referral to Holy Writ, or other traditional sources of conviction.

In an environment where movies have become bigger than real life and more convincing than the Bible, the internet has become the main engine for consumption, giving marketers the capacity to trace all dropped cookies back to their crumbling points of origin. It is now possible for a merchandiser to specify (and motivate) the preferences of each consumer, and to provide a whole panoply of goods and services she is likely to buy. The message is: A whole world is there *just for you* – if you can afford it. With enough money to spend, the depleted self's desire for recognition can be met, and whatever reality that self can imagine (or has been led to imagine), can be had – for a price. Or, if the fantasy is too expensive in real life, an imaginary identity can be tried on and then shed like a set of clothes in one of the multiplayer virtual universes that now exist online. Within this commodified and mediated environment, it seems that there are no preset limits, no naturalized roles one is required to assume, and no preconditions. Identity depends on what you choose to buy and display in order to represent yourself to others and to yourself. In contrast, in what are called traditional societies, roles were prescribed, and self-created identity spaces were few, yet 'everyone knew your name'. Culture existed, and persons existed in it, by it, and for it, without alternatives.

The modern extreme of self-construction through the consumption of goods and the manufacture of personalized virtual realities, which has reached its apogee in the computer revolution, began with a watershed event in marketing that occurred around one hundred years ago. It was then that huge department stores began to blur the contrast between elite and commoner. These new mass-market stores offered vast and appealing arrays of machine-made merchandise under one roof, attractively arranged in categories and available for all to see and perhaps to buy. As Daniel Boorstin writes, in these democratized "palaces of awakening desire . . . the consumer now was being persuaded not merely to become a customer but to join a consumption community. He was being offered something that was not just for him but for everybody like him."[6] Advertising in the mass market made everyone a member of multiple consumption communities, replacing, or at least providing alternatives to, more traditional fixed forms of collective and personal identity, thus allowing people to define themselves not by who they were, or who they knew, but by what they owned and how they displayed it.

This transformation occurred just as the first naïve thrill of buying, accumulating, and displaying a hodge-podge of flamboyant imitations was beginning to pall. Faced with an increasing number of manufactured goods and the potential for constructing an infinity of identity spaces, buyers began to realize that membership in vague communities of consumption did not provide them with either the respectability or the solidity they craved. The upwardly striving middle classes now wanted guarantees of the cultural value of their purchases, and sought instruction about what to buy and how to present both their acquisitions and themselves in society. Genteel opportunists were quick to provide popular guidebooks to taste and etiquette that were the precursors of the how-to-do-it manuals that continue to flood American bookstores. With this development, the golden days of unreflective imitation and exuberant ersatz were on the wane, displaced by anxious self-consciousness about the relationship between consumption and identity.

The Wasp upper crust in the United States strenuously sought to insulate itself from the status-climbing middle classes by the cultivation of an elite aesthetic style. By the end of the nineteenth century, good taste, signaled in the collection of art objects purchased from the accepted European centers of culture, had substituted for mere wealth in the self-definition of the select few seeking distinction in a progressively anonymous mass society. As Madame Merle remarks in Henry James' *Portrait of a Lady*:

> What shall we call our 'self'? Where does it begin? Where does it end? It overflows into everything that belongs to us – and then it flows back again. I know a large part of myself is in the clothes I choose to wear. I've a great respect for *things*! One's self – for other people – is one's expression of one's self; and one's house, one's furniture, one's garments, the books one reads, the company one keeps – these things are all expressive![7]

At the same time as the elite exhibited their taste by the collection and exhibition of refined and unique foreign *objets d'art*, American workers kicked industrial production into higher and higher gear, creating an unprecedented abundance of objects that had no pretense whatsoever of being either refined or unique. By the time production stopped in 1927 over 15 million model T Fords, all almost identical, had been built. Meanwhile, Ford's pioneering use of the assembly line and the influence of efficiency experts in the workplace accelerated the deskilling of American labor, making workers feel more and more like indistinguishable cogs in a vast and impersonal production machine. Reacting to the dehumanizing effects of mass (re)production and the rationalization of labor, the American general public increasingly strove to achieve some kind of secure identity space through the consumption and display of objects radiating authenticity, but standing in contrast to the Europeanized aesthetic pretensions of the snooty upper classes.

To meet the demand, mass advertisements began to promote "a paradise in which things were more real than in our everyday world."[8] As early as 1908 ads for Coke earnestly exhorted consumers to "get the genuine." This is only one example of manufacturers' efforts to persuade buyers that their brand was more natural, more located in history, or more pure, or more real, than anything

55

their competitors had to offer. Cigars from Cuba were the most genuine of all cigars, Hires Root Beer had "real root juices," and so on. Consumers who had the wherewithal could now surround themselves with products loudly proclaiming themselves to be real, true, and pure, and by doing so display and confirm the value of their own objectified identities.

The Dialectic of Authenticity and Imitation

As advertisers attempted to capitalize on popular disillusionment with the mechanical world of factory production by making excessive claims for product authenticity, a new generation began to resist Madame Merle's frank avowal of the mutual interdependency between the self and the objects that surround, protect, decorate, and exemplify it. Henry James' protagonist Isabel answers Madame Merle's soliloquy angrily: "Nothing that belongs to me is any measure of me; every thing's on the contrary a limit, a barrier, and a perfectly arbitrary one!"[9] In her protest, she expressed her repugnance for the specific conditions of modern capitalism which transform the external universe of things into an infinite array of goods and services, all available for purchase by anyone with money, all advertised as authentic and desirable, all therefore suspect as fake and detestable. Because of the implication of self-betrayal in the consumption and display of goods that have been produced and promoted for commercial purposes, it became more and more difficult for Americans to realize their identities unreflectively through objectification. Instead, like Isabel, some began to think and hope that there must be a deeper truth that was being stifled by the encrusted weight of possessions.

Many of the most influential artists and designers of the period were influenced by the dream of an inner reality hidden beneath the glittering materialistic surface of American life. To approach that deeper truth, some wedded American expertise with machines to the craft tradition hoping to produce an art that was uniquely American: artisanal, individualistic, true to itself and yet democratically available to all. In architecture, this ideal was expressed by transparently revealing the inner character of natural or constructed materials in order to achieve what Frank Lloyd Wright called the spiritual dimension of form. In photography, Edward Weston praised the camera as a machine that could produce aesthetic images "more real and comprehensible than the actual object."[10] Yet, Wright's quintessential American buildings became status symbols for the wealthy, while the power of the camera to infuse vitality into images was quickly appropriated by advertising. It was during this period that avant-garde artists, disillusioned by the commodification of creativity, gradually entered "the realm of aesthetic irony" by embracing postmodern parody, pastiche, and artificiality.[11]

But most ordinary consumers did not pursue this option. Like museum-goers who still believe, in spite of all evidence to the contrary, that art expresses the true, the good, and the beautiful, most Americans continued to believe in personal authenticity, though it became harder and harder to find and define in the onslaught of advertisements and promotions of 'the genuine' that were becoming characteristic of modern life. So, when rampaging commodification and expanding mediation made the relationship between external objects and personal identity ever more precarious and fraught, some Americans decided to step away from the outside world altogether. They followed the lead of tran-scendentalist philosophers like Ralph Waldo Emerson and looked for the truth *in* themselves, hoping to discover a transpersonal spirit hidden beneath veils of egoism and materiality.

Introspection, in the absence of recognized and secure connections to place and position, and in the absence of an accepted external model for, and verifi-cation of, authentic spiritual states, had a predictable outcome. Like the edge-workers described in the last chapter, seekers tended to believe that their inner states of attraction and repulsion, hope and fear, desire and contempt, were the only reliable revelations of the really real, rooted in the authentic emotional core of their selves.[12] However, these desires and aversions remained wholly abstract unless and until they were realized in the concrete universe of things. So, although commodification and the influence of the media rendered the external universe suspect and turned the gaze inward, the material world still beckoned – as it always has- as the location in which an objectified self-identity could be expressed and collectively validated. The difference between now and then is that in the past the solidity of the external world of things was unques-tioned, while in the present it is *known* to be contingent, manufactured, and manipulated. This means first of all that the objective world is regarded with unparalleled uncertainty. It also means that there is the new possibility of pur-chasing an objectified identity space that is different from and more expressive and convincing than whatever already exists. And so consumption has become a way to clutch at the chimera of a genuine and compelling reality that always slips out of reach because there is always another, potentially even more satisfying and convincing reality up for sale.

According to the philosopher Alasdair MacIntyre this pattern is so pervasive that the dominant philosophy of our time has become what he calls 'emotiv-ism', i.e., "the doctrine that all evaluative judgements and more specifically all moral judgements are *nothing but* expressions of preference, expressions of attitude or feeling, insofar as they are moral or evaluative in character."[13]

The sole rationale for any action, from this perspective, can only be: "I like it" or "I don't like it." An authentic action, therefore, must be the direct and imme-diate response to spontaneous feelings expressed in preferences. In this utilitarian faith there is no ultimate meaning to be found beyond knowing and pursuing what feels good *to you*, and knowing and avoiding what feels bad *to you*. Of course, the pursuit of authenticity through realizing one's felt preferences can be most directly expressed through consumption. In other words, commodified and media-saturated consumption has expanded to fill the void created by deep suspicions about the authenticity of commodified, media-saturated consump-tion, creating "a culture forever wedded to a dialectic between authenticity and imitation."[14] In our present-day culture, emotivism has become the conceptual engine of capitalism.

The expansion of the objectified domain of manufactured goods and of media influence in America and the ambiguities of the pursuit of authenticity within that domain has been characteristic of late modernity everywhere, but has naturally taken different trajectories according to cultural context and class position. As noted earlier, in the American setting, during the late nineteenth and early twentieth centuries many members of the American aristocracy, threatened by middle-class pretensions, sought to differentiate themselves from the vulgar masses and authenticate their elite status by accumulating art and other precious objects from the cultural centers of Europe, which were con-sidered to be far superior to the provincial products of the United States. By aligning themselves with the supposedly original and authentic high traditions of the European past, they set themselves apart from their rootless immigrant countrymen.

Financially unable to pursue the same project, less wealthy Americans responded by becoming connoisseurs of whatever popular arts and artifacts were available and affordable in the neighborhood marketplace. This was the beginning of the widespread American mania for 'collectables' such as commemorative coins, Barbie dolls, barbed wire, comic books, model racecars, or anything else that can be rescued from the rubbish heap of disposable goods proliferating everywhere. Avid collectors certify their found objects as 'genuine limited editions', put them in sequence with others of the same ilk, and display the whole assemblage proudly as an expression of personal taste, expenditure, and perseverance. Following the same impulse, other Americans involved themselves in folk arts and historical reproductions, repudiating high European art by waxing nostal-gic for the lost simplicity of the American past and striving to recapture the essence of what remained. The burgeoning appreciation of handmade objects inspired another very American phenomenon: the omnipresent 'do-it-yourself' hobbyists who firmly believe that despite any rough edges and uneven legs, a table hammered together in the garage workshop is better (that is, more authentic) than a mass-produced version because it has been produced at home (where a man can be himself) by a specific (real, genuine) individual.

Who Buys What in the Marketplace of the Soul?

But perhaps the most interesting and significant twist in the dialectic between authenticity and imitation occurred in recent years with the rise of a new class of American consumers who have heavily influenced the larger culture. These are the highly educated professionals the journalist David Brooks has entitled the bohemian bourgeoisie (bobos).[15] Their style of objectification is directly correlated to their anomalous class position. In the latter part of the twentieth century this well-educated, hard-working, and ambitious new class replaced (or at least challenged) the old hereditary Wasp aristocracy.[16] Their ascendancy was based primarily on intellectual ability; they attended the best schools, studied hard, excelled, became professionals, and succeeded (at least temporarily) in an open-ended meritocracy. In principle, their elite status did not derive from heredity or personal connections, but from continuous achievement in a fluid, risky, and fiercely competitive economy. As Brooks has described them, the bohemian bourgeoisie combined the rebellion and creativity of bohemians with the monetary success and conservativism of the bourgeoisie. "This is an elite that has been raised to oppose elites. They are affluent yet opposed to materialism. They may spend their lives selling yet worry about selling out."[17]

The unlikely blend of countercultural values with economic power resulted from shifts in the economy during the 1970s and afterwards away from factory production and toward service industries and businesses based on the creation of knowledge and dissemination of information. These types of businesses (and others influenced by their now-dominant paradigm) focused on innovation and favored a lack of hierarchy and an informal, playful atmosphere in the workplace. Management in these new industries, searching for novel ways to make a profit in a rapidly evolving marketplace, typically spewed out countercultural slogans about 'thinking outside the box' and habitually praised misfits, artists, and rebels. As Brooks wrote, "the dirtiest word in the corporate lexicon is *mainstream*; every company in America seems to be an evangelical enterprise rocking the establishment."[18] Within this ostensibly antiauthoritarian context, values of travel, learning, adventure, self-discovery, and personal authenticity were touted; corporate heads presented themselves as spiritual gurus whose main objective was furthering the creativity and expressivity of their employees.

Boredom, drudgery, and conformity were publicly detested. At the same time, jobs in this sector were notoriously insecure due to the dreaded specter of outsourcing. Workers were expected to be available '24/7' and to drop their personal commitments at any moment in order to keep jobs that were supposed to be fun and self-enhancing. In this internally contradictory setting, ambiguity about work, about identity, about the social world, became pervasive character traits.

When employed, the bohemian bourgeoisie were very well paid, and could afford to construct an objectified identity space that expressed their ambivalent positions as establishment rebels. To affirm their distinctiveness and counter-cultural status, and to provide themselves with feelings of connection so markedly absent in their work lives, they took a unique approach to consumption and authenticity: "the new elite disdains all the words that were used as lavish compliments by the old gentry: delicate, dainty, respectable, decorous, opulent, luxurious, elegant, splendid, dignified, magnificent, and extravagant. Instead the new elite prefers a different set of words, which exemplify a different temper and spirit: authentic, natural, warm, rustic, simple, honest, organic, comfortable, craftsmanlike, unique, sensible, sincere."[19] For example, where once smooth and silky texture denoted status, for the new elite roughness became stylish; even bread had to be grainy, sugar unrefined. Similarly, handmade or exotic items had an aura of authenticity that was prized by the new elite. All were reckoned to be more primitive and more pure, therefore more authentic, therefore good.

Industrial-looking objects were also favored for their aura of the genuine: stainless steel regulation prison toilets, costing ten times the standard, became a fad in stylish homes; gold Rolex watches could be purchased easily (if one had the money) but in 2001 there was a five-year wait for more authentic-looking steel versions.[20] The new elite was drawn to every sort of utilitarian item of professional quality, such as upscale hiking gear, sports utility vehicles, and kitchen equipment. "Only vulgarians spend lavish amounts of money on luxuries. Cultivated people restrict their lavish spending to necessities."[21] The new elite especially desired apparently inexpensive ordinary objects that were actually made specifically for them (or that seemed to be), and that demonstrated their down-home credentials while also revealing their taste and wealth in subtle ways discernible only to a select few. This 'narcissism of small differences' meant that a simple tee shirt could cost $300 or more. The distinctions marking it off from a cheap tee shirt from Wal-Mart were miniscule, but were identifiable by cognoscenti. The owner of the expensive/ordinary tee shirt thereby gained membership in a small club of those who, like him, were studiedly modest, but still knew real quality when they saw it.

Advertisers also successfully marketed other stereotypical indicators of genuineness. For example, they realized that products associated with a particular location were more valuable because they fed into taken-for-granted assumptions about the authenticity of origin. Swiss watches and Thai silk sold better and cost more than products of exactly the same quality from elsewhere. Items from the past were more valuable, even if the past was very recent, because such items radiated an aura of genealogical authenticity, and so were especially desirable. And, of course, it had long been recognized that a testament to the value of products by a trusted individual was a route to higher sales. If the person testifying was believed to be stating her sincere preferences, her word was trusted.

But the marketers selling to the new elite found that anti-establishment professionals were very cynical about the veracity of paid advertisements. Instead, they trusted expert local enthusiasts ('alpha consumers' or 'mavens') who were personally involved in researching, trying, and buying new products in order to display their own good taste and status as members of the fashion vanguard. These 'connoisseurs of consumption' sometimes even became paid sales staff themselves, such as the elegant *karisuma* (charisma) shop assistants hired to influence customers in Japan. However, when this occurred they began to lose their credibility, since now they were being paid for what had previously been spontaneous. In the language of marketing, buzz then became hype.[22] Buzz is defined as spontaneous excitement leading to the contagious spread of chatter about a product and a boom in sales. Hype is the commercialized version of buzz, The aim of modern marketing is to use hype to generate buzz, which requires disguising the marketer's manipulated creation of fake enthusiasm. Or, publicists can discover what is generating buzz and jump aboard. This strategy runs the risk that commercial involvement, if noticed, will immediately make genuine buzz seem like fake hype. The contradiction faced by publicists is the same one faced by tourists, artists, collectors, fans, and other seekers after the genuine, that is, to try to reconcile authenticity with commodification.

The best option to resolve (or disguise) this contradiction is to locate alpha consumers and subtly persuade them to try out new products. This can be achieved by using ever more sophisticated computer tracking methods to find and manipulate potential trendsetters, turning their enthusiasm into a marketing tool. If these efforts succeed, and hype is magically transmuted to buzz, then those who look to alpha consumers for inspiration will buy whatever they see their expressive idols wearing, using, listening to, or watching. This means that products valued by trendsetters because of their quirky distinctiveness quickly become mass marketed, old hat, uncool, and out of fashion. Fashion mavens then come up against the Yogi paradox mentioned earlier ("Nobody goes there anymore. It's too crowded") and restlessly move on, in a never-ending cycle of enthusiasm, appropriation, imitation, and exhaustion. This process, in which a craving to be recognized as unique leads to conformity and an obsession with style, is a powerful force in maintaining a high rate of conspicuous consumption among Americans anxious to objectify their self-identities as authentic individuals who stand out from the masses and are always on the cutting edge.

Merchandisers successfully catered to the anxious new professional's desire for distinction and recognition in other ways as well. An ever-expanding proliferation of choices (at the time of writing Snapple has 50 different flavors) was a marketing strategy that allowed individuals to develop comforting 'tastespaces' they believed were unique to themselves. These tastespaces could also be created by computers that tracked purchases, correlated them, and then formulated options tailored to each individual consumer's preferences. Pursuing the same goal, upscale stores organized themselves to look like spontaneous flea markets, with enormous ranges of products open for inspection by shoppers who enjoyed seeking out and discovering for themselves that special something which cried out "that's me." For example, Estée Lauder markedly increased sales by removing glass counters and letting customers browse and try out products without any intervention. Marketers focused on the lucrative new elite consumer thereby attempted to turn the onerous chore of shopping into a therapeutic expression of self-affirmation, choice, and control in a world that was increasingly perceived as anonymous, impersonal, and chaotic.

According to this model of consumption practices, shopping areas with an informal, non-mechanical, personalized look give customers the sense of entering a friendly informal spot, neither work nor home, where they can socialize without commitment. A spatial consumption community lacking any significant content besides shared taste was desirable for the highly mobile and educated new professionals who were trained to value their own self-actualizing autonomy and uniqueness above all.

> [I]ncreasingly distrustful of any authority, political or moral, that would constrain their freedom of choice... they also want a sense of community and the good things that flow from community, like mutual recognition, participation, belonging, and identity. Community has to be found elsewhere, in smaller and more flexible groups and organizations where loyalties and memberships can be overlapping, and where entry and exit entail relatively low cost.[23]

These new low-involvement, highly transient communities are places like coffee shops, upscale health clubs, new-style bookstores, and other casual 'third spaces' where a variety of goods and services are provided and an atmosphere of informality prevails, so that customers can just 'hang out' in a space that is both homey and anonymous at the same time.

The consumption attitudes of the professional elite consumer soon filtered into the mainstream value system, dominating marketing there as well, at least among an urban, upwardly striving clientele. Even Burger King, the bastion of industrialized fast food, proudly proclaimed, "Sometimes you gotta break the rules." But probably the best corporate example of the influence of the bohemian bourgeoisie is Starbucks, which made a fortune by producing Americanized versions of Milanese espresso bars. Starbucks works very hard to offer its customers an experience more involving than just drinking a cup of coffee. As its founder, Howard Schultz, explained: "The companies that are lasting are those that are authentic. If people believe they share values with a company, they will stay loyal to a brand."[24] In pursuit of this aim, Starbucks developed a policy of changing décor from one shop to the next, giving each a different, unique, ambiance, providing the appearance of creative distinctiveness so valued by the bohemian bourgeoisie. But while different, they were also all comfortingly alike. Each was decorated in inviting earthy hues; customers were always seated at small tables which test marketing had found provided a desirable sense of intimacy; there was always a supply of seemingly handmade wicker baskets of newspapers; coffees were given exotic Italian-sounding names (a double espresso with milk was called a doppio macchiato) that appealed to those in the know, or who wanted to be in the know. Like members of the new professional class, Starbucks' workers were called 'associates'. They owned stock in the company and were expected to be committed, enthusiastic, and cheerful. Above all, they were supposed to believe wholeheartedly in the value of their product, and to convey that belief to the customers.

However, Starbucks' studied efforts to appear different, casual, and genuine, combined with its aggressive absorption of local coffee shops worldwide, soon made it the target of angry protests. By trying so hard to give an impression of authenticity, to some it became a symbol of modern inauthenticity, far more offensive than MacDonald's, which has no pretensions of being anything other than an efficient, cheap, and clean fast-food venue. This reactive ideology has been appropriated as a political platform which proclaims that real Americans are not the over-educated, ironic, conflicted, affluent, secular bohemian bourgeoisie who sip café latte or doppio macchiato; instead, they are the humble, plain, down-home folks who unselfconsciously wear baseball hats and tee shirts with product labels on them, vacation in the Ozarks, shop happily at Wal-Mart, contentedly munch white bread and baloney, slurp instant coffee, drive an old Ford truck, listen to country music, work hard for a living, know who they are, believe in God, love America, and vote Republican. According to political analyst

Thomas Frank, the conflation of consumption practices and character means that class divisions have now become "primarily a matter of *authenticity*, that most valuable cultural commodity. Class is about what one drives and where one shops and how one prays, and only secondarily about the work one does or the income one makes."[25]

However, the populist blowback against bohemian bourgeois attitudes has not given pause to other entrepreneurs who have cashed in on upwardly striving middle-class American anxieties about identity and a deep-seated yearning for convincing objectifications of the really real. As advertising consultants David Lewis and Darren Bridges note:

> For many New Consumers the purchase of products and services has largely replaced religious faith as a source of inspiration and solace. For an even larger group, their buying decisions are driven by a deeply rooted psychological desire to develop and enhance their sense of self. Their choices are shaped by those core constructs from which identity and esteem are formed.

Consumption of various forms of commodified authenticity has provided these anxious buyers with feelings of autonomy, control, community, as well as feelings of distinction, status, and self-actualization in a risky and anonymous society. There is a hidden psychic price tag, as pervasive mediation eats away at all unreflective immediacy, leading to more and more consumption in order to fill the inner void. But whatever its personal costs, therapy through consumption has been very good for capitalism, since the cure never ends; there is always something new, something cool, something different and more desirable to be purchased, used up, thrown away, and replaced by a more exciting, trendy, and self-enhancing version. Bridges and Lewis conclude: "consumption begets more consumption until it becomes both a compulsion and a way of life. *The Soul is the Marketplace – **The Marketplace is the Soul**.*"[26]

Chapter 5

Authenticity and the Self

Marketing Feeling

As mentioned in the last chapter, the dominant trope for personal authenticity in modern America is emotivism – the notion that feeling is the most potent and real aspect of the self. People in non-modern societies would have found this strange. Living in a more integrated, less media-saturated world, they generally were not interested in exploring or heightening their feelings. Instead, emotions were mastered in order to live up to the roles imposed by religion and society. For example, among the Pukhtun of northern Pakistan, men concealed all feeling behind stoic faces so as not to offer opponents any advantageous evidence of a man's inner states.[1] The Yanomamo Indian warriors put on a fierce expression to give themselves the courage to fight their many enemies,[2] while in Bali a perpetual smile hid feelings of fear and sadness.[3] In the Court of France's Louis XIV emotions were a resource to be controlled and strategically deployed, never revealed without careful monitoring. As the courtier La Bruyère attests in his memoirs: "A man who knows the court is master of his gestures, of his eyes and his expression; he is deep, impenetrable. He dissimulates the bad turns he does, smiles at his enemies, suppresses his ill-temper, disguises his passions, disavows his heart, acts against his feelings."[4]

Today we are likely to think such mastery and role-playing is self-destructive and fraudulent. Instead, we want to *discover* and *express* our essential selves in rapturous church services, in charged therapy sessions, in risky sports, in intense personal relationships, and in the clubs and nightspots where the impulsive 'nocturnal self' is encouraged to emerge. The inclination toward a spontaneous mode of expressive self-revelation correlates with the collapse of reliable and sacralized institutional frameworks that once offered meaning and succor.[5] Cut away from the stability of an integrated community and subject to the instrumental, impersonal, and pitiless demands of the market, individuals struggle to find satisfying and convincing ways to authenticate themselves. Under these circumstances, private feeling is likely to be thought more real than public role-playing. The content of the self then consists of personal preference based on subjective desires and revulsions. The main thing is to be sure one's preferences actually do express one's truest desires, not cultural conditioning or parental moralizing. To avoid self-delusion, what is required is 'getting in touch with the inner child' – that is, with the genuine and spontaneous emotional forces of attraction and repulsion existing beneath socialized roles and customary behaviors.

This is not as simple as it seems at first glance, since our emotions are actually ambivalent and often self-contradictory; even choosing between chocolate and vanilla ice cream can be complicated. With more complex and intense feelings, looking deep within may lead to the unpleasant and perhaps unacceptable discovery that we simultaneously love what we detest and detest what we love, or find ourselves taking pleasure in pain and feeling misery in joy. So when we do get in touch with our real preferences, they may be conflicting, incomprehensible, overwhelming, and frightening. To put it another way, before we try to get in touch with our inner child, we ought to recall what infants are really like.

Furthermore, turning inward to discover one's true inclinations has become increasingly difficult as emotions themselves have become marketable items. This occurred in the latter part of the twentieth century as the boundary between workplace and home became increasingly blurred. Until then (and still often today), expressive authenticity was mainly to be found in the home, the "haven in a heartless world,"[6] where, ideally anyway, mothers loved their children for 'who they are' not for what they accomplish, and where breadwinners could just 'be themselves'. According to the traditional division of emotional labor, women as homemakers had special access to the intimate realms of feeling that are the hallmarks of expressive authenticity. But as the economy shifted and women increasingly filled jobs in sales and service, the gendered restriction of emotion to the home was extended into the workplace. Female workers were expected not only to do their jobs, but also to present a warm and friendly face to customers.

This trend rapidly spread to previously purely instrumental and traditionally masculine service jobs. Employees were expected to offer customers stereotypically feminine expressions of acceptance, sympathy, and nurturance. The gas station attendant who once simply wiped the windscreen and pumped gas became 'Mr Goodwrench' who supplied 'service with a smile'. As a result of this shift, feelings that were once private began to "fall under the sway of large organizations, social engineering, and the profit motive."[7] In service and sales professions, which are more and more the norm, the worker is constantly required to wear an expression of welcome, enthusiasm, charm, and seductiveness. Emotions outside this range are not part of the job description. For example, Starbucks' employees are not only expected to *look* attentive, eager, and warm. They are expected to *be* attentive, eager, and warm.

The psychic consequences of manipulating one's feelings in the service of the corporation are outlined in Arlie Hochschild's research on airline stewardesses who were required to project a warm, nurturing, and sexy aura to their customers. To accomplish this goal, the workers generally used one of two possible acting techniques. Some of them simply performed their parts on the surface, without any effort to stimulate concordant inner feelings. The price for this was cynicism and burn-out as a result of the constant effort to smile. Others followed the company line and actively tried to convince themselves that they truly wanted to be nurturing, seductive, and charming to their sometimes obnoxious or exasperating customers. Rude passengers were reconceptualized as children needing care; soothing irate drunks was interpreted as helping the weak and needy, like a nurse or teacher.

By investing themselves in the emotional labor of their job, these workers avoided the conscious inner split suffered by those who stayed on the surface. However, the psychological consequences were even more severe, due to the cultural assumption that heartfelt and spontaneous emotional expressivity constitutes the core of the authentic self. Therefore, when the stewardess tried her best to feel the emotions required by her job, she had to conceal her management of her expressivity from herself, for fear of turning her deepest reality into a thing to be manipulated. The result was profound confusion about identity. As Hochschild concluded:

> When the product – the thing to be engineered, mass-produced, and subjected to speed-up and slowdown – is a smile, a mood, a feeling, or a relationship, it comes to belong more to the organization and less to the self. And so in the country that most publicly celebrates the individual, more people privately wonder, without tracing the question to its deepest social root: What do I really feel?[8]

Ecstatic Religion and Improvised Style

Some escapes from this condition are possible. One is through an inward journey toward spiritual revelation. This pathway is manifested most spectacularly in the rapidly expanding 'world affirming' charismatic religions which are the fastest growing branches of Christianity in the United States.[9] Similar annunciations have blossomed elsewhere throughout the modern world outside of the Christian tradition. To name just a few: the multitude of 'New New' religions in Japan, the Ciji movement in Taiwan, and the international Sai Baba movement.[10] Despite many theological differences, these religions all attempt to reconcile the modern quest for a felt emotional truth with their doctrinal precepts. To accomplish this goal, the charismatic leader facilitates the believers' immersion in an ecstatic collective emotional experience which then is interpreted as indisputable evidence of the leader's divine mission and the truth of his or her dogma.

William James called these optimistic experientially based faiths the religions of the 'once born' and predicted they would supersede tragic belief systems of suffering and redemption.[11] According to the hopeful doctrines of the once born, existential ambivalence, painful memories, guilt, and anxiety are surface phenomena – mere delusions hiding the true face of God. Beneath shifting appearance, in the depths of each individual's soul, shines the constant flame of the universal cosmic self. By following the various mental and physical disciplines prescribed by their leader the believers hope to achieve release from "the cultural trance, the systematic self-delusion, to which most of us surrender our aliveness."[12] After being 'deprogrammed' away from attachment to personal history and cultural context the convert then can experience ecstatic union with the eternal. "After I realized that I knew nothing, I realized that I knew everything. . .I didn't just experience Self, *I became Self*. . .It was an unmistakable recognition that I was, am, and always will be the source of my experience. . . I was whole and complete as I was."[13] Or, as Yeats puts it, the liberated soul "learns at last that it is self-delighting, / Self-appeasing, self-affrighting, / And that its own sweet will is Heaven's will."[14]

In America, and elsewhere too, the pursuit of connection with a deep inner spiritual essence has spread into popular culture, as can be verified by walking down the aisles of any bookstore. The shelves are weighted down with advice from New Age gurus, feel-good clerics, and helpful therapists who instruct readers on how to express their deepest needs, reach a higher spiritual plateau, find a power source, heal themselves, free the thin person within the fat one, or play better tennis. What is characteristic of these self-help books is that the techniques offered are not simply the means to achieve a particular end, but aim to help the readers connect immediately with their authentic selves. Having achieved this ultimate goal, what will necessarily follow is clarity of thought, happiness in relationships, success in business, a cure for angina, a slimmer figure, or a better backhand.

The flowering of world-affirming ecstatic religions and therapies can be seen as a direct reflection of the modern delegitimization of any shared sacred social order. As Durkheim predicted, the fragmentation of the cosmically ratified premodern universe leaves only the individual as the ultimate object of worship: "Since human personality is the only thing that appeals unanimously to all hearts, since its enhancement is the only aim that can be collectively pursued, it *inevitably* acquires exceptional value in the eyes of all. It thus rises far above all human aims, assuming a religious nature."[15]

Durkheim said little about the actual substance of the inevitable religion of the individual, but according to the normative premises of emotivism, the crucial *content* of individual personalities is to be found in their experiential capacity for ecstatic connection with an inner emotional truth, hidden beneath the weighty bulk of cultural conditioning, parental restrictions, self-consciousness, and guilt. Like the adrenaline rush that motivates the edgeworker, feelings of heightened reality and communion validate the authenticity of the experience of the real self within.

To achieve the goal of reaching their core, seekers must tear away the masks of repression, eliminate falsity and self-delusion, and allow the 'inner child' to express the genuine yearnings of the soul. Many techniques (monitored self-interrogation, ascetic practices, disruption of the central nervous system, and so on) are employed to strip away cultural and personal conditioning in order to reveal the eternal inner truth. But, like Edmund Burke, one can wonder what remains after "all the super-added ideas, furnished from the wardrobe of a moral imagination, which the heart owns, and the understanding ratifies, as necessary to cover the defects of our naked shivering nature, and to raise it to dignity in our own estimation, are. . .exploded as a ridiculous, absurd and antiquated fashion."[16] What may remain after the process of tearing away the wardrobe of cultural conditioning and personal history is an inchoate and infantile welter of fears and desires waiting to be shaped by the charismatic leader's will, which, because it is experientially ratified by ecstatic states stimulated under his or her influence, is irrefutable.[17] The immediate sense of touching the ultimate that occurs in these emotionally charged circumstances can be more than adequate recompense for the 'programmed' individuality stripped from the disciples when they submit to the commands of their leader.[18]

The opposite pathway for escape from the anxieties of anomie is to become someone whose own self expands to encompass the selves of others. Such individuals are archetypical charismatics: rare people who firmly believe that their subjective reality is heaven-sent and immutable. A related attitude, necessarily less excessive and confident, is characteristic of the creative artist whose expressive public performance momentarily provides an audience with a shared experience of transcendence. But what I want to concentrate on here is the banal version of the prophet or artist. This is the 'alpha consumer' – the one to whom others look for lifestyle tips, the one who knows the newest dance steps, has the up-to-date hairdo, uses the cool new technology, listens to the hottest music, wears the trendiest clothes. Like prophets or artists who mold their acolytes into copies of themselves, the tribute of imitation is awarded to those who are first with the latest. But there is nothing 'behind' chic; no need for tastemakers to seek their inner selves or uncover deep spiritual truths in order for them to buy hip new shoes. Instead, their purchases and performances are simply a momentary and directly pleasurable expression of immediate personal taste.

According to Daniel Miller, an aesthetic and sensual concern with personal style is especially characteristic of the poor and marginalized who have "come up against the problematics of modernity with a particular jolt, having had stripped away many of the traditions and structures which would mediate this relationship elsewhere."[19] They are, in other words, those who have been left with only "their naked shivering nature" to fall back on. But naked nature has its own inner resources, most markedly the capacity for enjoyment and expansion. Miller takes his example from Trinidad, where many of the young, the outsiders, the poor and disreputable, as well as a wide range of ordinary people, are deeply invested in stylish self-display. Miller calls this the position of transience and opposes it to the mainstream position of respectability and tradition, which looks backwards to origin and inwards to spiritual essence. This fundamental division is locally symbolized as a split between "people who live only for the event, spend their money out, emphasize style but know how to enjoy life, [and]... those who can plan and save, but are mean and oppressive, who can be true to their families but exclude others."[20] The contrast harkens back to the division between those who authenticate art by immediate recognition, and those who authenticate it by tracing its genealogy, or the difference between romantic and historical musical performance.

While the respectable see the style-conscious as superficial and immoral, for lovers of transience the respectable are pretentious frauds who pretend to be superior beings, but are unable to dance, play, or have good sex. For the transient soul, real life is not lived in the inner depths; interior quests, self-questioning, and deep feelings are devalued in favor of spontaneity, sensation, fashion, and entertainment. The best response to misfortune is to ignore it, and introspective people are considered self-indulgent and absurd.[21] Coolness, not commitment, is the ideal; leisure activities define a person; freedom and expressivity, not responsibility and insight, are sought. Constant excitement, change, and ephemeral becoming are the only worthwhile values, and the highest goal is to create a glittering, always new, public impression of wit, élan, and eye-catching physicality. Recognition and imitation reward success, but at the same time, the thrill of immediate physical expressivity is its own reward – a bodily pleasure that has no need for explanation or external validation.

In Trinidad, carnival is the most potent expression of the pluralistic, anti-structural assumptions of transience. It is a bacchanal, a public enactment of status reversal that tears away the thin façade of respectability to expose the true chaos and scandal lurking behind the scenes. Anarchic brightly costumed dancers, fueled by rum, spin and grind, music pounds, and singers gleefully satirize the hypocrisy and pretensions of those in power. For those attracted to the transient view of life, carnival is the most genuine and most compelling part of the year, the time when roles are put aside and they can be immediate, sensual, stylish, heedless, and exhilarated. Like spiritual seekers, the celebrants of transience rip away the masks of repression and constraint in order to experience the really real. But instead of turning inward, they find their rapture in public performance.

The forces of authority and respectability seek to control and direct carnival, making it a festival in honor of tradition and the state; political rebels want to turn it into a protest march; businessmen see it as a commercial resource.[22] All of these interests are in play during the performance and its preparation, but the real carnival, the adherents of transience believe, is not a commemoration of history or the nation; it has nothing to do with reforming the political process, making money, or pursuing an ideal. Nor can its meaning be discovered by looking deep within. Rather, it is a public, shared performance of ecstatic immediacy, a celebration of the pleasures and beauties of the body in a world where official authority has been discredited, and where history makes no sense. As Miller writes, for the celebrants, "nothing can be taken for granted any more; identity, like liberty, is intrinsically an act of forgery."[23] The really real exists for the transient only in the instant it is concretely manifested through the style and attitude of the player engaged "in a perpetually improvised unfolding."[24] There is no core, nothing eternal – just the charged aesthetic enjoyment of the moment, just the dance. Although the ideologies and styles are completely different, this type of authenticity shares an underlying similarity with others that are equally ecstatic and experiential: for the edgeworker there is only the adrenaline rush of total engagement in a dangerous task, for the charismatic devotee there is only the rapture of moments of communion, for the fan there is only the transient nocturnal excitement of the show. All alike find an authentic reality in the undeniable but fleeting truth of intense emotion.

Saving the World for Pleasure

Can the quest for personal truth in the transient pleasures of the body have implications beyond just igniting "one free explosion after another"?[25] To answer this question, I am going to consider how some pleasure-loving epicures have escaped from anomie by exercising their aesthetic taste, just like any other trendsetting alpha consumer. But by virtue of their rarified consumption, they also claim access to a transcendent moral truth. In a creative reconciliation of exterior and interior modes of authenticity, the pleasures of the palate have become the ideological basis for a permanent spiritual revolution.

The story begins with the development of new and controversial technologies of genetic engineering, the propagation of hybrid crops, the extensive use of growth hormones and other chemicals, the development of industrialized techniques to produce meat, fruit, and vegetables, and the cloning of disease-resistant plants and animals, among other innovations. However safe and beneficial these novelties may prove to be, they nonetheless challenge taken-for-granted notions of the naturalness of what we eat and drink. All of this has led toward a vastly heightened concern in the developed world with authenticity in the growing, producing, and preparing of foods and to the rise of social movements dedicated to the purification of food production and the preservation of distinctive local cooking. In Europe in particular, fears of genetic engineering, bureaucratic rationalization of production, and other 'EU horrors' led to massive protests and the development of a new global, aesthetic and consumption-oriented turn in the search for authenticity.

It began in the provincial town of Bra in the Langhe region of northern Italy. Bra is a backwater industrial city once well known for leatherwork, for the pervasive sour smell of tannin in its streets, and for its many voluntary associations. In the 1970s and 1980s, with the leather industry disappearing after a long eclipse, tourism was the only option available for economic development in the area. Food and wine loving young members of ARCI, the Italian national recreational association of the political left, responded by forming the Free and Praiseworthy Association of the Friends of Barolo (later self-styled as the Arcigola or 'archgluttons') with the aim of increasing awareness and consumption of local fine wine. Italy had already been the home of gourmet societies, but this was something new. Where the earlier groups had been apolitical clubs exclusively for gourmandizing elites, the Arcigola united a leftist ecological, anti-globalist agenda with a populist message stressing the political and economic utility of reclaiming authentic local traditions in the production and preparation of foodstuffs.

The Arcigola gained widespread public recognition in 1986 when it protested against construction of a McDonald's near Rome's famous Spanish Steps. Calling themselves the *nuovi edonisti* (new hedonists) and the *golosi democratici e antifascisti* (democratic and antifascist gluttons) the members, led by their charismatic president, Carlo Petrini, handed out bowls of penne pasta to illustrate the difference between prefabricated meals and local food. From this protest the Slow Food label was born, with the snail as its logo. Ever since, the movement has rapidly expanded, and has gained an international membership. Its manifesto, ratified by members from 15 countries in 1989, stated that "Fast life. . . disrupts our habits, pervades the privacy of our homes and forces us to eat Fast Foods." These depredations can only be opposed by "a firm defense of quiet material pleasure" which will "preserve us from the contagion of the multitude who mistake frenzy for efficiency."[26]

At present, Slow Food's approximately 80,000 members in 100 countries are gathered in loosely organized voluntary groups called conviviums. Their task, Petrini says, is to save "historical and localized" producers, foster good taste, educate the public, and "reconstruct the individual and collective heritage" by "offering the world the hope of a future different from the polluted and tasteless one that the lords of the earth have programmed for all of us."[27] Participants in the conviviums believe that the protection, production, and pleasurable consumption of authentic traditional food and drink is a precondition for the development of good taste, a moral value that is capable, Petrini says, of "saving the world." The assumption is not simply that industrialized fast food is nasty, impure, and dangerous; even worse, its production ruins genuine communal identity and the legacy of history, as revealed in the venerable food traditions of the countryside. If we do not eat proper food grown and prepared in the original manner, we cannot experience the powerful ancestral links that bind us together. Fast food and existential anomie go together. Yet, the Slow Food manifesto does not favor returning to the localized rural world of yesterday when people ate the same things throughout their entire lives. Though healthy, that would be just as tedious as a diet of McDonald's hamburgers, and would destroy the pleasurable transient experience of taste. Therefore, the Slow Food initiate must always continually seek diversity. As Petrini proclaims, "to eat a different kind of food in every street in the world is the best answer to fast food."[28]

But for the Slow Food gourmet only a certain type of variety will do if a newly discovered taste is to be truly delicious and not indulgently clever or otherwise inauthentic. In the first place, whatever the revolutionary pleasure-seeker swallows, it must be made with the highest quality, certifiably purest ingredients, cooked in a traditional simple and unpretentious manner reflective of the unique *terroir* where it belongs. Authentic consumption also requires extensive knowledge of the varied historical, cultural, and ecological background of local comestibles. Petrini informs his readers that "in order to learn how to find slow pleasure, one has to travel, read and taste, abandoning the temptation of entrenched isolation." It is hard work to be a revolutionary eater. Having cultivated diversity and explored exotic traditions self-aware gastronomes become "allies who think alike while respecting one another at a distance." They are members of an association that is "heterogeneous but strongly cohesive... an elite without excluding anyone." The hoped-for end result is a world that "singles out, highlights, and values difference" but is unified at the deepest level by ecologically sound and aesthetically satisfying food production and preparation.[29]

The Slow Food Movement is based on a number of taken-for-granted assumptions. Firstly, the new hedonism is a highly moralistic enterprise. At the very least, pursuing authentic food is thought to lead to a shared concern for the environment, empowerment, knowledge, and social responsibility. At most, it will revolutionize the world, eradicating exploitation, pollution, and alienation. Secondly, the true gourmand must be a transient who leaves the familiar and continually searches the world for new and pleasurable tastes. Diversity and novelty, the celebration of difference, is a value in itself. Thirdly, authenticity is conceived to be a seductive and self-ratifying personal experience that naturally unites origin and identity: when food is grown and prepared in the original way, it tastes as it *should* taste, and vice versa. Finally, and most importantly, authenticity is judged by enjoyment. If comestibles are authentic, they are *ipso facto* more pleasurable to consume than those that are inauthentic, and so are intrinsically worth searching out. From this perspective, enjoying a McDonald's hamburger is not only a moral failing; it is also, more insidiously, a lapse into bad taste, a betrayal of the heart's deep desire for the transient truth of pleasure, and evidence of inauthenticity. The fundamental premise is that pure (and purified) preferences are the basis for judging the truth of experience, taste, reality, morality, and relationships. As Petrini puts it: "we catch barely a glimpse of the fundamental concept that ought to underlie all these projects: that of 'feeling good' with oneself and with others."[30]

Freed from cultural conditioning by a never-ending education of the palate, Slow Food initiates become (ideally anyway) authentic connoisseurs of transient pleasure whose cultivated and purified inclinations determine what is genuine in the world around them. Kept afloat by what they believe is their good taste, they are not washed away by the waves of modernity; they surf on them. And so a universalizing social movement has been created out of the fleeting and intimate aesthetic experience of personal pleasure.

Part II

Collective Authenticity

Chapter 6

Authentic Cuisine and National Identity

Inventing Real Belizean Food

The previous chapters were concerned primarily with the pursuit of personal authenticity. But, as the Slow Food movement demonstrates, the search for personal authenticity can have collective ramifications as well. The following chapters will analyze this aspect of authenticity, beginning with the case of the *gibnut*, which is a shy, guinea-pig-like rodent who lives peacefully in the dense jungles of the tiny country of Belize, formerly known as British Honduras. American tourists are unlikely ever to see this elusive animal, but the more adventurous of them may eat one, since a roasted, stuffed gibnut is proudly advertised in local restaurants as the 'Royal Rat' and as a prime example of authentic Belizean food. The story of how this unlikely creature gained such notoriety tells us a great deal about the ways an authentic national identity is imagined and constructed in the modern era.

Belize is a Central American/Caribbean nation of 200,000 people that gained its independence from Britain in 1981. Once a logging colony, it is now primarily a tourist destination known for its great natural beauty and eco-friendly attitude. It is inhabited by a Creole population of mixed European, African, and American Indian ancestry. Spanish-speaking migrants from the neighboring countries enter into the mix, and there are numerous other ethnic groups resident as well, including Mayan Indians, South Asians, and Chinese. These ethnic divisions are crosscut by class differences and kinship ties, though the elite are mostly white or Creole. Regardless of class, Belizeans are remarkably well traveled. At least 30 percent of the population resides in the United States, and Los Angeles is the second-largest Belizean city. Seventy-three percent of adult Belizeans have been abroad, 34 percent have lived outside the country for more than three months. Belize also plays host to a huge number of tourists every year (140,000), and has been heavily influenced by television, videos, and other cultural imports from elsewhere in the Caribbean and, even more, from the United States. For example, Belizeans are fervent fans of the Chicago Cubs because Cubs' games were the first live professional sports to be broadcast there. When some Cub players visited the country in 1984, the crowds who turned out for them were more numerous than those who greeted the Pope the previous year – and this in a predominantly Catholic country.

In sum, Belize is completely immersed in the international marketplace. Yet, Belizean eating habits have not become Americanized; instead, the reverse has occurred. Although Coke and McDonald's are certainly popular, new restaurants have sprung up serving local clients a mélange of what are proudly advertised as "authentic Belizean dishes – Garnachas, Tamales, Rice and Beans, Stew Chicken, Fried Chicken;"[1] a mixture that reflects the hybrid character of the population as a whole. And in this mélange, the Royal Rat has a central place as one of the most authentic representatives of real Belizean food.

One might imagine that the paramount position of the shy gibnut is the result of some long-standing taste for it among the local populace, and that its regal status is ancient. Appreciation of the culinary virtues of the gibnut, however, is a very recent phenomenon, as is its royal designation. In fact, the very idea of authentic Belizean cuisine is recent. During the colonial era, the Belizean upper classes never ate the gibnut at all. Instead they purchased and ate expensive European imports as a way of affirming their elite status positions. When they did eat local products they picked those they could prepare following European recipes. For instance, the large local clawless crustaceans were called lobsters; they were prepared in European style and eaten as a luxury dish. Meanwhile the poor also ate the local lobsters, as well as gibnuts and anything else that they could catch or grow, preparing their meals according to their own traditional recipes. Caught between these two extremes, the small but upwardly striving middle class tried to separate themselves from the poor by imitating elite tastes, but at a lower level of expense and sophistication; feast food for them was imported corned beef, white bread, and tinned sardines. Seeing the local lobster as food of the poor, they despised it as trash . . . though later they learned to appreciate its qualities. Even as late as the 1980s, the food at a wedding party for the daughter of a prominent local politician consisted of "American butterball turkey, Honey-Baked ham, Stove-Top stuffing, white-bread sandwiches filled with canned Armor Deviled Ham and Hellman's mayonnaise, potato salad and almost as an afterthought a small scoop of Belizean rice and beans."[2]

Food in Belize was primarily an internal symbolic boundary marker, dividing the classes from one another in a relatively stable hierarchy of taste with the elite as the sole arbiters of what was or was not a proper meal. Some variation was added when the Belizean middle class consumed 'Spanish' dishes from the north as a "safely exotic option – associated neither with the class below nor the class above."[3] During the colonial period, there was no unifying authentic Belizean national cuisine and no concept of one. But all of this began to change when Britain granted Belize a degree of local autonomy. As part of its campaign to stimulate a sense of Belizean national identity, the fledgling government made efforts to promote the consumption of local fish and other produce. At first this initiative was met with strong opposition. Middle-class Belizeans were repelled at the thought of eating 'bush food' instead of the imported tinned sardines, canned ham, soft drinks, mayonnaise, and white bread to which they had grown accustomed and which they associated with higher status and international sophistication.

Resistance began to evaporate after the visit of Queen Elizabeth in 1985, the first time a British monarch had ever come to the ex-colony. This was a major event for the young nation, and every effort was made to impress the Queen with local culture. It was at this point that the Royal Rat made its fateful entrance. At a state dinner, the pièce de résistance was a stuffed, roasted gibnut. The Queen, who has dutifully eaten many odd dishes in her travels, showed no surprise at her unusual main course (though it is reported that she didn't eat much of it). But the British tabloids, sensing a scandal, "carried outraged headlines, on the theme of 'Queen Served Rat by Savages.'"[4] These sensationalist and racist press reports emanating from their former colonizers stimulated an outraged reaction among middle-class Belizeans, most of whom had never eaten, or thought of eating, a gibnut, but who now proudly defended the previously despised rodent as a tasty national treasure. Ever since, it has been served in restaurants as the Royal Rat and has become so popular that it is in real danger of being hunted to extinction. Although unfortunate for the gibnut, this was the symbolic beginning of the Belizean rediscovery (or invention) of a distinctive national cuisine.

The Queen's visit was a catalytic event, since it occurred just as the newly independent Belize was searching for appropriate symbols to mark itself off as a unique nation. In a sense then, the new taste for the Royal Rat and the development of an authentic Belizean cuisine are expressions of a nascent state's growing need to differentiate itself from its neighbors and so inculcate loyalty in the populace, serving much the same purpose as the new flag, the nation's new name, the national anthem, and state sponsorship of folk music and indigenous dances. The appearance of real Belizean food also occurred alongside the first really massive influx of tourists into the country. The local people soon discovered that their wealthy visitors did not come to Belize in order to eat meals consisting of Seven-Up and canned ham on white bread. From this experience, Belizeans became conscious that an authentic local cuisine was expected and valued by the visitors whose respect and dollars they craved. At the same time, as a result of massive out-migration and the pervasive media invasion from abroad, Belizeans became more discriminating and savvy consumers themselves. Having lived in the United States, and having become increasingly aware of the vapidity of mass-produced American culture, they were no longer unduly impressed by the mere existence of imported goods. They also became conscious of, and proud of, the specificity of their own foods and cultural production.

As Richard Wilk has beautifully documented, because of these changes the old binary colonialist divide between inferior backward local goods and superior modern foreign goods rapidly began to erode, as did traditional internal hierarchical distinctions of class-bound taste. In the new post-colonial world of the nation-state, all Belizeans, whatever their status, class, or ethnicity, have become aware of the necessity of defending (and sometimes manufacturing) their own local culture, which is now understood to be under siege, whereas previously it was not even known to exist. As Wilk puts it, "everyone in Belize is now concerned with foreign influence, local authenticity, and the interpretation of various kinds of domination and resistance."[5] In response, a taste for a recently discovered Belizean national cuisine has grown up in the shade of McDonald's Golden Arches, and the Royal Rat has become the local rival to the butterball turkey.

If Real Italians Eat Pasta, Do Real Indians Eat Curry?

The connection between the invention/recovery of an authentic local cuisine and the development of a national consciousness is not only found in tiny and remote Belize. Italy is a case in point. The Italian state only came into existence in 1860, gaining a relatively feeble hold in a society that still favors familial ties over civic duties. After the formation of Italy, people continued to speak their varied local dialects and to identify themselves as Piedmontese, Neapolitans, and Milanese first, Italians second. To this day, even small villages are proud of their own distinct identities. In these circumstances, food, and especially pasta, has been one of the few things that Italians feel they share and that mark them as a specific people. But despite Italian's own beliefs, the identification of true Italianness with pasta is not ancient. On the contrary, it is largely a result of the huge outpouring of poor Italian immigrants in the nineteenth century. In lieu of other obvious national markers, these workers were identified as, and began to identify themselves as, pasta eaters. The connection between being Italian and eating pasta was then carried back to the home country by returnees.[6]

Pasta is a uniquely apt symbol for the fragmented Italian nation, since it is manufactured in a seemingly infinite number of shapes, sizes, and textures (one expert catalogues 298 different types of dry pasta[7]), is prepared with a huge range of sauces, and cooked and served in many different ways. Each combination is rigidly codified and reckoned to be characteristic of a region, locality, and even a family. At the same time, all are recognizable as pasta, and so as quintessentially Italian. As Erick Castellanos and Sara Bergstresser put it: "The general concept, pasta, is shared nationally, while its specific forms allow for local identity to be represented."[8] Local variety is subsumed into national taste, which can then be contrasted to outsiders' inability to make pasta properly or to recognize the standards regulating variation. For most Italians, being Italian means making, eating, knowing, and loving pasta in its multiple local forms, though mama's is always best.

A more complex and incomplete construction of an authentic national cuisine has occurred in India, where linguistic and cultural distinctions between regions and even between villages are much greater than in Italy. These distinctions are also overlain by caste restrictions on food that make the development of a national cuisine a difficult project indeed. This extreme differentiation coincides with an oral tradition of local culinary traditions and the historical absence of any pan-Indian style of cooking, though there was a strong, shared consciousness of the prohibitions on sharing food between caste groups. In the sixteenth century the invading Muslim Mughal regime did develop a high cuisine that foreigners recognize as Indian, although actually it only blended the culinary traditions of the Afghan invaders and the peasant foods of north India. Later the British colonialists and their Anglo-Indian allies began to develop a truly subcontinental food regime of 'curry', based on their own standardization of recipes. This is the type of cooking that is labeled authentic Indian cuisine in South Asian restaurants throughout the world. But in India, multiple local styles of cooking attest that there is an infinite plurality instead.

This is now changing due to the efforts of two linked upper-middle-class groups, which are both products of increased social and spatial mobility in modern India. The first are itinerant international professionals who have returned to their home country, and who nostalgically hope to recapture the culinary traditions of their forebears by researching and writing 'regional' cookbooks that codify the 'standard' dishes; the second are members of the indigenous urban middle class who want to publicize and raise the status of the cuisines of their native localities; they too are writing standardizing regional cookbooks. As a result, certain regional dishes and styles are becoming recognized as a set of generalized images which codify and legitimate certain aspects of local foodways.[9]

At the same time, members of these new mobile classes have also begun to write cookbooks that mingle food from a number of regions, developing what might be called a conglomerate cuisine. These books mix together a variety of supposedly typical regional dishes within an imported Western framework of a 'menu' consisting of a series of apparently natural but actually quite arbitrary categories: rice dishes, breads, lentils, vegetables, sweets and savories, pickles and chutneys, and sometimes beverages. These cookbooks are responses to an increasing fascination among urban Indian consumers for food variety. Today, computer engineers who flock to the software export center of Bangalore can not only eat conglomerate international Indian cuisine, but also pizzas, Thai noodles, or Mexican burritos (among other international cuisines), as well as food from every part of India.[10] For these mobile urban consumers, eating exotic foods is an adventure and a way to demonstrate their cosmopolitan tastes.

However, the same restless middle-class professionals who avidly consume exotic dishes and internationalized Indian food also read regional cookbooks and buy prepackaged 'authentically prepared' foods that remind them of home. Catering to this 'gastro-nostalgia,' a number of restaurants in Bangalore now specialize in the traditional preparation of local foods for middle- and upper-class clients. As one reviewer says, the aim is to conjure up "lip smacking memories of a cuisine unsullied by instant mixes and powders. Of firewood, smoky kitchens, and bustling women fragrant with the aroma of food."[11] So, as they pursue variety and assert their cosmopolitan tastes, the new professional classes try as well to recapture their lost roots. Conflicting desires to be international sophisticates, Indian citizens, and authentic indigenous people are ambiguously reconciled by incorporating recipes and foods from many regions and local traditions into a mélange designated as 'Indian', and imagined to be the equivalent of the codified cuisines of other nations.

In India, as in Italy and Belize, a mobile, transnational population of the burgeoning middle class has had the central role in recovering and instituting food traditions that are then taken by them to be authentic and characteristic of the nation as a whole. In Italy, this process has focused on pasta: a single food item that permits infinite local variations. In Belize, a simple set of foodstuffs has been taken as typical and is now consumed by everyone. In India, there is no single overarching category of national foods all people recognize as authentically Indian. Instead, what is most valued is maintenance of local traditions, which can then be brought together into a varied menu that is 'Indian' in its inclusiveness. And while Italian pasta and 'real Belizean food' have been wholly integrated into popular consciousness as symbolic representations of national identity, in India the audience for national and regional menus and prepared foods is overwhelmingly from the same class of people who wrote the cookbooks: the transnational migrants and upwardly mobile professionals uprooted from the countryside, striving to overcome their feelings of "exile, nostalgia and loss."[12]

Terroir, Power, and French Cuisine

A different interlinking of authentic cuisine and national identity has taken place in France, but in this instance it was neither colonialism nor mobility that stimulated awareness of the national significance of local food and drink. It was the French Revolution. When it began in 1789, only 20 percent of the population spoke 'proper' Parisian French; 30 percent could not understand it at all. It was therefore necessary, as Eugen Weber famously put it, to "turn peasants into Frenchmen," a laborious process akin to internal colonization.[13]

The French response to internal diversity intimately linked consumption and cuisine to national identity in a unique way. This model of nationhood was first proposed around the turn of the twentieth century by the French geographer Paul Vidal de la Blache, whose theories were adopted by the Third Republic for inclusion into state approved textbooks, and as a result became deeply engrained in French culture. This is partly because his ideas played upon France's already existing image of itself as the world's cultural arbiter. Vidal argued that France was the natural geographical center of all the civilized peoples of Europe. According to him, "the diversity of people within France, reflected in regional identities, gave the nation a unique ability to assimilate and transform what it received."[14] In other words, because the French (or at least French intellectuals) perceived themselves to be at the crossroads of cultures and geographical regions, they believed that France could synthesize the universal and the particular – thus fulfilling its world-historical mission by harmoniously creating an aesthetic unity out of what nature had divided.

Vidal argued that the sacred national destiny of France was revealed concretely in its *terroir*. Originally referring to a wine-growing region, the notion of terroir was expanded after the *belle époque* to mean "the combination of natural factors (soil, water, slope, height above sea level, vegetation, microclimate) and human ones (tradition and practice of cultivation) that gives a unique character to each small agricultural locality and the food grown, raised, made,

83

and cooked there."[15] For Vidal, the various terroir of France provided both the source and the expression of French historical memory; together, the various terroir comprised the soul of the nation, unifying the provinces that had been liberated by the Revolution.

What this meant in practice was that France could be conceptualized as a nation that is quite literally a set of interlinked cuisines, each derived from a specific terroir. All the populace could then enjoy these various flavors and be united in shared appreciation of one another's typical food and drink. In this context, it makes sense that the French term *la carte* means not only menu but also map. From Vidal's point of view, listing regional specialties on the menu of a restaurant reinforced the natural links between cuisine and nation; consuming these specialties embodied France in the citizen-cum-gastronome. Wine, in particular, was regarded as the "the realization of . . . French *esprit* in the material world." "[T]he same words [are used] to describe both the qualities of Frenchness and the qualities of French wines. Wines and national identity become so intertwined that it is difficult to invoke the one without eliciting the other." As one enthusiast remarked about champagne: "This wine resembles us, it is made in our image: it sparkles like our intellect; it is lively like our language."[16] French national identity, as understood by the French themselves, consists in large measure of knowing and appreciating French wine.[17]

Vidal assumed that the properties of each particular terroir actually formed the fundamental character of those who lived and worked on it, ate its foods, and drank its wines. Rural people were authentic expressions of their soil, diverse in essence, like the produce of the land itself, but alike in their genuineness and aesthetic appreciation of local food and drink. This meant that bureaucratic divisions of France into regions should reflect real differences of terroir, and not be arbitrary limits imposed by a central government. Therefore he testified in favor of redrawing old regional boundaries to confirm to the natural geography.

However, the governmental effort to reformulate regional boundaries according to Vidal's theory of fundamental natural organic principles was hardly apolitical or disinterested. Huge amounts of money were at stake in the designation of certain towns and villages as the only appropriate environments for the production of registered foods and especially wines and liquors. Producers in the designated region could claim that only theirs was the real Bordeaux, burgundy, or champagne and charge consumers accordingly. Legends were fabricated to substantiate these claims. For example, Dom Pierre Pérignon, a monk at abbey of Hautvillers, is said to have invented the process for manufacturing champagne sometime between 1668 and 1715. However, it is known that the story of Dom Pérignon was invented in 1821 by another monk from Hautvillers seeking publicity for his monastery. The legend was quickly adopted and artfully embellished by the champagne industry. By 1860, the saintly long-dead Dom Pérignon had become blind, but in compensation was blessed with the subtle sense of taste and smell that enabled him to perfect the champagne process. In 1899 he was declared the father of sparkling wine, and in 1910 a monument was built to him, where pilgrims can pay their respects. All this is part of the French champagne industry's very successful marketing campaign to maintain its monopoly over what is, after all, one of the first intrusions of industrial factory production into agriculture.[18]

More convincing are the authenticity claims of *grand cru* wines, such as Bordeaux, which actually do use grapes from specific estates, which are then bottled in an artisanal manner. The assumption is that each officially recognized appellation has the best natural terroir for a specific grape and type of wine production, with Bordeaux at the peak. However, up until the twelfth century wine from the high regions of southwest France was considered much superior to wine from around Bordeaux. It was with the English invasion of France that Bordeaux gained prestige, mainly because its wine could be easily transported across the Channel. "The importance of Bordeaux wine is not based on climate but on their better organization of marketing to Northern Europe."[19] The authority of Bordeaux increased due to the growers' strategy of developing grand cru or elite wines using old rootstocks, with smaller yields, and longer aging, all of which were said to improve the quality of the product, but which also required very considerable capital investment as well as an intensification of labor, leading in turn to a proletarianization of the workforce and the monopolization and consolidation of the fields in the hands of a small number of producers.

French lawmakers supported the elite growers' strategy of developing expensive wines, and in 1855 officially codified the grand cru classifications that favored single-domain production. Meanwhile, wealthy vignerons built replicas of aristocratic chateaux and pictured them on the labels of their bottles, reinforcing claims to noble status for themselves and ancient lineages for their wines (although after the phylloxera epidemic at the turn of the century all French wine has been grown from rootstock imported from the United States). The question of whether the wines of these grand chateaux are 'better' in any absolute sense can never be answered, but they did have great snob appeal due to their rarity, their cost, and their association with luxury and aristocratic heritage. The combination of chateau production, manufactured aristocratic lineage, and state-sponsored certification of the authenticity of wine grown on the great estates worked against the remaining small vignerons who, in regions like Médoc, are likely to occupy vineyards bordering directly on those of a grand cru, grow exactly the same grapes on the same soil and with the same techniques. Nonetheless, their wine sells for very much less, since they cannot claim an elite designation. As Robert Ulin says, the designation of appellations "takes for granted the social construction of authenticity, quality, and taste, and therefore tends to naturalize the social and historical conditions that have long differentiated winegrowers."[20] Terroir, it turns out, is not transparently natural, and authenticity in French wine is a matter not only of geographic origin, but also of power and money.

This method of authentication has been extended to foodstuffs as well. For example, French cheeses are divided into complex categories and subcategories, each attached to specific regions and modes of traditional production. Most famous is Camembert, which is both a symbol of France and a runny cheese from Normandy, protected from imitation by a governmental appellation. Like champagne, Camembert has its own legend of origin, supposedly being the invention of Marie Harel, a Norman farmer's wife. Like Dom Pérignon, her grave too is now the site of a monument, and is visited by tourists and dignitaries alike who honor her memory. That this entire story is unsupported by any evidence whatsoever has not prevented Camembert from becoming a beloved symbol of French taste.[21]

A more recent example of the same very French authentication process can be found in the transformation of French artisanal chocolate production, which was in retreat due to increased competition from low-cost Belgian importers. Responding to this threat, chocolatiers in France began to claim that their expensive chocolates actually derive from different South American terroirs and are blended in a manner reminiscent of grand cru wine. By relying on exquisite craftsmanship in the production of ornate chocolate confections and on tastings, which instruct willing laymen about the supposed purity, special qualities, and authenticity of these expensive products, a new elite industry has been manufactured. This is despite the fact that all chocolate is actually exported in mechanically produced blocks, which are then distributed to buyers, whether they are French or Belgian, great or small, industrial or artisanal.[22]

From these examples, it is clear that the development and appreciation of authentic cuisine is full of paradox and ambiguity. The story winds through labyrinths of resistance, pride, entrepreneurship, power, money, and imagination. But it is especially intertwined with nationalism. Pasta is the quintessential Italian dish because it takes so many forms, and so can unite specific and general in a fragmented society; Indian cuisine is manufactured by nostalgic and mobile cosmopolitan elites hoping to wed tradition and novelty in their complex homeland; real French food and wine originates not only from a varied terroir, but also from political negotiations and masterly public relations that unite people in their love for a shared cuisine. In every case, ingesting food and drink that is certified as authentic is, quite literally, a direct way for citizens to taste their immediate communion with that most potent of modern secular religions: the nation.

Chapter 7

Authentic Dance and National Identity

Collective Identity and the Speech That Cannot Lie

While food serves as a particularly potent symbol of collective identity, dance has an even stronger capacity to merge personal and group consciousness. This capacity is a product of the nature of dance itself. American dance pioneers Ruth St Denis and Isadora Duncan both "considered that the function of dance was to celebrate and reveal, through body movement, the inner emotional life which stems from the soul."[1] Their follower, Martha Graham, later declared that "movement is the one speech that cannot lie."[2] This notion has a long history in Western iconography, where so-called savages, from whatever place, were always depicted as capering wildly, lost in mass hysteria. As the 1788 edition of the *Encyclopaedia Britannica* explained: "As barbarous people are observed to have the strongest passions, so they are also observed to be the most easily affected by sounds, and the most addicted to dancing."[3] Émile Durkheim's famous description of the corroboree of the Australian aborigines owes much to this image of savage dance: "the passions released are of such an impetuosity that they can be restrained by nothing...The sexes unite contrarily to the rules governing sexual relations. Men exchange wives with each other. Sometimes even incestuous unions, which in normal times are thought abominable and are severely punished, are contracted openly and with impunity."[4]

But for Durkheim the sensual dance of the aborigines had a profoundly positive significance. The ecstatic passions unleashed in dance were the fundamental source for the "collective effervescence" that he saw at the heart of social life and religious faith (which for Durkheim are the same thing). Dancing together, rhythmically mirroring one another's movements in the contagious rapture of mimesis, the performers lose their individuality and are carried away into a collective state of ecstasy:

> Feeling himself dominated and carried away by some sort of external power which makes him think and act differently than in normal times, he naturally has the impression of being himself no longer. It seems to him that he has become a new being. . . . Everything is just as though he really were transported into a special world, entirely different from the old one where he ordinarily lives, and into an environment filled with exceptionally intense forces that take hold of him and metamorphose him.[5]

For Durkheim, such depersonalizing and energizing collective rites have priority over all systems of meaning. They provide the real and immediate experience of a felt truth that is beyond ordinary life, and in so doing *create* the bonds that give society its compelling sacred power over the individuals who make it up. For him, a social world without some effective forms of collective participation must inevitably collapse in alienation and anomie. In the modern world, where organized religion has lost much of its hold, inspiring collective power is largely located in nations, which very often legitimize themselves through dance – the most potent embodied form of collective participation and worship.

The overt integration of dance with national interest became common in Europe during the nineteenth century. For a populace suffering from precisely the sense of meaninglessness that Durkheim feared, the folk dances of peasants and rural people offered the unifying inspiration they craved – less sexual and frightening than the capering of savages, but equally binding on the community. These folk dances were soon employed as symbolic validations for the new collective of the nation, to be performed in the company of flags, anthems, and other iconic expressions of significant difference. Today, similar state-sponsored folk dances, complete with government-approved folk costumes, are a feature of almost every national celebration in every country. But which dance is chosen as the symbolic representation of the nation is a matter of historical, cultural, and political circumstance, as is the manner and degree to which the dance form is accepted as an authentic expression of collective identity.

For example, Dominican Islanders have been famous in Latin America and the Caribbean for their love of dance since the early eighteenth century. Of late, one local dance, the meringué, has become extremely popular on the island, among Dominican expatriates, and on the international dance circuit, where it presently is one of the two or three preferred dance forms for young people.[6] Dominicans are justifiably proud of the success of meringué, and see it as the direct expression of Dominican national character. But in reality meringué is just one genre of dance from one region of the country: it arose in Cibao in the northern part of the island. Originally it was a peasant dance, looked down upon by the local elites who favored the polka-like mazurka. Meringué and mazurka were parts of a complex of regional and rural Dominican dances, each equally rooted in its own particular area and class. As a heavily orchestrated and urbanized meringué has predominated as the most representative form of Dominican dance, these other indigenous dance styles have almost been forgotten. At the same time, African influences on meringué have been denied while its Hispanic heritage has been foregrounded.

The rise of the meringué is a consequence of the cultural policies of the dictator Rafael Trujillo, who ruled the island with an iron hand from 1930 to 1961. Trujillo wished to weaken the rural oligarchy in Cibao, and so officially promoted meringué as a symbolic blow to the cultural pretensions of the local elite. However, Trujillo also understood meringué to be a specifically Spanish dance form, unlike the Polish mazurka. It was therefore chosen as the official dance in order to support his cultural policy of *hispanidad*, that is, the assertion that what is authentically Dominican is its Hispanic heritage. This policy specifically contrasted the Dominican Republic with Haiti, which is on the other side of the island. Haiti is famous as the first modern nation to be ruled by black people, and it has a strong and self-conscious connection to its African past. In fear of contamination of its Spanish inheritance by Haitian/African influence, the official Dominican construction of its national identity has systematically been oriented toward the colonizing culture of Spain, which was presented as culturally superior to the African heritage of the former slave population. In Dominican schools there is little acknowledgement of any African legacy, nor is there any state-sponsored effort to come to terms with the history of slavery and its effect on the culture at large.

Despite the official version, dance historians say that meringué is far from purely Hispanic; rather, it is a Creolized form combining African and Spanish styles. As such, it is not very different from many other new world dances which are cultural hybrids exhibiting strong African influences, particularly in terms of rhythm. The African aspect of local dance genres has been embraced elsewhere in the region, but 500 years of contact have obscured awareness of which traits belong to which tradition, and it has been possible for Dominicans more or less to ignore the complex genealogy of meringué and to stress instead the aspect which has the most status, and most clearly marks the Dominican nation off from Haiti.

However, the official narrative is now meeting with resistance from the many Dominicans who immigrated to the United States and came in contact with black power and anti-colonial discourse. On their return to the island, they were no longer convinced by the old hispanidad rhetoric. Their new oppositional consciousness coincided with the decline of regional and rural folk dances in favor of the energized version of meringué suitable for the international market. Newly aware of rapid cultural homogenization and radicalized by exposure to alternative models of local authenticity, some performers began to redefine what it means to be a Dominican by learning African-influenced and obscure local dances. As we shall see in the next chapters, this type of reaction is widely found whenever people become aware of authenticity as a form of symbolic capital, to be used in asserting power.

Without Rumba There Is No Cuba

The establishment of rumba as the national dance of modern-day Cuba followed a very different trajectory from meringué. As Yvonne Daniel informs us, "since the revolution of 1959, rumba has emerged as a symbol of what Cuba stands for among its own people and what Cubans want the world to understand when the international community envisions Cuba and Cubans."[7] Yet this was not preordained. In the nineteenth century, rumba was one of four typical Cuban dances – the others are conga, *danzon*, and *son* – and more have developed or been imported since then, including *casino* and salsa. According to dance historians, rumba evolved from several dances that originated in western and central Africa. Like its African forebears, it features pairs of dancers entering a circle of onlookers where they perform to cheers or jeers. In some types of rumba the man imitates a cock chasing a hen while his partner adroitly attempts to avoid being 'vaccinated'. Or the dance may be one of rivalry between men, as each dancer demonstrates his ability to respond creatively to the riffs of the drum.

Traditionally the word 'rumba' simply meant a street festival; a gathering with music, drinking, and improvised dancing to a number of different rhythms. This spontaneous 'rumba event', still known as the 'real' rumba, was a feature of Cuba's black slums. It was highly competitive and sometimes ended in violence; middle-class people generally avoided these potentially dangerous affairs. While rumba events still occur, most rumba today is a much safer, more controlled affair, featuring professional artists who perform carefully choreographed dances at specified times and places under government auspices.

The rise of professionalized rumba coincided with the Cuban revolution. Previously, the Cuban government supported ballet as its contribution to the international dance world. Heavily reliant on tourism, pre-revolutionary Cuba looked to Europe and the United States for its cultural validation; local dances were considered uninteresting, crude, and – in the case of the sexually explicit forms of rumba – embarrassing. This was despite (or because of) the fact that Cuba under Batista was known as a wide-open country, where gambling, corruption, and prostitution were rampant. Caught in a demeaning situation in which their Europeanizing ambitions were belied by the sordid facts of post-colonial exploitation, elite Cubans wanted to demonstrate that they too could produce artists who could enter the international stage and excel in the most prestigious arenas of classical dance. The ability to compete in the highest European art forms compensated for the degraded reality of Cuban life in the pre-revolutionary era.

After the revolution, this attitude was completely reversed. The Castro regime prosecuted prostitution and gambling, embraced Communism, and sought to overturn Cuban cultural dependence on elite Western art forms, which were denounced as bourgeois. As part of the revolutionary project, it chose to support rumba as the dance characteristic of all those who had been most ignored and oppressed during the previous regime: the impoverished black laborers of the city. So, where meringué gained state approval in the Dominican Republic because it was thought to be Hispanic, white, and European, rumba was selected for the opposite reasons: it was supported as a vehicle expressing solidarity with downtrodden workers, as a mark of the reconciliation between light- and dark-skinned people, as a turn toward Africa, and as an acceptance of overt sexuality over effete refinement. The official endorsement of rumba was a symbolic statement to Cubans and to outsiders alike that the revolution would right the wrongs of the past, and would embrace the sensual African heritage that had previously been denied. What had been too black, too low, too vulgar, was now realigned with dignity, equality, recognition, and inspiration. Rumba and the revolution were symbolically united. This confluence is captured in a well-known rumba lyric:

> Now the people are happy and long live the drums. The kid goes to school. Let's read. I'm Cuban and I love Cuba and I die for my flag. . . . Havana is the leader as the blessed Capital. There you can find everything that you need, from a fine, hot flirtatious babe who can turn you on, to the highest authority in the country. Education of the people is the first thing you have to learn.[8]

Yet the mere desire of the state to make retribution for past wrongs and establish its socialist bona fides cannot quite explain the degree to which rumba was popularly accepted as the most genuine dance of the Cuban nation. After all, it is more difficult to learn than other Cuban dances and cannot be performed correctly by everyone; nor is rumba a collective dance, like conga or casino, and so it cannot easily be understood as the direct symbolic expression of the Communist ideals of the Cuban state. Most extraordinary is the fact that to this day the vast majority of Cubans do not dance rumba, and "exit quickly and politely when they are coerced to attend a rumba event." Instead of rumba, the most popular dances on the island in 1995 were son and salsa. Yet, as a song puts it, "without rumba, there is no Cuba; without Cuba, there is no rumba."[9] Why?

Popular acceptance of rumba as the most authentic expression of Cuban national character is partly a result of the success of the government's assiduous campaign to make it appealing to the international market. After the revolution the state-sponsored Folklórico Nacional developed a professional dance troop of *rumberos* that featured colorful costumes and intricate choreography. In 1980 rumba Saturday was initiated, primarily as a tourist attraction, though many Cubans also attended. For rumba Saturday, national rumba festivals, and other tourist-oriented public performances, the dance was speeded up, the music was made more percussive, and the choreography more sexually explicit. Performance was moved from small local spaces to large public plazas. Where formerly only one couple danced, now several danced at once. Rumba previously ended only when everyone was tired, or with a fight; now they were put on a tight schedule. Competitive elements were emphasized while the possibilities for actual violence were minimized. The intensification, rationalization, and professionalization of the form succeeded: tourists came to Cuba not only to watch rumba but also to learn how to dance it. As prestigious foreigners increasingly identified rumba with Cuba, and as public performances became more polished, middle-class Cubans also came to recognize rumba as their national dance, even though they might not dance it or even listen to it themselves.

Probably even more important for the general Cuban identification with rumba has been the way it has represented idealized elements of the culture. In rumba, the black worker, ordinarily marginalized in the light-skinned, middle-class, literate Cuban world, is placed in the center of the communal circle to dance the always-enthralling drama of flirtation. The audience identifies with this story, in which men are the pursuers, while women are both coy and sensual, but also more than able to hold their own. Rumba proclaims to the audience members that they too are sensual and exciting; and that differences of race and class can melt away, as the Communist dream promises. At the same time, the dancers are not lost in a mass nor are they isolated; the performers express their creativity within the admiring circle of the group, so that individualism and collectivism are reconciled. The state confirms its benevolence and popularity by sponsorship of an exhilarating and involving art form that is collective and egalitarian *as well as* individualistic and charismatic.

State-supported efforts to preserve and promote rumba as the national dance have been remarkably successful, but in consequence new issues of authenticity have arisen. This is because the Cuban folkloric authority demands that the elite cadre of government-trained dancers must "guard and protect the established representations of Cuban folkloric traditions."[10] As a result of the state's overriding concern with maintaining historical authenticity, professional rumba is in danger of suffering what Yvonne Daniel calls "performance death," as the rumberos go through their highly skilled, but soulless and repetitive, motions in order to preserve the form that has been designated as authentic. The national desire to favor one form of authenticity (genealogical origin) is in danger of eliminating the other (personal expressivity).

This risk is offset by the performances of amateur local dancers who still feel free to combine elements and innovate spontaneously, according to personal mood. Foreigners also insist on changes to the traditional forms, such as the use of female musicians, and these changes are often allowed in order to keep the paying customers happy. But the question then arises as to whether these transformations are genuine rumbas. Do they still retain the meaning and flavor of the original dance, or have they forfeited historical accuracy in pursuit of tourist dollars? This is the quandary not only for rumba, but also for all professionalized and state-supported folkloric arts, where the civic effort to express national identity through traditional forms inevitably comes into conflict with individual creativity.

Tango: The Dance of the Scream

Although the rumba and the meringué are deeply connected to Cuba and the Dominican Republic, the dance that is most intimately associated with national character is the tango, which is recognized everywhere in the world as a uniquely Argentinean product and also as the archetypical expression of lost love and seduction. Argentines agree. According to them, only they have the melancholy stoicism and smoldering sexuality of the true *tanguero*; only they are marked by *el mufarse* – bitter introspection, leavened with self-indulgence, depression united with cynicism – required for the tango. They like to imagine that the tango is "incomprehensible but immutable, the result of a tragic geographic distribution of mood."[11] However, tango's mood is anything but a mere consequence of geography; it is a product of a specific historical and cultural configuration.

Tango was originally the creation of the poor and excluded. Although its origins are shrouded in mystery and subject of impassioned debate, it is agreed that its earliest forms appeared in the slums of Montevideo and the underworld of Buenos Aires in the middle of the nineteenth century. The heroes of the classic tango are tough guys with soft hearts, immigrants to the city who are destined to suffer, betrayed by the women they love and yet mistreat. Its heroines are rebellious femmes fatales, sensual and untrustworthy. Both are seeking to rise in a world that is hostile and alien; both will be destroyed for their efforts. As one lover of tango writes, the plot of a typical tango lyric is: "A patio in the slums. . .A chick, an abuser; two knife-wielding ruffians, seduction, passion, crash, jealousy, discussion, challenges, stabs, confusion, runaways, help, cops. . . Curtain!"[12]

The tango contrasts starkly with the more Africanized dances that are typical of the Caribbean and Latin America. These utilize complex but steady percussive polyrhythms and hip and shoulder rotations; the partners often dance apart within a circle of observers, matching complementary steps in playful competition. In tango, the rhythms are jagged, percussion is minimized, the hips of the dancers are completely immobile, their shoulders stiff; they are alone, locked in a tense erotic embrace as they glide together across the floor, with the woman bent back under the domineering control of her partner. It is, on the surface, a much more European dance genre than others of the area. And, in fact, only tango has been totally integrated into European formal ballroom dance; other dances from South America and the Caribbean – like meringué and rumba – are placed into the mixed category of 'Latin'. This makes symbolic sense, since Argentina prides itself on being the whitest and most European of Latin American nations. It has a minimal Indian population and few black people. Although Spanish in heritage, it looks to France and England as the sources of the high culture to which it aspires. And, in tango, it has apparently succeeded in its aspirations, as Europeans (as well as Japanese, Americans, and other Latin Americans) flock to Argentina to learn the authentic version.

Until the early twentieth century, however, middle-class Argentines regarded tango as the property of the disreputable and impoverished. It was only adopted as their national dance after Parisians, Londoners, and New Yorkers had taken it up (in a sanitized and commodified form) as a dance that combined sensuality and control in a new and enticing fashion. The popularity of the tango in this period was a response to what Sigmund Freud had called 'civilized neurosis'. According to this view, savages were closer to happiness than the civilized because they could express their desires immediately (no doubt this is why tribal dances were thought to be so rampantly sexual). But the complexity of

95

the civilized world made repression an unfortunate necessity for which there was no cure.[13] However, for many ordinary people, the answer to cultural pessimism was obvious. Throw off the stultifying conventions of morality and indulge in more primitive behaviors – at least momentarily, with the option to return to the security of repression if matters got out of hand. Dance was one way this goal could be reached, but modern dance, stiff with self-conscious intellectualism, appealed only to a small avant-garde; pageants, cabarets, and spectacles provided the masses with much more accessible escapes from the necessary constraints of civilization.

At the turn of the century, impresarios organized popular entertainments that played to bourgeois fantasies of the untrammeled sensuality of natives, slum dwellers, peasants, black people, and others who were thought to be in touch with the natural forces of life, love, and liberation. In this era, tango shared the stage with a variety of sexy and exotic genres: hula, flamenco, Russian folk dance, jazz, and almost anything else that seemed primitive, foreign, and novel. All were reckoned to express and inspire the powerful emotional experiences that could cure civilized boredom. However, the tango had some advantages over the other styles. It was not *too* different from what was already known; the dancers were white, or almost white; they came from a country known primarily for exporting its wealthy playboys. The dance was erotic, but not vulgar – no obscene hip movements. Tango was titillating, yet amenable to domestication. The British soon organized tango teas where imported dance masters taught proper young ladies how to tango with decorum; in the United States Rudolf Valentino became a matinee idol.

In its prestigious new guise, tango returned to its homeland as the truest expression of the soul of the Argentine nation. To affirm their ownership, Argentines purged tango of its tainting foreign additions; only *they* really knew how to tango – it was, they said, in their blood (repressing the fact that only a transfusion of European and American appreciation had allowed it to re-enter the national bloodstream). Earlier connotations of class warfare and racial tension were also edited out, and tango became wholly focused on the (supposedly) universal sexual war between men and women.

The psychoanalytically inclined often believe that a repressed sexual story lurks beneath all symbolic expressions. But in the tango, sex is on the surface. The tortured portrayal of desire and repulsion in the dance also can be seen as an expression of Argentina's self-contradictory colonial identity. Tango is the Argentine response to the projected fantasies of Europeans about the passions of the periphery; fantasies which are then internalized and performed in the act that Marta E. Savigliano calls autoexoticism. The urge to autoexoticism is more compelling the more the colonized identify with the colonizer, as is the case for

Argentines, who imagine themselves to be the most European of all Latin American countries, yet are seen as exotic by Europeans. As Savigliano writes: "Exoticism seduces both the colonizer and the colonized. . . The counterpart to the colonizer's fascination is the taste of empowerment experienced by the colonized. For the colonized, exoticization often means being recognized, noticed, and identified, but this glamorous recognition is also objectifying and binding."[14] As another commentator and dancer writes, the tango's drama of seduction and refusal reveals "a passionate desire to comply with the requisites of Europe; a passionate rejection of those same standards; a passionate immersion in a bitterness derived from Europe's rejection of Argentine attempts to imitate their way into a reality about which they are so deeply ambivalent."[15]

Tango is a dance that expresses sexual desire and estrangement, but it also represents the contradictions of self-imposed autoexoticized identities of the Argentines, portrays their resistance to those identities, and expresses the solitude and heartbreak that result. In its jagged fits and starts, images of attraction and rejection, complicity and antagonism, in its almost schizophrenic movement, tango is Argentina's most poignant symbol of its own fractured national identity. For these reasons, a tanguero tells his pupil that if she wants to dance a truly authentic tango she must "dance a tango that screams."[16]

Chapter 8

Modes of Authenticity in the Nation-State

Primordial Nationalism

Castro's proclamation of rumba as Cuba's official dance, state promotion of French champagne, the appearance of the gibnut on the Queen's menu, Trujillo's sponsorship of the meringué, are all examples of the use of concrete symbols in nation-building. Every modern government appropriates indigenous aesthetic productions in order to give itself an aura of legitimacy, continuity, and embodied reality.[1] Unlike earlier republics, kingdoms, and empires, contemporary nation-states are not content with mere control over a territory and the right to collect taxes. As the modern replacements for the sacred institutions of the past, they want to be both obeyed and worshipped.[2]

The concept of nationalism as a secular religion owes much to Émile Durkheim, who famously argued that religion consists of "a unified system of beliefs and practices relative to sacred things, that is to say, things set apart and forbidden – beliefs and practices which unite into one single moral community called a Church, all those who adhere to them."[3] As I mentioned previously, according to Durkheim, active participation in collective rituals allows individuals to become greater than themselves. Their elevation is not due to any supernatural force commanding and instructing them, but arises because they actually feel the powerful uplifting force generated by the group gathered together for dance, song, and worship. It is a kind of rave theory of the divine, where self-transcendence through participation in the united congregation is the deepest reality human beings can know. For Durkheim, the group is a God who *actually* exists, as proven by experience.

Many different kinds of collectives – religious, ethnic, political, aesthetic – can provide this experience, but the nation-state is one of the most potent existing today. To accomplish its mission of establishing a sacralized connection with its citizens, every emergent nation-state not only selects, codifies, and publicizes indigenous aesthetic productions as concrete expressions of the national soul; it also writes its own history books recalling its mythical origins, designs a distinctive flag-totem, composes an anthem praising itself, establishes holidays, pageants, and pilgrimages celebrating its glorious past, and constructs all the other standard symbols of the nation-state. In each school in every modern nation, children are taught from an early age to revere these symbols and celebrations and to love their nation as a surrogate family. If this effort succeeds, the nation-state is stabilized and legitimized, and can make a claim for membership in the international community of countries that have already followed the same path. Success is hardly guaranteed, however, as the number of 'failed states' shows, nor is the eternal loyalty of the citizenry guaranteed, as the collapse of the Soviet Union demonstrates.

Durkheim argued that the cult of the sacred nation is appealing in the modern era because, when the social world has been desacralized, and roles are without moral significance, then the individual is "no more than a lifeless cog, which an external force sets in motion and impels always in the same direction and in the same fashion."[4] Under these alienating circumstances, people feel that their acts, emotions, and relationships have no connection with any fundamental reality. The consequences are high rates of suicide, mental illness, criminality, and other socially destructive behaviors. However, within a healthy and convincing nation-state the individual is redeemed from meaninglessness and can feel the sense of belonging that has been transposed from tribe to nation, from clansman to citizen, from role player to free agent.

This is, of course, an unrealistically idealistic picture of the modern nation-state. But the unifying psychological force of nationalism should not be underestimated. Even when the state's governmental apparatus itself is disliked and repudiated, the nation, as the sacred half of the nation-state equation, is likely to be conceived as the fount of a unique and authentic collective identity. For example, as Michael Herzfeld documents, Greeks, who harbor a great deal of well-warranted animosity toward their state, are simultaneously deeply loyal to their nation and strongly believe that all Greeks share a distinctive national character of "warm-blooded and amiable villains."[5] As a result, Greeks are confident (wrongly, as it turns out) that they can automatically pick out other Greeks from a crowd of mixed nationalities. The firm belief in innate mutual recognition linking all fellow countrymen provides Greeks with feelings of intimacy, solidarity, and belonging that are felt to be natural and organic, growing out of deep roots of shared blood and common experience.

If the nation is a refuge from modern anomie, the question then arises as to who has a right to that refuge. One paradigm for citizenship, which makes the socially constructed nation-state appear deeply rooted in nature and history, is that individuals whose forebears were born into the nation all share a primordial identity with those who have the same biological ancestry and therefore the same primeval collective experiences. Those who are outsiders and newcomers can never be wholly accepted, no matter how much they identify with the nation. The pre-eminent (though hardly the only) case of a modern nation where citizenship was based primarily on this type of genealogical-historical paradigm was Germany. When a unified German state was created in 1871 the constitution asserted that all Germans everywhere were members of a homogenous ethnic *Volksnation*, despite the fact that many who were designated as German citizens lived outside the new national boundaries, spoke no German, and were citizens of other states. In contrast, those without proven German genealogy were hard put to gain citizenship, no matter how long they lived in the country or how assimilated they had become.

This concept of the nation as a primal genealogical entity is a nineteenth-century biologizing transformation of the romantic nationalist ideology most powerfully expressed in the writings of J. G. Herder (1744–1803), an eighteenth-century German philosopher who believed that every culture was worthy of respect, and that none deserved to be enslaved or dispersed. For him, the "understanding of man was intended to blossom and bear fruit in all its varieties."[6] However, the reverse side of his faith in the value of authentic local cultures was contempt for those that had lost their original purity. Herder opposed conquest and colonialism not only because of the destruction meted upon the defeated nation but also because the pristine integrity of both victor and victim would be compromised by exchanges of ideas and customs and by intermarriage and concubinage. Trade also mixed cultures, and led to a loss of spiritual integrity, as did the onset of social complexity and the evolution of a learned elite whose rationality and acceptance of universal principles of logic and rights alienated them from the primordial sources of their heritage. This type of adulteration led to the malaise of modernity.

From Herder's point of view, states in his era had lost their collective souls by permitting foreign immigration, absorbing foreign influences, and succumbing to the disenchanting pressures of modernization, industrialization, and commerce. Only among the isolated rural folk (not in the polyglot modern city) did the vibrant heart of the primal culture still beat. Its pulse could be heard in the simple dances, songs, myths, and legends that arose spontaneously in popular consciousness, resurrecting the *Gemeinschaft* of the original *Volkish* community animated by poetry and intuition, not logic and reason. Motivated by this vision, ever since Herder generations of historians and their philological and folklorist cousins have dedicated themselves to seeking, recapturing, and disseminating what they believed to be the essence of the aboriginal national culture, cleansed of all spurious and exogenous elements. As Eric Hobsbawm has written, "the historian is to the nationalist what the poppy-grower is to the opium addict."[7] Each supplies the stuff of dreams.

Herder's narrative of an untainted past, though not racist in itself, had what Max Weber would call an elective affinity for mythopoeic romantic German nationalist fantasies of reconstituting the primitive folk community as it was before it had been degraded by modernity, mechanization, capitalism, and foreign influence. Those who felt their society had lost its coherence and meaning in the face of modern challenges imagined in compensation an idealistic image of Germany as a mystical unity animated by a potent collective life-force. Contrasting "their own deep inner life of the spirit, the poetry of their national soul, the simplicity and nobility of their character, to the empty, heartless sophistication of the French," these nationalist intellectuals and artists rejected a modernity that privileged reason over feeling, universal principles over local traditions.[8] German essence, they said, was embodied in 'a nation of people' (volksnation) and not in what the French Enlightenment thinkers had called a 'nation of citizens', which Herder and other German romantics despised as a recipe for alienation, since it put the individual on a pedestal, cut off from the community.

As German romantic nationalism evolved into ever more essentialist new forms, the folkloric quest for primal origins easily blended with emergent popularized notions of race, which asserted shared biological ancestry as the ultimate and incorruptible source of cultural authenticity, counterpoised against the Creolizing and dehumanizing trajectory of modernity.[9] In this racist version of nationalism, only true Germans, born of Germans with impeccable German genealogies, could transcend corrupting modern influences and recapture the fading national gemeinschaft. Of course, this was not the only direction that a folkloric idealization of the nation could take. The Grundtvigian movement in Denmark, for example, was essentially romantic in nature, but led to a nationalism based on democratization and resistance to fascism.[10] And in Germany itself, there was by no means a 'straight line' leading from romantic nationalism to cultural essentialism to Nazi racism. It is well to recall that Kant and Goethe were extreme universalists who would have been appalled at Hitler's bigotry.

But for many complex cultural and historical reasons, which cannot be elaborated here, the racist implications of a genealogical version of citizenship, derived intellectually from a particular reading of Herder and propelled by threatening social circumstances, found their apotheosis in the Salvationist doctrines of the Nazis, which arrived "complete with Messiah, a holy book, a cross, the trappings of religious pageantry, a priesthood of black-robed and anointed elite, excommunication and death for heretics, and the millennial promise of the Thousand Year Reich."[11] The Nazis, motivated by resentment against successful rival states and by fear of attack and disintegration, worshipped the nation rooted in German blood and soil as the most authentic form of life, and venerated Hitler as the nation's embodiment and redeemer. As one of the faithful put it, "Hitler was given by fate to the German nation as our savior, bringing light into darkness."[12] The Nazi movement became the Hitler movement; the Nazi salute, "Heil Hitler," was the national greeting. This process reached its apogee when Rudolf Hess told the great Party rally in 1934 that "Adolf Hitler is Germany, and Germany is Adolf Hitler." And in return, Hitler declared: "I know that everything you are, you are through me, and everything I am, I am through you alone!"[13]

The most powerful and compelling expression of the Hitler religion occurred during the great Party convocations, where tens of thousands of participants paraded and cheered, lost in an ecstatic collective worship of Hitler and the state. In Durkheimian fashion, these ritual occasions were standardized into a new liturgical calendar, with massive celebration of Hitler's birthday as the Spring Festival, All Saints' day replaced by commemoration of the beer-hall putsch, and so on. There were sacred objects as well, notably a venerated flag that was said to have been soaked in the blood of the martyrs who died during the beer-hall putsch. All new Nazi banners were touched to this sacred flag in order to absorb the mystical powers flowing from it. Similarly, parade grounds became sacred spaces, rallies became religious processions, and a whole panoply of shrines and pilgrimage centers sacralized the Nazi world around the catalyzing figure of the Führer.

For the faithful believers in the Hitler cult, any one who claimed to be German, but did not have a German bloodline, or anyone who transgressed what the Nazis defined as primordial German political or moral boundaries, was importing a cancerous hybridity into the pure soul of the nation. There were many who were defined in this way: Gypsies, homosexuals, the mentally ill, black people, and so on. But the most hated were the Jews, who were pictured as an amorphous and floating population, exiles without roots, duplicitously changing shape to adapt to their environment. They even looked, talked, and acted like Germans! They mixed licentiously with real German people, hiding their own polluted identities while seducing the innocent in order to produce monstrous offspring. According to this ideology, the Jews were fluid, formless, and uncanny, spreading promiscuously and tainting the blood of the German nation like a lethal virus, destroying its honor, weakening its will, and ruining its future. Hitler's anti-Semitism had deep resonances with German popular culture, where Jews had long been portrayed as subversive, money-hungry, and generally despicable.[14]

According to Hitler's polarizing worldview, the Jews had to be destroyed for the authentic German nation to prevail. "Two worlds face one another – the men of God and the men of Satan! The Jew is the anti-man, the creature of another god." The cataclysmic confrontation between these two forces is, Hitler said, "in truth the critical battle for the fate of the world."[15] The cosmic struggle took precedence over military logistics, as resources were channeled away from hard-pressed German armies at the close of World War II and devoted to speeding the elimination of the Jews, whose vile interventions were said to be responsible for any German defeats.

Repellant as Hitler's movement was, it had a goal we can recognize. As Fred Weinstein reminds us: "Hitler was concerned with the fall from perfection, with human limitations, with freeing people imprisoned in a world of moral and bodily restraints. He wanted to break through to a new reality, the true one, he thought, and one more consistent with human potentiality and desire."[16] His messianic ambition was to repudiate the complex, industrialized, and alienating modern world and recapture the authentic racial essence flowing in the veins of the natural folk ennobled by their Aryan blood. By eliminating the amorphous Jews and other degraded populations, Hitler hoped to protect the purity of the German heart and soul. And so he precipitated the Holocaust.

Who Belongs?

The form of citizenship that is authenticated on the grounds of shared ancestry is especially convincing in the modern world where genealogy is given priority as 'natural' and therefore unequivocal. But it is not the only option. Alternatively, the right to be recognized as a citizen can emanate from the individual's deep personal faith in the particular beliefs and values of the nation.[17] Both forms of authentication (origin and content) always exist in tandem, although they are weighted differently and shift over time. For example, today Germany has completely retreated from its previous genealogical standards for citizenship, and now awards citizenship to every child born in Germany whose parents have been law-abiding residents for eight years. In fact, the constitutions of most nations today define citizens by their rights and duties, not by their bloodlines or birthplace. The official emphasis on citizenship is particularly characteristic of new nations, which are made up of immigrants who have no claims to racial purity. At the same time, immigrants who arrived earlier often do make claims to a kind of racial superiority as 'first settlers'. This seemingly irresistible impulse is evident in the long history of prejudice against newcomers to the United States.

In Europe, the universalistic and incorporative model of citizenship has been most clearly exemplified in post-revolutionary France, where a citizen is anyone who embraces the fundamental French Enlightenment values of individualism, reason, equality, democracy, and *laïcité* (secularism), regardless of race, ethnic origin, or religion.[18] Within this framework, France defines itself as "a political community to which newcomers are admitted providing they accept the political norms and national culture. In principle, it does not recognize the right of minorities to make claims for cultural recognition and social rights on the basis of their group identity."[19] Because the incorporative French nationalist creed rejects the concept of a minority with its own political identity, in principle it also ignores any potentially disruptive or exclusivist primordial ethnic, religious, or racial differences. This philosophy would seem to be a formula for tolerance, but instead the French ideology of national identity based on shared *civilisation* ran aground because of its inability to accommodate alternative claims for authenticity and identity expressed by Muslim immigrants.[20]

The official French doctrine is that the unitary liberal state would compromise its own reasons for being if it were to recognize foreign characteristics and loyalties. In deference to this assumption, the French census did not include information on ethnic or racial backgrounds of respondents, for "fear of giving even verbal recognition to the settlement of people seen as enduringly different from the indigenous majority."[21] This is the case despite the fact that for the last two centuries France, in line with its civic ideal of inclusion and openness, has accepted more immigrants into its boundaries than any other European nation. In 1995 immigrants, children of immigrants, or grandchildren of immigrants made up about 14 percent of the population. Among these the most numerous are Muslims, mostly from North Africa, who have turned Islam into the second largest religion in France. Yet, whatever their origins, all were officially conceived to be French citizens who simply happened to have non-French ancestors and who therefore required no special categorization or attention.

As late as 1993 the report of the High Committee on Integration repeated the litany that France "does not recognize any ethnic or religious communities" and that all French citizens are equal free agents, participating voluntarily in the national project. At the same time the report paradoxically recommended that special attention be paid to "immigrant communities," and particularly to "Muslim and Algerian communities."[22] The committee's reluctant acceptance of the existence of minority enclaves within the national framework was a response to a new situation in France. Previously, immigrants and other marginalized groups had rarely contested the state's version of what it meant to be a French citizen. But after the late 1970s some North African immigrants, resentful of their marginalization and impoverishment in the *banlieues*, began to affirm their own cultural and religious minority identities and vigorously demanded collective recognition from the state, in defiance of the assumptions that are at the base of French civil society.

The opposition between the French national creed of equality, secularism, and individualism and the demands of Muslim immigrants for collective recognition took center stage in 1989 when three Muslim girls refused to remove their headscarves in a state high school, stating that Islam required them to veil in public.[23] This seemingly minor symbolic act caused a major uproar, as it was seen as a direct challenge to the French secular religion of laïcité. The "*affaire du voile*" soon escalated. The issues were whether the girls were being forced to wear veils against their wills, and whether they needed protection by the liberal-democratic state against the despotism of their parents and the irrational demands of a fundamentalist Islam. Was the schools' mandate to teach Republican virtues of secularism, individualism, and loyalty to the nation fundamentally undermined by the religious and political symbolism of the headscarf? Did the presence of the veil in school endanger the respect for spiritual and cultural differences that is necessary in a unitary nation-state? Was veiling the first salvo in what would eventually become a civil war between secularist French nationalists and immigrant Muslim zealots?

Such alarmist cries of subversion led to the convocation of a government commission to study the issue. Various ameliorative proposals were made advocating respect for religious beliefs, but on March 15, 2004, President Jacques Chirac accepted only the recommendation that outlawed all forms of conspicuous religious symbolism in the state school system, infuriating many Muslims who interpreted the ruling as a direct attack on their community and their religious beliefs. The burning and looting that took place soon afterwards in the banlieues was generally understood as a result of outrage against this decision, though there were certainly many other issues in play, not least of which was the state's failure to address poverty and joblessness among the Muslim population.

Obliged by circumstances, France has covertly but pragmatically forgone its earlier faith in the inevitable assimilation and integration of immigrants into a secular and incorporative French society and has initiated a policy of 'insertion' in which Muslim and North African cultural and religious groups are recognized and supported by the state, justifying this apostasy against the official creed on the Durkheimian grounds that participation in voluntary associations is a valuable step toward citizenship, regardless of the content of the association. A policy of accommodation aims to draw Muslims gradually into civil society by first giving them a taste of collective responsibility. But, as critics have been quick to point out, this policy "runs the risk of essentializing and freezing timeless cultural differences within the boundaries of homogeneous ethnic groups."[24] Muslims and North Africans who wish to escape from the grasp of French secular universalism are likely to find that the price of participation in a minority community is submission to the commands of self-styled cultural/religious leaders who ironically have often been granted official legitimacy by the very state they oppose.

Meanwhile, in response to the Muslim outcries, French ultra-nationalists retorted that only people with French blood deserve French citizenship. This racial claim has a long history. France itself, of course, is named after the Franks, a Germanic-speaking people who established the Merovingian dynasty in the fifth century AD. Afterwards the French nobility and royal family claimed these invaders as their ancestors, tracing the birth of the nation, and their own lineages, to the Frankish king Clovis and his attendants. According to this ideology, the rest of the French population was descended from the local Gallo-Romans who were defeated by the Franks (Rome conquered the native Iron Age Celts in the first century AD). Prior to the Revolution, the elite used this ancient ethnic division between the master race of Franks and the subservient race of Gallo-Romans to justify their continuing domination over an increasingly restive populace.

During the Revolution, the notion of racial origin as the essential characteristic of a true French citizen remained, though the values were reversed. As Michael Dietler recalls, the revolutionary theorist Abbé de Sieyès urged an ethnic cleansing of all those with Frankish blood so that the new French republic would be "constituted solely of the descendents of the Gauls and Romans."[25] Unusually, not just one ancestral line is invoked here, but two: the local barbarian Gauls, characterized by their bravery and tribal honor, are placed alongside the invading civilized Romans, known for their discipline, imperial past, and urban sophistication. The tension between these two imagined ancestors has been continually played out in post-revolutionary French history. Institutionally, the multinational, legalistic, and rational Roman Empire has generally provided the appropriate civic model for the universalistic ideals of the Republic, but the popular emotional appeal of a substrate of vigorous tribal Celtic/Gallic blood has remained potent, especially in times of crisis. For example, Napoleon I justified his campaign of expansionism on the grounds that he was reuniting the ancient land of the Gauls, just as Hitler would later justify his conquests as reclamation of the Aryan heartland. When

Napoleon's ambition stretched beyond the hypothetical borders of the ancient Celtic world, he turned toward the Roman imperial model. The court painters and sculptors thereafter portrayed him as a Roman king, and Roman imagery prevailed in his empire.

In 1865, a symbolic return to Celtic roots took place, as Napoleon III had a massive statue of Vercingétorix, the near-mythical Gallic leader of resistance against the Roman invasion, erected at the site of Rome's final victory. Significantly, the statue's face was modeled after Napoleon's own. According to Dietler, by honoring the indigenous Gauls while at the same time recognizing the benefits of the Roman conquest, Napoleon III sought to unite the two strands of French racial identity. Simultaneously, he subtly justified the expansion of the contemporary French empire in Asia and North Africa as a necessary step in world civilization just as the Roman conquest of France had been in its time. Afterwards, and in the wake of French defeats by the Prussians in 1870, Vercingétorix (who had been more or less unheard of previously, and about whom very few facts are known even today) became an ubiquitous national symbol, and French schoolchildren (as well as their colonized counterparts) have been obliged ever since to study "our ancestors, the Gauls."

Following upon the resurgence of the biological model of Frenchness, many genealogically inclined historians and popularizers throughout the late nineteenth and twentieth centuries expended a great deal of time and energy attempting to describe the exact physical characteristics of the ideal dark, short, brachycephalic 'Celtic type' which was contrasted to the lighter, taller dolichocephalic 'German race'. The purest Frenchman, it was said, could be found in the Auvergne, the rural area at the center of the nation – not among the debased and cranially challenged inhabitants of Paris. Contemporary anthropologists do not accept these fanciful attributions. As Dietler writes: "It is doubtful that the peoples of these diverse societies ever had a cohesive collective identity or ethnonym, and they clearly never constituted a unified political community"[26]

A lack of historical accuracy has had little effect on French romantics and conservatives who are opposed to the universalistic national values of individualism, reason, equality, inclusive democracy, and laïcité. From their perspective, the rationalism of the Enlightenment was a depraved attack on French (and human) spiritual integrity; the Revolution finished the job by annihilating traditional authority, destroying regional autonomy, undermining local character, and imposing a soulless and abstract state, bound to crush any human values in pursuit of the chimera of equality. In its place, they argued for "the idea of the encompassing totality" which would recognize each nation's unique "collective soul."[27] Obviously, this model of the nation is parallel with the organic philosophy of German nationalism, as it developed from Herder's theory of authentic folk culture. The main difference is that here the folk culture referred to is not German, but French; not Aryan, but Gallic.

Missionary Politics[28]

A comparison of case studies shows some of the characteristic patterns of the primordialist model of national authenticity, as it has developed in the modern era. In France, the standard-bearer for the fight against modern liberal universalism was Jean Marie Le Pen, the charismatic leader of the populist National Front, whose anti-immigrant stance and ardent support for a blood-based French identity gained him a small but ardent following. Le Pen's argument against the predominant French value system was framed within a narrative of a larger struggle against what he termed the destructive twin forces of cultural homogenization and biological hybridization. His messianic political oratory is typical of the rhetoric of a worldwide movement favoring blood and heritage over citizenship based on values of equality and participation.

Like the cultural conservatives who were his inspiration, Le Pen rejected the Enlightenment ideal of the state as a community voluntarily tied together by shared beliefs and by participation in a democratic polity. In Le Pen's view, the Enlightenment values of disinterested reason, secularism, inclusion, equality, and individual choice destroyed cultural integrity. His heroes were not the leaders of the Revolution, whose aim, he said, was to declare the Rights of Man while eradicating the Rights of the Soul. Instead, the National Front hailed Joan of Arc, who martyred herself to defend the French nation against England, just as Le Pen claimed to be sacrificing himself to save France from the homogenizing and technocratic forces of globalization, capitalism, Islam, Americanism, and the international mercantile/political elite.

In Le Pen's apocalyptic eschatology there were many enemies and few friends. Only he and his loyal followers, he said, realized that France had fallen victim to a massive plot hatched during the Enlightenment, carried through in the Revolution, culminating in the modern era. According to him, the French majority had been so seduced by capitalism that they had forgotten their fundamental values; meanwhile, faith in impersonal science had dissolved moral judgment, local traditions had vanished under the pressure of globalization, and the nation had begun to lose its racial integrity due to massive immigration. As a result, France was in deadly danger of being absorbed into a spiritually bankrupt world empire dominated by the multicultural deracinated capitalistic behemoth consisting of the United States and its allies, which included the International Monetary Fund, the World Bank, the Trilateral Commission, Jews,

Freemasons, and other conspirators promoting an artificial, homogenous, anti-human New World Order.

To allow Le Pen to speak for himself:

> [We have] borders that disappear, local and cultural specificities that blur to the advantage of a universal culture, an ideology of human rights elevated to the rank of Holy Gospel, an appearance of democracy, a planetary market economy, one currency (why not the dollar?), and the belt is buckled. The World Village is not a whim anymore. We witness..., a true totalitarianism [that is] much more vicious than communism and much more destructive.[29]

According to Le Pen, in this brave new world,

> men and women will be sacrificed to Humanity and the self-appointed experts will define and organize their happiness. This happiness will be the same on all the continents....In order to accomplish this Orwellian project it is necessary to uproot the people and to dissolve the familiar, religious, civic, social and associational links...that is why the family and the Nation are their main targets. The family because it is the material link of the transmission of life and moral values. The Nation because it is a superior principle of effective solidarity, dignity and security.[30]

Only a religious crusade can avoid this dire outcome. "Materialism, rationalism, scientism, will be defeated by a formidable aspiration for a spiritual renewal...a vital reaction against the programmed death of the human civilization in all its diversity."[31]

In Le Pen's messianic vision, the National Front was destined to be the inspiration for a general uprising of authentic local cultures worldwide against the disintegrative universalistic principles of global capitalism and the corruptions of modernity. However, the revolution against the Enlightenment could only be realized if the nation purged itself of foreign influence and returned to its authentic genealogical essence. As a result, the National Front pursued an anti-immigrant, anti-Muslim, anti-Semitic agenda.

Le Pen's urgent defense of primordial national identity was far from unique. The same missionary rhetoric has been proclaimed by minority nationalist parties of both the right and left throughout Europe and, indeed, in the rest of the world. For example, Umberto Bossi, the leader of the Northern League in Italy, declared that his country was under the sway of the *partitocrazia*, an unholy alliance of political parties, media, and money, which was supported by a sinister global conspiracy to bring the "birth of a multiracial society, of identical men with the same ambitions and without traditions. In sum, the big consumer, fat from hamburgers and drowned in a sea of Coca-Cola." The League's mission was "to stop globalization and to prevent everything from being made into a product, to prevent man from being reduced to a thing, always the same, *homo economicus*, without soul and identity."[32] According to Bossi, immigration was just one tactic in the effort to substitute artificial forms of life for all natural affiliations and local traditions. The end result, he said, will be a human being reduced to a cipher, without community, culture, or family, eating manufactured foods, living manufactured lives, impotent to resist the massive forces arrayed against him.

But, rather than calling for a purification of the entire nation, as Le Pen had done for France, Bossi wanted independence for his homeland of 'Padania' (former Lombardy), which he said was culturally, genealogically, and histori-cally linked to central Europe, not to Italy. For Bossi, Lombards were only attached to Italy because of historical contingencies, which the state proclaimed as inevitable to disguise its own self-interest. But like Le Pen, Bossi had a higher goal: to "liberate the peoples of the peninsula – and Europe – from the yoke of the State... For this it was born, for this it has grown and fights without mercy against its eternal enemies. If successful, it wins its historical battle. If not, it fails. There is no middle ground."[33] His argument was that individuals every-where can only preserve their true identities in small, historically rooted, cul-turally and ethnically homogenous communities. To avoid destruction of the human soul, all authentic local collectives must fight against the universalizing ideology of the modern state and its evil companions of homogenization, Americanization, capitalism, and rational bureaucracy.

A messianic call to resistance is not the sole property of political reactionaries. For example, in France the National Front's right-wing rhetoric of a shared Gallic/Celtic ancestry was mirrored by leftist Breton nationalists, who declared that Bretons must be freed from the same French state that Le Pen wanted purged of non-Gallic influence. For the Breton nationalists, most Frenchmen and women (including Le Pen and his followers) were not actually Gauls at all; the only *real* Gauls and Celts lived in Brittany and in Cornwall, Ireland, Scotland, and Wales, where some form of Celtic language was still spoken. For them, France was an enemy that had denied an authentic identity to its own culturally oppressed Celtic peoples; these peoples should be reunited with their tyrannized Gallic brethren across the Channel.

The appeal of this trope has been truly astonishing. Even the faceless bureau-crats of the European Union (EU) have recently enunciated a primordialist narrative of authenticity in an attempt (mostly in vain) to gain the love and loyalty of its citizens. This is despite the fact that the EU is the quintessential cultural offspring of the Enlightenment, convened precisely in order to provide the practical benefits of economic justice, legal order, and institutionalized rationality that romantic nationalists detest. Its universalistic and formal character is perfectly symbolized in the EU currency, which features semi-abstract architectural drawings, without reference to any existent object, place, or person. To offset its image as the main agent of soulless conformity in Europe, the EU has tried to present itself as the rightful heir of the ancient Celtic culture, portrayed as the first civilization that included all of present-day Europe within its boundaries. EU sponsorship of archeological exhibits on the Celtic heritage of Europe has been marshaled to substantiate this dubious claim.

Whether associated with an existent state, or with localized independence movements, or with linguistic-cultural collectives that cross state boundaries, or even with the abstract universalistic bureaucracy of the EU, all of these ideologies have drawn upon spiritualized narratives of peoples united by shared blood and heritage. And, in pursuit of primal origins, they downplay or even deny outright the possibility of a collective bound together by a common belief in the principles of liberalism and the practice of secularism and political individualism. This is a worldwide phenomenon. Assertion of a primordial authenticity of blood has provided the rationale for nationalistic, ethnic, racial, religious, or tribal anti-modernist and anti-universalistic social movements everywhere, often with dire consequences. As proof, all one needs to recall is the Tutsi genocide in Rwanda, or the murderous ethnic cleansing in Darfur.

Chapter 9

Israel and Authentic Jewish Identity

Defining Jews, Founding Israel

The story of Israel, which proclaims itself as "the only place in the world where an authentic Jewish culture can flourish"[1] is a particularly complex example of how the quest for an essential authenticity has been intertwined with the rise of a nation-state, and how both have been transformed over time due to internal and external circumstances. Israel defines itself as the ancestral homeland for God's chosen people, who have been humiliated, defeated, massacred, and scattered to the four winds ever since the destruction of the Second Temple in Jerusalem and the loss of Jewish sovereignty in 70 AD. From then onward, Jews everywhere have prayed daily for the ingathering of exiles in Zion, where they can re-establish their physical connection with their sacred place of origin, and, some believe, move toward the eventual realization of God's promise of ultimate redemption. In the aftermath of the Holocaust, many non-Jews also supported Jewish repatriation – despite the troublesome presence of Palestinian Arabs who said the land had belonged to them from time immemorial.

The primordial connection between Israeli citizenship and Jewishness was articulated early in the nation's existence in a speech delivered to the parliament (the *Knesset*) by prime minister David Ben-Gurion, who explained that

> it is not this state which grants Jews from abroad the right to settle in it, but that this right is inherent by virtue of one's being a Jew. . . . This right preceded the state of Israel, and it was this right which built the state of Israel. This right originates from the historical bond between the fatherland and nation, which was never severed.

In this paradigmatic statement Jews are presented as linked to one another and to Israel in an elemental fashion, so that "legislation simply expresses what is natural, organic and true."[2] But the apparent simplicity of the Jewish/Israeli connection hides a convoluted debate about who actually does count as Jewish, and how Judaism itself should be defined.

The question of who is a Jew is a very modern one. Prior to the end of the eighteenth century, European Jews assumed Judaism was a solidary combination of belief, practice, and a common spiritual and genealogical essence. Judaism meant belonging to a God-given community that defined itself in reference to the central body of Jewish law, the *halakha*. It also meant being born of a Jewish mother, though it was also possible (with great difficulty) to convert and become Jewish.[3] Because Judaism was regarded not only as practice but also as an innate state of being, one could never cease being a Jew. As a halakhic principle states, "Israel who has sinned is still Israel." For this reason, a Jew who converted to Christianity did not need to reconvert to become a Jew again – only to repent. At the same time, there was no possibility of becoming a secular Jew; that was an identity that did not yet exist. The only option for those who did not follow the law was to leave the fold entirely and join another religion. Nor were there any identity issues caused by variation in practice, since it was assumed that all Jews everywhere followed – or at least referred to – the same fundamental set of halakhic principles.[4]

All this was to change when the advent of Emancipation led to a revaluation of the nature and essence of Judaism. Freed from old restrictions by the Enlightenment values of equality and participation, and inspired by the rise of the universalistic and incorporative secular nation-state where all people could become citizens, many Jewish reformers[5] ceased to pray for restoration of the homeland and dropped usage of Hebrew in their prayers, seeking instead greater connection to the places in which they lived. They also began to redefine Judaism as a personal religion, chosen and voluntary, and therefore not in conflict with citizenship. For example, the philosopher Moses Mendelssohn, Kant's contemporary and the founder of the Jewish reformation movement in Germany, argued that German Jews should be regarded as Germans of the 'Mosaic persuasion'. Some modernizers even dropped religious practice altogether in favor of socialism and Marxism, but still claimed to be Jews by virtue of their identification with the Jewish people. They were 'Jewish, but not Jews'. All this took place alongside public debate and doctrinal splits within the Jewish community about the relationship of man to God, the content of the law, and the interpretation of practice. As the cohesion and certainty of the community melted away, "Jewish existence became questionable. The Jews had to embark on the weary business of self-definition."[6] But self-definition had a positive side too, as many Jews began to think they could hold their destiny in their own hands and escape from anti-Semitism and European pogroms by taking action, instead of passively waiting for God's intervention.

From this upheaval the idea of Israel was born. Although Israeli ideology places Jewishness at the very center of its existence, the Israeli state was not inaugurated by the efforts of the pious. To the contrary, many Orthodox Jews opposed (and still oppose) the foundation of Israel on religious grounds as premature and presumptuous. According to them, Israel could be united only after the arrival of the Messiah. Israel's founders were mostly secularized European Jews who were heavily influenced by Herder's essentialist German romantic theory of nationalism. Theodor Herzl (1860–1904), the charismatic leader of the international Zionist movement, was a secular Austrian journalist of Jewish descent who was shocked into activism by the rabid anti-Semitism evidenced in the Dreyfus trial in France and by the widespread harassment of Jews in eastern Europe. At the same time, Herzl was ashamed of and repelled by the religiously conservative Jews of the urban ghettoes with their pallid skins, old-fashioned piety, and foreign-looking sidelocks and yarmulkes. They clearly did not fit into the progressive modern world he lived in, and their appearance and attitude seemed to invite repression. Herzl and his companions believed these problems could be solved by giving Jews their own independent state, which at first was planned not for Israel, but for Uganda. He and the other founders assumed that Jews with their own state (wherever it was located) would transcend their status as despised minorities and become equal members of the community of nations. Furthermore, in a new homeland, "our pants-peddling boys could be transformed . . . [into] agile, courageous riders."[7]

The Zionist dream of agile Jews on horseback was finally realized after World War II, when the Balfour declaration proclaimed Palestine the national homeland for Jews. In 1948 Israel was born. Herzl wrote a revealing utopian novel (*Altneuland* or 'Old-New Land') about his hopes for the new state. In his book, he imagined the future Israel as a socially progressive, economically advanced place where Passover is celebrated with uplifting songs about the state; human happiness is produced by bumper crops, industrial growth, and clean streets; religious, national, and ethnic pride are replaced by Enlightenment values of universal human rights.[8]

Zionism was, in short, a very Western and very modern project, based on assumptions that Israel would resemble, more than anything else, an advanced social-democratic European nation-state, but with a Jewish (rather than French, German, or Italian) citizenry. It was thought that traditional Jewish religious life would play a distinctly subordinate role in the nascent homeland, which would be a place where Jews could give up their tainted urban occupations as middlemen, tailors, and small-scale entrepreneurs. Instead, they would work their own farms, become healthy, handsome, and virile, eliminate the contemptible traits that made them easy targets for persecution, and find their true identities as free men and women actively creating a collectivist utopia. As Ben-Gurion's statement makes clear, this project was based on the conviction that Jews everywhere had a primordial shared identity derived from genealogy, character, and outlook. This primal unity, which had been submerged and distorted in the diaspora, would flower in Israel, making it easy for the new nation to integrate and establish a solid identity in the world community.[9] In this formulation, little attention was paid to the varieties of Jewish practice, the multiple ethnic and cultural backgrounds of Jews worldwide, or to the ethnocentricism of secularized intellectual Ashkenazi Jews who led the Zionist movement and who took their worldview for granted. The ingathering of exiles (*kibbutz galuyot*), it was thought, would inevitably be followed by *mizug galuyot*, the fusion of exiles.

Jews on Horseback

As Herzl predicted, in the early years of the Israeli state Zionist nationalism did indeed become the dominant faith, suppressing all alternatives.[10] This process was aided by the violent beginnings of the new nation. Within the cult of Zionism, the soldiers who died in battle were consecrated as martyrs for the holy cause. Ubiquitous shrines to the sanctified dead became centers for pilgrimage and for rituals associated with national holidays; Yizkor, the memorial prayer, was Zionism's declaration of faith, and the memorial anthologies were the equivalents of national prayer books. Jewish religious rituals were recast to retell the story of the nation's struggle for existence – for example, Passover (Pesach) shifted from a celebration of the greatness of God to a commemoration of Jewish independence; traditional holidays were supplemented by memorials to heroic Zionist history; nationalistic songs about the homeland served as a substitute liturgy, while a new version of the traditional male Hasidic dance (the *hora*) was transformed into the dance of the barefoot kibbutzim youth celebrating their unity by circling together, hands joined in ecstatic solidarity. The nationalization of religion was graphically symbolized in the festival of first fruits, which were ceremoniously bestowed not on the rabbi, but on representatives of the Israeli government.

In the Zionist eschatology a striking new embodiment of Israeli/Jewish authenticity developed. These were the Sabra[11] – the native-born "agile, courageous riders" foreseen by Herzl. Though this personality type has now lost much of its allure, it represented the living essence of the nation in the public imagination from the 1930s to the 1960s. The term Sabra is taken from the Arabic word *tzabar* (*sabbar* in Hebrew), the prickly pear cactus, which became a symbol of Israel (ironically it was originally imported into the region from Central America).[12] Like the tzabar, the ideal Sabra was said to have a prickly and tough exterior, concealing and protecting a delicate and sensitive sweetness within. The Sabra's unique character was believed to be a result of "growing up, so it was said, naturally, 'without complexes,' in their true homeland."[13] As memorialized in innumerable romanticized accounts and portraits, the archetypical Sabra were native-born, kibbutz-raised Israelis of Ashkenazi descent, well educated and imbued with strong belief in their own innate moral and physical superiority. The ideal Sabra was poetic and tender, bold and athletic, tousle-headed, confident, casual, insolent, tanned, handsome, and European looking, the exact opposite of the stereotypical urban Jewish shopkeeper of the old country.[14] The Sabra clothing style was simple, even slovenly: sandals, khaki work pants, and shirts that were wrinkled and untucked. Sabra women did not wear makeup or jewelry. Even on formal occasions the Sabra flaunted their monastic simplicity, their energy, their self-conscious primitivism, and their contempt for all forms of sophistication, which they saw as masks for weakness. They disparaged Jewish refugees from Hitler for their passivity and referred to them as 'human dust' or 'soap'. Oriental Jews were laughed at for their piety and backwardness.

The Sabra modeled themselves expressly on the heroes of American cowboy movies and on the local Bedouin horsemen, even wearing Arab headdresses. Herzl's virile "courageous riders" cherished the easy egalitarian camaraderie of camping, hiking, and adventurous marches deep into the hinterland. "We worship the land as a man worships his God" one Sabra wrote.[15] The central ritual of the Sabra was the evening group *kumzitz* (come sit) in which a group of buddies (male and female) gathered around the campfire to sing Hebrew nationalist songs and drink coffee from a primitive pot made of tin cans. Eating charred potatoes and onions with their hands under the stars, slurping from the communal coffee tin and joking together, far away from the city and its decadent civilization, the Sabra saw themselves as natural and genuine, connected to their ancestral homeland and to one another in a deep and intimate way, much like they imagined the native Bedouin to be. This romantic vision was linked to the notion that Palestine was fundamentally a wilderness, inhabited by savages.

In their pursuit of the simple life, the Sabra did away with conventional etiquette. Among them there was no polite 'please' or 'thank you'. A pat on the back sufficed. Hebrew was spoken with a blunt and sarcastic slanginess, called *dugri*, a term taken from Arabic, signifying straight, accurate.[16] Among the Sabra it came to mean without affectation, devoid of religious references; it also meant confrontational, non-deferential, bluntly assertive, and, most importantly, the direct expression of the speaker's own true attitude regardless of the feelings and opinions of others. The Sabra's distinctive aggressive style of straight talk was a self-conscious negation of the style of the diaspora, which was despised as intellectual and obsequious. The Sabra also rejected romantic notions of self-discovery through painful soul-searching. For them, the true self was already known; authenticity was a matter of saying exactly what one feels and thinks, and then acting according to one's words. As Tamar Katriel brilliantly demonstrates, in their "accent of sincerity and the attitude of antistyle" the Sabra asserted their autonomy, their 'naturalness' and, paradoxically, their collective solidarity.[17] The assumption was that self-assertive confrontation reaffirms the larger unity of 'those who speak dugri', who are inherently honest, true, and straightforward, and who can therefore be trusted to defend the nation bravely.

The final socialization into the Sabra ideal came mainly through participation in the much-feared commando forces, the Haganah, and Palmach, and, after the formation of the state, by membership in other elite combat units. Small and exclusive, bound together by shared danger and a strong sense of the values of the collective, these military units undertook glamorous clandestine attacks where fatalities were high. Intense hazing and numerous secret rituals helped to instill deep ties of loyalty and affection among the men and women of these close-knit groups. Under the constant threat of death and accustomed to killing, they cultivated a defiant, unsentimental, and ironic demeanor and were famous for their irreverent attitudes and supreme self-confidence. In keeping with general ethos, the Sabra senior officer wore no insignia and dressed and acted like everyone else. For example, Moishe Dayan "walked to his general's office without a hat or insignia and in sandals and gave friendly slaps on the shoulder to those who came to see him there."[18] Ideally, such a leader inspired love and admiration by character alone; he was imagined to be a poet/warrior who would willingly die to protect his men. Above all, the Sabra leader was authentic, which in this context meant speaking and acting dugri, without artifice, hard-boiled, true, honest, brave, self-sacrificing, tough, and direct – a natural leader and a 'real person'.

For nationalists, the Sabra, as the embodied exemplars of the besieged Israeli state, represented a reborn, self-confident Jewish people who had finally found their true, virile, yet sensitive inner essence after generations of toadying, introspection, and effeminacy.[19] In their mode of speech and their collective rituals the Sabra invented a new Israeli Jewish identity that was based on deep emotional

117

bonds and strong feelings of communion, as well as on self-assertion and pride. In this constellation, the expression of personal authenticity and the defense of Israel mutually reinforced one another. It was a kind of identity that was well suited to nation-building in a pioneer environment that was highly contested, dangerous, fluid, and unstructured. These tough new Jews knew how to defend themselves against their enemies, and deserved to fly their flag proudly. That they were also almost all Ashkenazi Jews with European backgrounds went more or less unnoticed. Also unnoticed was the implicit denigration of all who did not belong to their mystical band of warriors.

The Poly-Ethnic Theme Park[20]

This attitude did not last. After independence, new modes of collective identity based on ethnicity and religiosity quickly appeared to compete with Sabra dominance. To understand this, we need to recall that, despite the official rhetoric of fundamental and innate Jewish unity, the Jews are by no means a homogenous group. For thousands of years, the diaspora spread the Jewish population all over the world. As a result of this long historical process, even though Israelis still consciously identify themselves firstly as Jewish or as Israeli, they also identify themselves secondarily by their various places of origin and ethnicity.

The major division among Jews in Israel is between the Mizrachim (Middle Easterners, Spanish Sephardim, and Asians) and the Ashkenazim (northwestern Europeans);[21] but there are internal divisions as well, as Yemeni Jews differentiate themselves from Bukharan Jews, Iraqi Jews are distinct from Moroccan Jews, Russians differ from Poles and Rumanians, and so on. These divisions often are marked by significant symbolic and cultural differences in practice, belief, identification, marriage, and residence. The Mizrachim also have tended to be poorer, more religiously inclined, and less influential than their Ashkenazi cousins. It is also important to note that Israel is the youngest society in the world, and has the highest proportion of citizens who were not born in the country (40 percent in 1990). Only 21 percent of Israelis are third generation or more.[22] Israel then is a very new, very young, pioneer nation of great internal diversity, populated by relative newcomers with varied cultural practices, languages, religiosity, and physical appearance; these distinctions often coincide with wide gaps in power, wealth, and influence. As noted, for the founding generations, such differences were simply overlooked, since the essence of Israeli identity was assumed to be Ashkenazi, modern, and European – like the Sabra who served as its ideals. As Eliezer Ben-Rafael and Stephen Sharot write: "In a largely unconscious fashion the Europeans tend to regard cultural amalgamation as unidirectional; the norms and styles of European Jews are taken for granted, and non-Europeans are expected to behave in conformity with them."[23]

Things began to change in the 1950s, 1960s, and 1970s as Mizrachim, who had long been stigmatized by the European Ashkenazim, began their massive immigration into Israel from Muslim countries. The resident Ashkenazim saw themselves as having 'high culture' (*tarbut*) while the incoming Mizrachim had more primitive 'folk culture' (*moreshet*) and were organized in 'tribes' (*edot* – singular *edah*).[24] The very fact that the dominant and mostly secular Ashkenazim portrayed themselves as the 'real' Israelis and expected the rest to 'modernize' and become 'non-ethnic' led to a reaction among the proud Mizrachim, who emphasized their specific ethnic practices and identities, and focused on religiosity as the core of Israeli identity. In response, in the 1980s many young Ashkenazim began to exhibit a new awareness of their heritage of Yiddishkeit, which had previously been denied or suppressed because of its shameful association with the *shtetl* and the Holocaust.

As a result of these processes, 'culture' was increasingly reified as an objective and valuable essence capable of being counted, owned, and evaluated; following the German romantic tradition, ethnic identity was imagined as genealogical and territorial. According to this definition, authentic culture is expressed in language, music, food, dance, and folklore. It can flourish or degenerate, be fostered or oppressed. But only individuals who organically 'belong' by virtue of birth have a legitimate claim to an ethnic/cultural heritage; only they have the right to tell its stories, sing its songs, or found museums celebrating its past.

As the nationalist Sabra ideal eroded, Israel had to discover some way to integrate these various potentially hostile separate cultural/ethnic Jewish collectives (edot) into the state. This was accomplished through an ideological model that traces present differences back to their mythical beginnings in the primordial Jewish/Israeli nation. The story is that the Jews were originally divided into 12 equal yet distinct tribes, each with its own territory, color, name, and character. After scattering in the diaspora, each tribe remained unique, but each also retained its fundamental identity as part of Israel; their present 'ingathering' fulfills Ezekiel's prophecy and reconstitutes Israel as a community of varied peoples who share common ancestry and religion. From within this symbolic framework, extensive borrowings by diaspora communities from the surrounding non-Jewish world are not seriously taken into account; rather, the habits, customs, and traditions of the exilic groups are seen as independently achieved, reflecting each group's inherent tribal nature. These differences are then defined according to halakhic law as *minhag ha'makom*, the custom of the place, allowing the members of all edot to affirm and celebrate their cultural differences while remaining united at the level of religion and blood with all other Israeli Jews.

In this idealized symbolic system, each edah recalls its immigrant past, proclaims its own value as successful participant in the Jewish collectivity, and applauds its specific cultural practices. The ultimate goal

> is not revolution or segregation. It is integration. The values of those at the top are only mildly questioned. Culturally they seek to add rather than to supersede. . . . Heritage is presupposed, people turn to it in their search for raw material for 'Israeli society,' and yet whitewash enough of their differences so that all that's left are differences in local color.[25]

The result is a "supermarket ethnicity" where a relative indifference to variation predominates since there is an assumption of unity at a deeper level.[26] Of course, this unifying ideology is much more convincing under threatening conditions, since Israeli Jews then identify with the nation and ignore internal divisions. It is for this reason that an Arab leader is reputed to have said: "We should support total peace between the Israelis and the Arabs, because then the Israelis will kill each other."

However, even under the stimulation of a permanent Arab threat, the ideal of unity within difference is difficult to maintain in instances where differences are extreme. The most famous examples are the black-skinned Ethiopian Jews who are commonly and pejoratively known as Falasha, and who call themselves Beta Israel. The Beta Israel believe that they were cut off from the rest of the Jewish community over 2000 years ago but retained their Jewishness despite persecution in Ethiopia, where they were at the bottom of a caste-like social structure. Although they were illiterate and did not have the Talmud, the Falasha were nonetheless recognized by Israeli religious officials in 1975 as members of the lost tribe of Dan and were permitted to immigrate into Israel under the Right of Return. However, when many thousands were airlifted to Jerusalem to save them from annihilation during Ethiopian civil wars in 1981 and when thousands more demanded repatriation, their integration into Israel became a controversial project. Citing deviations from standard ritual practice and the absence of the Talmud, many rabbis argued that the Beta Israel were not proper Jews at all. They demanded those who had already immigrated be officially converted to Judaism according to the Orthodox code – which meant submitting to religious instruction and a ritual bath in the presence of three witnesses. Furthermore, after the initial influx, the majority of Beta Israel remaining in Ethiopia, who had converted to Christianity many years ago (they are called Falas Mura) were prohibited from migration to Israel except for humanitarian reasons.

By questioning the Jewish identity of the Beta Israel, the religious authorities of Israel asserted the right of the state to judge the authenticity of the Jewishness of peoples on the periphery. This exclusivist assertion is contradictory to the inclusive egalitarian 12 tribes paradigm in which cultural differences are encompassed under the umbrella of a mythical shared ancestry. In contrast, the judgmental model assumes that the Israeli state rabbinate is the fount of genuine spiritual knowledge and practice, which deviant diaspora communities must learn, accept, and emulate on penalty of expulsion. However, historically there is no certainty as to who exactly *does* wield final religious authority among Jews. There is, after all, no Jewish Pope, and many competing centers of Judaic spiritual learning have existed over time and continue to exist today, each making its own claims to be the source of proper interpretation of the law. Jews on the margins have always had their own places of learning, as well as their own wise men and scholars.[27] Thus, when faced with the stipulation that they convert, some of the Beta Israel acquiesced, but others refused, on the grounds that they were already Jews, faithfully following the teachings of their own religious leaders. The outcome of this controversy is not yet resolved.

This would be a purely doctrinal debate, save for the fact that in Israel religious authorities are part of the state, and those found in violation of their demands can be deprived of their official status as Jews, which can have many negative effects. In the Beta Israel case, the doubts of the Orthodox rabbinate coincided with the state's pragmatic anxieties about the difficulties of incorporating 80,000 Ethiopians, whose cultural and racial differences and lack of marketable skills do not make them the most desirable of immigrants. Meanwhile, the South Asian Bene Israel, also a dark-skinned and exotic group, have been officially recognized by the Israeli rabbinate as wholly Jewish, and permitted to marry anyone within the Jewish community. To some extent, this is because the Bene Israel have a tradition of literacy and Talmudic scholarship, but it also reflects their high skill level and their relatively small numbers, which make them much easier to assimilate. On the opposite end of the spectrum, a large number of recent Russian immigrants are wholly secular in outlook and practice and have mixed or vague genealogies as well, but their right to be recognized as authentic Jews has never been seriously challenged. Partially this is because their ethnic classification as Ashkenazim links them historically and genealogically to the founders of Israel; perhaps it is also because they are relatively well educated, and so are valuable immigrants, unlike the poorly educated and unskilled Beta Israel. Evidently, the legal validation of Jewish authenticity and Israeli citizenship is a product of many factors, not all of them purely doctrinal.

Other more individualized cases illustrate further complexities in the deter-mination of who is officially entitled to be defined both as a Jew and as an Israeli citizen. One celebrated example mirrors the efforts by French Muslims to be recognized as both French *and* Muslim. In 1962 a Carmelite monk named Brother Daniel applied to be admitted to Israel as a Jew, despite the fact that he had converted to Christianity and was wearing monk's robes. He invoked the Right of Return on the grounds that "a Jew, even if he has sinned, remains a Jew." The Israeli Supreme Court concurred that this was indeed the halakhic view, but argued that for the man in the street "a Jew who has become a Christian is not called a Jew." The court ruled that "whatever national attributes may be possessed by a Jew living in Israel, whether he is religious, non-religious or anti-religious, he is bound by an umbilical cord to historical Judaism, from which he draws his longings, and from which he derives his idiom."[28] A Christian con-vert, the court argued, cannot experience this same nationalist sentiment, and so ought not to be awarded a Jewish/Israeli identity. The court thus moved away from the strict genealogical definition of a Jew as anyone born from a Jewish mother, and invoked instead a notion of personal commitment as the marker of authenticity. The finding was popularly welcomed, but was ulti-mately overturned by the minister of the interior who affirmed that matrilineal descent is the ultimate source of Jewishness. From this point of view, one could be both Christian *and* Jewish – *if* one had a Jewish mother.

The linkage between genealogy, nationality, and religion was challenged from another direction in 1968. In this case, an atheistic Israeli navy lieutenant commander named Benjamin Shalit was married to a non-Jewish woman. The question then arose as to the religious/national identity of their children. Shalit argued that the equation of nationhood and religion was repressive, and, fol-lowing the court finding in the Brother Daniel case, he claimed that religious affiliation was a matter of personal choice, not of heredity. He wanted his children's identity cards to read "nationality Jewish, religion none." In other words, he wanted them to be Israeli *but not* Jews. Religious members of the government threatened to resign if Shalit's claim was accepted. However, the Supreme Court ruled in Shalit's favor, accepting his argument about the subjec-tive and voluntary nature of religious affiliation.

The heated debate that ensued rotated around two points: on the one hand, the Orthodox declared that accepting a subjective and secularized nationalistic vision of Jewishness would lead religious Jews to withdraw from public life, since they could never be certain whether those they were interacting with were genuine Jews or not; on the other hand, secularists stated that the ingathering of exiles was the supreme value for the nation; therefore, as Golda Meir is reputed to have said, anyone who calls himself a Jew should be welcomed as a

Jew. The end result was the enactment of a law confirming the halakhic principle that "'Jew' means a person born to a Jewish mother or who has become converted to Judaism, and who is not a member of another religion." Blood and orthodoxy triumphed, though a Christian Jew was now impossible. But a loophole remained permitting non-Orthodox conversions, while non-Jewish spouses and children were incorporated in the Law of Return. This meant the creation of a new class of immigrants who could become citizens, but who were not technically classed as Jews, and so were not 'returning' at all. Despite this ambiguity, the state accepted the fundamental halakhic legal principle that Judaism (and Israeli citizenship) is a spiritual essence, impossible to lose, that is passed down genealogically through the mother. In so doing, the state sought to retard the burgeoning growth of multiple subjective modes of authenticating Jewishness and focused instead on what seemed most natural and real: blood and birth, while still providing a space for belief. The two forms of authentic belonging (origin and content) were thus maintained, though the former was given official priority.

The legal definition of Jewishness in Israel continues to evolve in response to external influences and political arrangements. For example, after the Oslo accord in 1993, it seemed as if peaceful relations with surrounding Arab states were soon to be achieved. The easing of tension led to renewed debate about what it means to be a Jew and how Israel ought to define itself. Some reformers argued that the entire notion of a Jewish state should be set aside, and that Israel should become a 'normal' nation based on the Enlightenment values initially promoted by Israel's secular founders. The Law of Return should be abolished and citizenship should be based on loyalty and participation, not blood.[29] However, when the Oslo accord failed and Arab resistance to Israel increased there was a return to the identification of Israeli citizenship with Jewish descent.

The reader may well ask what the place of the Palestinian Arabs is in this discourse of authenticity. At present, Arabs, whether Israeli citizens or residents of the West Bank and Gaza, remain a ubiquitous, mistrusted 'other' who "are not 'relevantly similar'" to the Jewish populace, and who therefore do not enter significantly into the official discussion of Israeli identity.[30] It is against the ominous backdrop of fanatical suicide bombers and massive Arab resistance that Israelis today construct their own fraught national identity. The assumption is: whatever differences we have among us, we are Jews together, united against terror. Yet solidarity against the Arabs is rendered problematic by the evident racial, cultural, and structural similarities between Mizrachi immigrant Jews from the Arab Middle East and the Muslim and Christian Arabs living in Israel and its environs. These very similarities make many in the Mizrachi communities, already anxious about their place in a society dominated by Europeanized

Ashkenazim, even more concerned to differentiate themselves from the Arab 'others' whom they so resemble. They therefore are likely to see religious practice and genealogical heritage as the fundamental core of Israeli identity. In contrast, more secularized Ashkenazi Jews, unworried about being mistaken for Arabs, can conceptualize, at least in principle, an Israel that is more inclusive. The fundamental question remains: can Israel incorporate non-Jewish indigenes into its narrative of collective authenticity, or will the Promised Land remain forever defined, and divided, by their exclusion? Of course, this leaves aside the equally vexing question of whether Israel's Arab neighbors will ever accept the existence of a Jewish state in their midst, or whether they too will continue to be enchanted by their own vision of a primordial purity.

Chapter 10

Authenticity On the Margins

Genes Make the Tribe

So far, I have discussed how aesthetic productions such as cuisine and dance have been marshaled to buttress the authenticity of nation-states, and I have also outlined the way citizenship has been authenticated in several different contexts. In this final chapter, I will consider the issue of collective authenticity from a different angle, asking how those who are rejected or marginalized or simply divergent from the center construct, maintain, and cultivate their own specific forms of collective authenticity. As with the nation, for the excluded the default position is the assertion of a common genealogical heritage (origin). Extreme forms of the genealogical option seem to be especially appealing for discreditable minorities[1] who do not stand out from the mainstream in any obvious way, perhaps because the group never was particularly distinctive in the first place or because any real differences have long been buried under generations of 'passing'. But when shame changes to nostalgia, the stigmatized collective can be exhumed and reaffirmed through the discovery of lost ancestors and common lineages.

Nowadays, in the United States, the quest for a pedigree has gone beyond compiling and consulting written histories and oral records. Seekers after the past can contact commercial genetic websites such as FamilyTreeDNA.com, which offer various kinds of complex chromosomal analysis for a moderate cost. These analyses can be used to test for paternity, or to discover a relationship with a famous ancestor. The most well-known example was the effort by a black family to demonstrate their descent from Thomas Jefferson and his slave mistress Sally Hemings.[2] Such tests have also been used to find evidence of ethnic/racial/religious identity. Clients include African-Americans who hope to discover their original tribal affiliations, individuals and groups seeking to prove their Jewishness, and others who, for various reasons, want irrefutable evidence of their ethnic or racial inheritance.

Genetic testing is especially appealing to Americans for two reasons. The first is that it uses sophisticated, rigorous, and, most importantly, scientifically proven technology. In the modern world where science – and particularly biology – is reckoned to be the ultimate arbiter of reality, laymen generally presume that scientifically valid findings are solid and real, not conjectural or contextual. The second, related, reason is that in an environment where collective and personal identities are felt to be unstable or at best ambivalent, an individual's biological-genealogical makeup is understood to be not only irrefutable but also fundamentally real at the deepest level. As Paul Brodwin sums up: "New genetic knowledge. . .adds the cachet of objective science to the notion that one's identity is an inborn, natural, and unalterable quality. Rapid advances in sequencing and analyzing the human genome have strengthened essentialist thinking about identity in American society and elsewhere."[3]

The techniques for probing one's ancestry rely on the proven fact that some genetic material is passed unchanged from parent to child, and so can be traced back in time if comparisons can be made across equivalent populations to determine significant similarities. There are two routes for hunting down one's lineage: in the first, particular alleles, or mutations on the Y chromosome, can be followed from fathers to sons; in the second, variations in mitochondrial DNA, inherited by children from their mothers, are tracked. There are severe limitations to both of these techniques, not least of which is the fact that at most only two lines can be traced out of a number that double with every generation (two for parents, four for grandparents, eight for great grandparents, and so on ad infinitum). Nonetheless, experts have discovered some startling links between people today and their ancestors. For example, English scientists have used Y chromosome evidence to argue that a South African tribe, the Lemba, have a Semitic heritage, validating the Lemba's own oral tradition of Jewish ancestry.[4] So far, Israeli law has not tested this claim, since the Lemba have not (yet) asked to become Israeli citizens under the Right of Return.

A more germane case recently occurred in the United States. Known for at least a hundred years as a mysterious 'lost tribe' inhabiting the southern Appalachian region of northeastern Tennessee and neighboring areas of Virginia and Kentucky, the Melungeons were described by anthropologists as a mixed-blood enclave of Indians, whites, and blacks thrown together as a result of the discrimination they suffered from their neighbors.[5] Local whites used the term to insult poor people with suspected black ancestry. It also carried implications of backwardness, inbreeding, and laziness. Naturally, few people admitted to being Melungeon themselves; the real Melungeons were always those primitive people living deeper in the backwoods or further down the creek. People denying that they were Melungeon generally called themselves Porty-ghee (Portuguese) instead, thereby explaining their dark complexions.

In 1966 two economists who had been asked by the state to investigate ways to bring some income into this impoverished region recommended a tourist development that would feature a drama about the Melungeons and the marketing of local 'Melungeon' handicraft items. The play, entitled "Walk Toward the Sunset: The Melungeon Story," told a romantic tale of the suffering and resilience of the Melungeon people through two centuries of prejudice. Although the tourism boom did not occur as planned, there was another, unforeseen result. After seeing the play, people in the area began to take pride in their ancestry and to identify themselves publicly as Melungeon for the first time. This re-evaluation occurred during the civil rights movement and coincided with the explosion of rights language and multiculturalism in the United States. In this revisionist context, it now became both interesting and potentially advantageous to discover membership in a deprived minority.

The turning point in the modern rehabilitation of the Melungeon came in 1994 when the vice-chancellor at a local college published a popular autobiography that told how he overcame a crippling disease, experienced a spiritual rebirth, and cast off shame at his Melungeon past. Using the rhetoric of the gay rights movement, he said he wanted to bring Melungeons 'out of the closet' to "embrace our heritage – whatever it might be – and wear it like a banner."[6] Soon thereafter the Melungeon Heritage Association was founded and began yearly meetings. Membership rapidly expanded, as thousands of people from all over the country and from many walks of life claimed to be Melungeons; so many, in fact, that disputes soon arose over who was and who was not a real member of the clan.

As the formerly shameful Melungeon identity was transformed into a valuable scarce resource, various factions struggled to define just what it means to be Melungeon, since no traces remain of the original culture – whatever it may have been or whether it existed at all.[7] In this vacuum, the speculative pursuit of ultimate origins flourished. Some Melungeons stressed their Indian descent and sought official (and potentially very profitable) recognition as an Indian tribe. Others were interested in discovering their European heritage and employed a professional geneticist who could compare Melungeon DNA with DNA from Portugal and with other darker-skinned ethnic groups such as Moors from Spain or Turkey.

However, collecting an adequate statistical sample of DNA proved difficult, since those who define themselves as Melungeon are extremely varied racially and physically; at the same time, many of the people who have a typical

Melungeon surname do not identify themselves as Melungeon at all. Since the Melungeon do not constitute a genetic isolate, there was no DNA sequence or Y chromosome type characteristic of them, nor was there any particular reason to consider Melungeons to be direct descendants of the Portuguese, as many had hoped. There was evidence of black ancestry, American Indian ancestry, and some gene sequences matched with a South Asian sample, while a few others matched with samples from Turkey and Syria. As it turned out, the self-proclaimed Melungeons had a genetic baseline not significantly different from any random group of white Americans. The geneticist employed to trace Melungeon origins concluded that: "It's a cultural identity which is real and important, but it does not reflect any genetic basis."[8] This was not what the people who hired him wanted to hear. In response, a number of Melungeons immediately fixed upon the few South Asian matches and began to claim an exotic Gypsy heritage; others concentrated on the faint indications of a Turkish and Syrian background, while still others focused on their supposed American Indian ancestry. Proliferating Melungeon websites began to "turn a trivial genetic fact into an appealing identity claim."[9] Each group now claimed an essential reality, based on a genetic connection to a desired past, while disregarding alternatives.

This pattern, while extreme, nonetheless follows a typical American mode for constructing an essentialized ethnic/racial identity. As Mary Waters has shown, white Catholic Americans may firmly believe that they look, act, and are authentically Irish (for example). They may express their supposedly innate Irish identity by wearing green and marching in Saint Patrick's Day Parades, joining Irish Associations, contributing to Irish causes, eating Irish food, drinking in Irish pubs, and returning to Ireland to revisit the beloved homeland. Like the Greeks mentioned in chapter 8, self-proclaimed Irish also think they can instinctively recognize others with the same heritage. All this occurs despite the fact that the individual may have important ancestors who are not Irish at all, but Scottish (or English, or German, or Polish, or Serbian).[10] In other words, Americans with mixed heritages very often identify strongly with only one of their ethnic lineages, forgetting their other, less prestigious, bloodlines. By this act of selective remembering, white American Catholics, like the Melungeons, gain membership in a valued ethnic/racial community they believe is natural and therefore authentic.

First Nations: Identity and Identification

The Melungeon case shows what can happen when the actual content of a discreditable group identity has vanished, or perhaps never existed. For members who want to reclaim their heritage, the best that can be hoped for is the genetic recovery of a unifying pedigree. Other ostracized groups are equipped with a better awareness of their past, and therefore take different approaches to establishing and expressing what they believe to be their authentic collective character. This is particularly so with the colonized peoples who make up the so-called 'first nations' worldwide (an estimated 300 million people in 4000 different societies). These varied aboriginal groups have little in common aside from their claims to 'first-ness' and their appalling experiences of "state-sponsored genocide, forced settlement, relocation, political marginalization, and various formal attempts at cultural destruction" by the colonizing power.[11]

In order to redress these injustices, many indigenous rights organizations have joined together to petition international aid agencies for help. These global movements for aboriginal cultural expression and self-determination have been supported by anthropologists and others who believe strongly that powerless indigenous peoples should be able to decide their own fates, and who believe as well in the absolute value of maintaining cultural diversity. Their fear is that, like the Melungeons, first nation minorities will be obliged to fit in with the dominant authority. In so doing, they will become untrue to themselves, without a genuine culture or heritage to call their own. This is seen as an irretrievable loss to the first nations and to the world, which is becoming ever more impersonal, standardized, and meaningless.[12]

The salvaging of first nation cultural integrity, however, has had unforeseen and paradoxical consequences. As Ronald Niezen has shown: "The very process of trying to hold social integration at bay is a force of social integration."[13] The reason is partly structural. In their struggle to avoid absorption within the encompassing state, the first nations necessarily have recourse to the very same bureaucratic procedures, centralized hierarchies, and legal mechanisms that are characteristic of the state systems they are fighting against.[14] Because they must imitate their enemies, the various aboriginal groups come to resemble one another, and to resemble the governmental organizations they are resisting, especially if their resistance is successful.

The second reason for a loss of diversity and absorption into the mainstream has to do with the way the developed world tends to respond to the plight of indigenous peoples by invoking the inalienable right of human beings to be treated with dignity. This faith is predicated upon the accepted belief, derived from Enlightenment thought and characteristic of non-genealogical models of modern citizenship, that all individuals participating in civil society are legally and spiritually equivalent and that collectives ought to be voluntary associations, to be joined or left as the regent individual sees fit.[15] Well-meaning governmental agencies, non-governmental organizations (NGOs), and other helping organizations who accept these premises put their energies into alleviating indigenous poverty and discrimination, while encouraging education and enterprise. When these measures succeed, the outcome is likely to be precisely what first nation activists most fear; that is, integration of the members of aboriginal collectives into modern society, where they become free agents and good workers who just happen to have an exotic bloodline and a few odd customs.

A third reason for homogenization is that aboriginals, if they are to elicit guilty redress from the powers that be, must express themselves in ways that are not only bureaucratically efficient, but also emotionally compelling. Therefore, a very similar rhetorical appeal tends to be employed by first nations and their allies everywhere; one that caters to a romanticized nostalgia for a more simple time when people lived in harmony with themselves, with their friends and family, with their neighbors, with nature and with the cosmos. Native peoples, more primitive by definition, fit the bill as exemplars of a primordial halcyon existence, even though they have been corrupted by civilization. By playing into colonial fantasies of primitive authenticity the colonized peoples can gain the sympathy of their conquerors, but at the cost of smoothing over local particularities.

Evoking the myth of the pure past is not just a strategy engineered by native peoples intent on arousing feelings of nostalgia and remorse among their oppressors. Within the community of the subjugated, a recalled utopia also provides an empowering history that is the reverse of the degraded present. "We may be suffering," the narrative says, "but our original circumstance, in the world of our forefathers whom we recall and honor, was far more in touch with eternal truths, far more integrated, far more humane, heroic, and beautiful, far more genuine, than the world made by our oppressors, which we now reluctantly inhabit." The story is psychologically compelling to the excluded and marginalized even though it ignores or represses aspects of history that do not fit into the desired image of unity and harmony.

The various ways these external and internal narratives of authenticity and origin intertwine and are enacted can have a huge effect on the real lives of native peoples. For example, the San people (known also as Bushmen) of Namibia and South Africa are recognized by the outside world as the most impoverished and stigmatized ethnic group in the region. To protect their vanishing way of life, aid agencies have generously helped those San who are regarded as the most authentic, that is, those who continue to live the traditional lifestyle of hunting and gathering, isolated from the modern world and maintaining their ancient ways. These 'real San', however, are few and far between. Most members of the tribe are landless and impoverished farm workers toiling and suffering at the bottom of a repressive caste system. Because of their mode of life, aid agencies usually consider these workers to have lost their authenticity and to be ineligible for funding. The San cannot understand this discrimination; for them all people who call themselves San are members of the same tribal collective, regardless of how they make a living. Nonetheless, those who want to qualify for help must "conform to popular stereotypes" and act as they are expected to act by aid granters, which means wearing loincloths, tracking animals in the bush, and eating nuts and berries.[16]

In the San instance, stereotypical Western images of authentic primitivism have been imposed on the aboriginal people, trumping the San's own declarations of shared ancestry and culture, but the San still retain considerable cultural distinctiveness among themselves, and have not incorporated externally imposed images into their own definitions of their collective identity. Nor has it (as yet) occurred to them to wonder whether some San are authentic and others are not, and they have not (yet) developed counter-myths of who they really are to offset the stories told by outsiders. So at present, though impoverished and marginalized, they have no doubts about their group's intrinsic authenticity. The question, in fact, does not come up for them – only for outsiders. So we now have two extreme cases: the Melungeon, who have no identifiable heritage whatsoever, and who pay for scientific DNA tests to affirm (albeit shakily) some form of genealogically based unity, and the San, who are certain of their own collective identity, but who have not been recognized by an outside world obsessed with stereotypical images of primitivism.

Most cases are more mixed and occur where an identifiable and stigmatized native group has been partly (but not wholly) integrated into the larger society. This is what has occurred among the Maori of New Zealand, who know their country as Aotearoa. The vanishing of the old name is symbolic of the fact that the Maori have been reduced to second-class citizens in their own homeland, despite their proud history as warriors and conquerors. Maori resentment and desire for recognition have inspired a movement known as Maoritanga (Maoriness), which has a political, economic, and cultural agenda.[17] The former revolve primarily around Maori activists' legal demands to be compensated for the land taken from their ancestors by treaties with the white settlers. Coincident with lawsuits for reparation has come a new cultural attitude toward the larger society. Instead of seeking assimilation into Aotearoa/New Zealand's white majority, which was the goal of previous generations, the Maoritanga movement portrays white colonial culture negatively as cool, passionless, rational, instrumental, and mechanical; Maoritanga is portrayed positively as emotional, passionate, mystical, subjective, poetic, and natural. European romantics have contrasted the alienated modern world

131

with the authentic primitive world in the exact same manner ever since the eighteenth century.

Maori activists also appropriate academically questionable but appealing early anthropological theories about their origins and religion, which are then presented to Maori and to outsiders alike as genuine. At the same time they contest standard theories that contradict the self-image they wish to display and identify with. For example, the standard academic interpretation of Maori history has been that when they arrived they exterminated an earlier population, the Moriori. In response, the Maori argue that this is a settler myth designed to justify their dominance.[18] This development is a reaction to years of exclusion, cultural deprivation, and poverty. New narratives, whether objectively accurate or not, serve the very real purpose of offering the Maori a satisfying alternative history that they can affirm as their own. This then feeds back into their legal effort to be paid for the land they believe (with good reason) has been unjustly taken from them.

A comparable pattern has occurred on the other side of Polynesia, in Hawaii, where the local population has also suffered a long history of colonization and marginalization. Like the Maori, Hawaiians have mobilized themselves in a nationalist movement of resistance that is opposed to the overwhelming political and economic might of the occupying imperial power (the United States). Along with their struggles for political and economic power, both the Maori and the Hawaiian nationalists have tried to recapture the original culture of their people through resurrecting the traditional arts and crafts that set them off from the colonizers. These efforts portray precolonial life on the islands as egalitarian, pious, and generous, ignoring historical evidence of hierarchy, oppression, and cruelty. The same romanticization is also applied to village life, where "you *give*, don't sell," and where unstinting mutual aid, harmony, and unconditional love always prevailed. As Jocelyn Linnekin remarks, "Cultural nationalists often invoke a mythic past to legitimize and promote solidarity in the present."[19]

Hawaiian activists, like Maori activists. have also been strongly motivated by a mystical sense of their own connection to the land, which, they say, has been abused by white settlers. To validate these claims, activists rely not only on critical readings of historical records and on their own accounts of deceptive treaties and other tricks played by the colonists, but also on more encompassing notions of an instinctive native oneness with nature. Hawaiians style themselves the *kama'aina*, children of the land, similarly, the Maori are the *tangata whenua*, people of the land. As the Maori activist Ranganui Walker put it, among his ancestors: "the earth was loved as a mother was loved."[20] The message is that the aboriginal population are the proper and sole guardians of the spirits of the place.

The assertion of communion translates directly into demands for monetary reparations (in Aotearoa/ New Zealand, $1 billion has been set aside for
this purpose), but the affirmation of innate mystic ties to place is not simply
a ploy to induce lucrative feelings of guilt among the colonists; it is also deeply
felt. The claim to primordial connection restores (and revitalizes) a spiritualized collective sense of significance that has long been obscured and devalued, though never quite obliterated. As Jonathan Friedman says, this type of
revaluation "is not a question of semiotics, of sign substitution, of the intellectual game of truth-value and museological authenticity. It is, rather, a
question of the existential authenticity of the subject's engagement in a self-
defining project."[21] The Maori and Hawaiian nationalists refer to their roots
in order to attain a sacred identity that contrasts with, and is superior to, the
secularized identity of the powerful outsiders who have taken their culture,
their land, and their power from them. By spiritually reaffirming their roots
they explicitly hope to offset the epidemic alcoholism and depression that
have decimated them.

Like every such project, the definition of an authentic collective identity
poses perils for those who do not fit in. The question always remains: who is
(and who is not) one of us? Is membership in the tribe a biological essence,
unchanging forever – if this is the case, then behavior is irrelevant. If not,
how much behavioral change is permitted – and who decides on the limits?
Is the full-blooded Maori or Hawaiian who appreciates 'white culture' still
authentic? How authentic is a person who has only one grandparent with
Maori or Hawaiian blood, but who nonetheless speaks the native language,
knows the native crafts, and is a political activist? What, after all, is at the
heart of authenticity?

The Empty Center and the Tears That Bind

To explore (not answer) these questions and their ramifications, let me turn to
one final case study. The Salish and Pend d'Oreilles Indians are residents on the
Flathead Indian Reservation in rural Montana. Many of them know some of
the ancestral language and a few are even fluent; most practice some of the
ancient customs of their tribe; they still live in their historical homeland and
can directly trace their genealogies back to Indian heroes of the past. Like the
San, they are far from urban life and any semblance of political and economic
power. But, although they have retained more of their indigenous culture than
the Maori and the Hawaiians (though less than the San), they are nonetheless
extremely conscious of their alienation from their past. The reservation has one

of the highest rates of self-reported depression in the world: 80 percent see themselves as depressed – six times the national average. They diagnose their depression as a direct result of their present disconnection from the genuine culture of their forefathers. Having lost their authenticity, they say that they have lost their souls.

One of the problems for the Flatheads is that they do not see identity as fluid. Instead, they believe racial and ethnic categories are both rigid and essential for determining one's true being; pure-blooded Flatheads are considered naturally 'more Indian' than mixed bloods. This is partially because of the power of biological essentialism, but it also has an institutional basis. The Flatheads, like other recognized American Indian groups, enroll and exclude members on the basis of their blood quantum. Those who are reckoned full-blooded get a full share, half-blooded get a half share, and so on. United States government grants are also distributed to Indians in the same ratio, as are university scholarships set aside for them. This means that those not enrolled as tribal members by virtue of blood are not eligible for these benefits. In principle, membership can be rescinded for members who are reckoned not to be sufficiently Indian. This causes distress because, like most other aboriginals today, everyone on the reservation has family members who are designated as outsiders and almost all have non-Indian ancestors. One full-blooded Flathead even keeps a list of remaining full-bloods, which he calls the endangered species list.

Given that blood (and birthplace) are crucial for determining tribal membership among American Indians and other aboriginal groups, the assignment of authenticity, like the assignment of membership by blood quantum, is imagined by the Salish to consist of a set of concentric circles, with whites and others who have no Indian blood on the outside, real full-blooded Indians at the center, and various degrees of admixture in between. Those positioned on the outer reaches imagine that there are still some pure-blooded old-timers remaining at the core, keeping up the traditional ways. Those at the center, however, have a different perspective. The remaining full-blooded elders say that to be an authentic Indian is not just a matter of genes; it is also existential, a sense of identity and of connection with the community and the world that colonial influence has destroyed. Real Indians, the Salish old-timers say, no longer exist. As Theresa O'Nell, the ethnographer of the Flatheads, puts it: "The rhetoric of the empty center culminates in a message that contemporary Flathead identity is, in essence, inauthentic."[22]

Although the Flathead elders believe that no truly genuine Indians exist today, the construction of opposed ideal types (Indians versus whites) encourages individual Flatheads to compete to be recognized as *more* authentically

Indian than their fellows, even though none of them can ever be *completely* Indian. Because genetic notions are prior, this is accomplished most convincingly by establishing direct genealogical connections to pure-blood Indians of the past. Weaker claims can be made through learning to speak Salish or through practicing skills such as traditional beadwork. Best is to combine both. However, attempts to be more Indian than the rest can always be rejected by the community, and those who make the strongest claims risk the most rejection, because boldness and assertiveness are said to be 'not very Indian'. Even some of those who are known to be full-blooded Flatheads may behave in a manner reckoned to be 'less Indian' while some 'half-breeds' may behave in a more traditionally Indian fashion; some individuals may present themselves to outsiders as archetypical Indians dressed in feathers and beads, but may be considered rank imposters by the rest of the community; meanwhile, as noted, those who are praised as the purest and most authentic representatives of Indian blood and culture may see themselves as mere counterfeits of a world that is gone forever.

There are other problems in the never-ending game of Flathead identity construction. Since practicing Indian skills and traditions gives a person credibility and status as being closer to a really real Indian identity, people who hope to be recognized as approaching the genuine worry incessantly about whether the customs and practices they know are actually traditional. Are they following the true and correct original Indian way? As a result, some avoid participation in communal activities altogether because they fear they might make mistakes that would undermine their identity claims. In so doing, they lose the legitimacy they seek, since they no longer take part in the community as real Indians should. Ironically, ritual practices certainly varied considerably in the past, changing in accordance with individual skills and interpretations. Modern inflexibility is a result of heightened anxiety about authenticity within a very isolated and marginalized collective that does not have the capacity of the Hawaiians and Maori to engage in a struggle against the mainstream. Instead, knowledge and practice have been rigidified out of fear of not being Indian enough – a normal reaction to uncertain identity.

In the good old days, the Flatheads believe, things were much different. The question of authenticity did not arise. Instead, all the Flathead people wore proper Indian clothes, lived in teepees, and tied their hair in braids; they were hardworking, honest, and superb hunters and gatherers; they visited frequently, knew their relatives, and were always friendly and helpful to one another; women were modest, men were brave; everyone spoke Salish; animals and humans could talk to each other; people had magical powers. Most of all, there was respect and discipline. Children minded their elders and everyone obeyed

135

the chief. According to the story, the happy world of the past was ruined by assimilation and intermarriage with whites. Now the old ways are gone, and no one respects their seniors anymore.

One major aspect of this very common narrative is that people in the past were authentic precisely because they had no thoughts about their authenticity; they did not compare themselves with others, and they just *were*, without self-consciousness. However, recapturing this Edenic state is now impossible; colonialism and modernity have made everyone aware of displacement and alienation. This narrative has great appeal for the romantics in the colonizing culture as well, who see indigenous peoples as "canaries in the iron cage of modernity."[23] The Indian's fall from grace mirrors the colonizer's own laments about the loss of volkish collective solidarity and spiritual connectedness.

The standard narrative of corruption and disintegration creates an especially troubling double bind for the Flatheads (and for other marginalized people in similar weak and isolated situations). They wish to do their best to live as Indians ought to live, and to be really Indian means obedience to one's elders, but their elders say there are no real Indians left to obey. This insurmountable contradiction helps to heighten the omnipresent depression and despair that the Flatheads experience. It is a familiar enough tale of the psychological distress caused by marginalization and cultural disintegration. The Flatheads, weaker, less numerous, and more isolated than the activist Maori and Hawaiians, cannot assert themselves to revitalize their culture; they cannot confront their oppressors or make claims to a higher form of being. At the same time, unlike the San who retain their sense of cultural integrity, they have become conscious of their distance from their heritage. And so they have succumbed to anomie.

But the story is even more complex, and oddly hopeful. Although the Flatheads are indeed impoverished and marginalized in American society, their social world is actually relatively stable and strong; objectively speaking, the family structure on the reservation is healthy and the community is unified and supportive of its weaker members. Despite the real losses they have suffered, the Flatheads are far from being rootless weeds adrift in an empty sea. Nonetheless, the Flatheads talk incessantly about breakdowns, jealousy, resentment, fears of being 'abandoned, thrown away', and dwell on their own loneliness and misery. According to O'Nell, their omnipresent sadness and continuous complaints are caused not by the collapse of the tribe, but by its opposite: an intense emotional and moral investment in the collective and its traditions of interdependence. For the Flatheads membership in the tribe means above all recalling that among the genuine Indians who lived long ago, cries for help and understanding were always heard and responded to. The distressed were never rejected, never left alone, never denied love and kindness. And now the Flathead people "discipline their hearts to remember their pain."[24] Without mourning, their Indian identities, already diminished, would vanish altogether. Their sadness is an authentic reaction to the disenchantment of the modern world.

Conclusion

An Anthropology of Authenticity

My aim in this book is not to debunk authenticity as an illusion, nor to reduce it to a secondary phenomenon that can be explained by some other, more primal factor. I agree with Durkheim's wise words about the study of religion: "What sort of science is it whose principle discovery is that the subject of which it treats does not exist?"[1] I take very seriously the enthusiasms of collectors, fans, tourists, folklorists, genealogists, nationalists, adventurers, performers, true believers, and others avidly hunting the authentic. I share some of the same passions myself. But I did not write this book from the stance of the seeker. I wrote it as an anthropologist,[2] which I think gives me a special insight into the issues involved, as well as a method for investigating them.

Anthropologists are particularly concerned with authenticity because of the contradiction between their roles as observers and participants. This tension has existed from the earliest days of the discipline, ever since Franz Boas undertook his first research among the Eskimos of Baffin Land in 1883. During this and his later fieldwork, Boas became more than a scientific outsider and the people he studied became more than his experimental subjects; they were also his friends, confidants, protectors, and teachers. He admired them and wanted to convey their unique worldview to his audience. Henceforth, all anthropologists have been torn between these two positions: the empiricist observer and the romantic participant. Empiricists have tried to maintain detachment and scientific objectivity. Romantics have identified with the individuals who served them as interpreters and guides; they regarded their informants as not only the bearers of valuable knowledge but also the heroic creators of their own unique, beautiful, and compelling worlds. Romantic anthropologists then could envision themselves as transmitters of authentic spiritual wisdom to a decadent and fragmented Western civilization. All anthropologists continuously balance these two opposing modes within themselves, which inevitably challenges our certainty about exactly what it is we do, and why.

The solidity of the anthropologist's self-image has also been eroded by the way ethnographers are regarded in the cultures they study, where they are often seen as buffoons or, even worse, as spies, while simultaneously they are likely to be admired, envied, and exploited as wealthy travelers from the powerful West. Meanwhile, in the academic world, anthropologists are generally regarded as specialists in the marginal and exotic. Their research, between science and poetry, is thought impossible either to define or apply. At the same time, anthropologists are also sometimes imagined to be in possession of arcane knowledge that can be appropriated by other disciplines in search of new paradigms. The popular American stereotype of the anthropologist is equally ambiguous: sometimes envisioned as a romantic action figure like Indiana Jones, at other times portrayed as an arrogant fool or interfering snoop. All this ambivalence of perception makes anthropologists, as a collective, quite conscious of the contingency and contextual nature of their own identities and hyperaware of larger social problems of alienation and anomie.

Conflicted consciousness in the discipline is strengthened by the brute facts of the anthropologist's professional life. Much of our time is spent in foreign cultural worlds among people who have very different ways of living and of being. Our subjective certainty is challenged while we are in the field, where immersion in the culture and the requirements of participant observation oblige us to question the validity of our beliefs, acts, and values. But self-doubt really blossoms on return to the once-familiar homeland, which is likely to seem strange and alienating after the intense experience of fieldwork – this is the well-known phenomenon of culture shock. Having been transformed by our professional identification with 'the other', we are always at least partially disconnected from the taken-for-granted values of our own society, yet unable to become members of the cultures we have studied. This experience has its positive side, at least for me. As a semi-permanent outsider, I think I understand those who seek roots, and who struggle to find an absolute truth beneath the fluidity of appearance.

I do not believe, however, that my sympathy entitles me to serve as a guide for the perplexed who are embarked on a personal spiritual journey to discover their authentic being (if it exists). I take a non-committal stance because I consider myself professionally (and personally) obliged to detach myself from the values, goals, and hopes of those whom I am writing about and for, and to look at their works and lives from as objective and value-free a perspective as possible. On the continuum between objective and subjective, historical and emotional, I am inclined to the former. As inheritor of the Enlightenment faith in reason and free inquiry, I want to understand, not to proselytize, and so my ambition is to reveal empirical evidence and let the results speak for themselves.

Yet, I also realize full well that the value-free model of inquiry is itself motivated by values, and that my perspective is inevitably fashioned by my own character, by the culture and era that I live in, and by the professional discipline I follow. The objectivity I seek is ultimately impossible. But my awareness of the personal, historical, and cultural conditioning of knowledge does not oblige me to drop my ambition to develop a theory of human desires, ideals, and dreams; instead, it makes that goal all the more imperative, since my own desire, ideal, and dream is to come as close as possible to a portrayal of the human experience that would be applicable, understandable, and acceptable to people in other cultures. Psychologically, to motivate myself to try to accomplish this goal, I need to convince myself that it is indeed possible, at least to a degree.

To achieve the understanding I seek, I rely on comparisons of cultural systems across time and space, as they exist within the framework of larger global changes in economy and authority, carried by capitalism and by post-colonial and imperial ambitions. Although I recognize that that knowledge is always contingent and changing, nonetheless, I assume that by making relevant comparisons some relatively plausible truth(s) may be discovered and defended. It might be argued that even such a modest project is impossible because each social formation is necessarily crosscut by gender, class, and age, blurred and fragmented by migration, mingling, and the multiple identities of its members, so that there is really nothing in any cultural collective to serve as a foundation for comparison – only the varied lives of individuals – and even these, when looked at closely, are disintegrated and plural. From this point of view, culture (like every other collective identity) is an invention that serves to obscure both variation and similarity, and to sustain Western authority over exotic 'others' by visualizing them as different and inferior.

I agree that culture is never wholly unified or hegemonic and that there are many different crosscutting factors that complicate analysis. But it is also evident that people do strongly identify themselves as members of various national-ethnic-racial-tribal-religious collectives. The fact that such collective identities are historically constructed, internally complex, and inevitably divided does not make them any less real and compelling to those who belong to them. To deny the importance of collective self-identification would be to deny exactly what those in favor of the deconstruction of culture seek to assert: the rights of individuals to make their own decisions about what matters most in their lives. As Jonathan Friedman has written, "Culture is supremely negotiable for professional culture experts, but for those whose identity depends upon a particular configuration this is not the case. Identity is not negotiable. Otherwise it has no existence."[3]

Another critique of the comparative approach maintains that, even if such a thing as culture does have a subjective reality for participants and an objective reality for investigators, all cultures are unique, and so cannot be compared. I disagree. I see no problem comparing cultures, which, despite many differences, nonetheless share the same existential conditions. My fundamental ontological premise is that, as the 'unfinished animal', human beings are creatures of imagination. We invent the world as we go along, and as we do so, we collectively construct cultural frameworks of meaning that are external to us, existing as objective realities over time, and that are internalized through socialization, so that they become engrained in our hearts, minds, and souls. Without these frameworks, we are lost. To hold anomie at bay, every human culture must at minimum maintain its vitality by arousing a shared sense of transcendence and significance among its members. This process is integral to our mental and spiritual wellbeing, as necessary as food, water, and shelter, as real as the ocean is real to the fish swimming in it. So despite vast differences, every culture has as its basic concern the manufacture of a convincing definition of the identity of its members and an explanation of why they are who they are, what they belong to, and why they do what they do – that is, every culture must construct a convincing collective framework for belief and action.

At the same time, the stability of these cultural frameworks is fragile and incomplete. The imaginations of people within any social world are never exhausted by the possibilities offered. Individuals always dream of something more, always resist what is and fantasize about what might be, always seek the embodied miracle of ecstasy to overthrow the limitations of the ordinary. These challenges and alternatives become more compelling when the stability of the social framework is weakened by external forces and internal contradictions creating fragmentation, decay, and doubt. Today, the major external challenges to coherence are the global processes of late capitalism, including revolutions in media technology and its intrusion into our lives, and the development of the nation-state and other communities, with all their assorted and sometimes conflicting claims on our loyalty. These influences have a deep effect on everyone today, though of course in different ways and at different rates according to numerous factors, not least of which are the relative degrees of autonomy and maneuverability available to people, and the degrees to which they are dependent upon the wills and whims of the wealthy and powerful, both foreign and domestic.

As taken-for-granted meaning systems have been challenged from within and without, human beings everywhere have sought ways to recapture a degree of significance and stability, often enough by inventing or affirming a form of authenticity they can claim for themselves and share with others. These forms can be benign: cultivating a purist musical taste, drinking the best wine from the proper vineyard, or dancing ecstatically in carnival; they can also give nationalist, racist, ethnic, or religious fanatics reasons to subdue and destroy all who do not share their version of the really real. Al-Qaeda believers, like other zealots worldwide, see themselves as restoring authentic religion and a pure, genuine community to a disenchanted and corrupted humanity.[4] But whether the type of authenticity sought is socially malevolent, benevolent, or neutral, the quest is always of great significance to those who are swept up in the modern torrent of change, and who must try to spin a lifeline out of thin air in order to keep from drowning in the deluge.

Notes

Introduction

1 Friedrich Nietzsche (1969) *On the Genealogy of Morals and Ecce Homo*. New York: Vintage: 119. (Original publication of *On the Genealogy of Morals* 1886.)

2 Lionel Trilling (1972) *Sincerity and Authenticity*. Cambridge, MA: Harvard University Press. See also Marshall Berman (1970) *The Politics of Authenticity: Radical Individualism and the Emergence of Modern Society*. New York: Atheneum; Charles Taylor (1989) *Sources of the Self: The Making of the Modern Identity*. Cambridge, MA: Harvard University Press; Charles Taylor (1991) *The Ethics of Authenticity*. Cambridge, MA: Harvard University Press. These stay within a Euro-American context, but similar trajectories toward authenticity have been followed in other times and places, when parallel conditions prevailed. For examples, see Jonathan Friedman (1994) *Cultural Identity and Global Process*. London: Sage Publications.

3 René Descartes (1996) "Third Meditation." In René Descartes, *Meditations on First Philosophy with Selections from the Objections and Replies*. Cambridge: Cambridge University Press: 35. (Original publication 1641.)

4 Judith Shklar (1984) *Ordinary Vices*. Cambridge, MA: Harvard University Press: 75–6.

5 Ibid.: 76–7.

6 Lynn Hunt (1984) *Politics, Culture, and Class in the French Revolution*. Berkeley, CA: University of California Press: 44, 45.

7 Jules Michelet (1967) *History of the French Revolution*. Chicago, IL: University of Chicago Press: 10, 444. (Original publication 1853.)

8 Sigmund Freud (1962) *Civilization and its Discontents*. New York: Norton: 61. (Original publication 1930.)

9 Jean Jacques Rousseau (1954) *The Confessions of J. J. Rousseau*. Harmondsworth: Penguin: 17. (Written in 1765, original publication in 1781.)

10 Quoted in Berman, *The Politics of Authenticity*.

11 Jean Jacques Rousseau (1974) "The Social Contract." In Jean Jacques Rousseau, *The Social Contract and the Discourse on the Origin and Foundations of Inequality Among Mankind*. New York: Washington Square Press: 7. (Original publication 1762.)

12 Jean Jacques Rousseau (1974) "Discourse on the Origin and Foundations of Inequality Among Mankind." In Jean Jacques Rousseau, *The Social Contract and the Discourse on the Origin and Foundations of Inequality Among Mankind*. New York: Washington Square Press. (Original publication 1754.)

13 Jean Jacques Rousseau (1979) *Reveries of the Solitary Walker*. London: Penguin: 88. (Original publication 1782.)

Chapter 1   Authenticity and Art

1 Walter Benjamin (1969) "The Work of Art in the Age of Mechanical Reproduction." In Walter Benjamin, *Illuminations*. New York: Schocken Books.

2 'Primitive', 'savage', and other pejorative or problematic terms will usually be put in quotes when first mentioned and then the quotes will be dropped, with the assumption that my readers will not take these terms at face value.

3 Benjamin, "The Work of Art": 226, 246.

4 Émile Durkheim (1965) *The Elementary Forms of Religious Life*. New York: Free Press. (Original publication 1912.)

5 Durkheim's understanding of the intimate connections between 'art' and the sacred in Australian aboriginal society has been corroborated and amplified by later studies which demonstrate that aboriginal artworks, along with myths, rituals, and songs, are generally regarded as secret collective property, produced within the context of ritual.

6 See Paul Binski (1996) *Medieval Death: Ritual and Representation*. London: British Museum Press: 15.

7 Patrick Geary (1986) "Sacred Commodities: The Circulation of Medieval Relics." In Arjun Appadurai (ed.), *The Social Life of Things: Commodities in Cultural Perspective*. Cambridge: Cambridge University Press.

8 This definition follows David Phillips (1997) *Exhibiting Authenticity*. Manchester: Manchester University Press: 5–6.

9 Lionel Trilling (1972) *Sincerity and Authenticity*. Cambridge, MA: Harvard University Press: 98.

10 This transformation is documented in Charles Taylor (1989) *Sources of the Self: The Making of the Modern Identity*. Cambridge, MA: Harvard University Press.

11 For the opposition between singularity and commodity see Igor Kopytoff (1986) "The Cultural Biography of Things: Commoditization as Process." In Appadurai, *The Social Life of Things*.

12 Charles Taylor (1991) *The Ethics of Authenticity*. Cambridge, MA: Harvard University Press.

13 Phillips, *Exhibiting Authenticity*: 7, 93.

14 Benjamin, "The Work of Art": 223.

15 Quoted in Shelly Errington (1998) *The Death of Authentic Primitive Art and Other Tales of Progress*. Berkeley, CA: University of California Press: 75.

16 Howard Morphy (1995) "Aboriginal Art in a Global Context." In Daniel Miller (ed.), *World's Apart: Modernity Through the Prism of the Local*. London: Routledge: 214.

17 Errington, *Death of Authentic Primitive Art*: 71–2.

18 Molly Mullin (1995) "The Patronage of Difference: Making Indian Art 'Art, Not Ethnology.'" In George Marcus and Fred Myers (eds.), *The Traffic in Culture: Refiguring Art and Anthropology*. Berkeley, CA: University of California Press: 183.

19 Nelson Graburn (ed.) (1976) *Ethnic and Tourist Arts: Cultural Expressions from the Fourth World*. Berkeley, CA: University of California Press.

20 Michael Thompson (1979) *Rubbish Theory: The Creation and Destruction of Value*. Oxford: Oxford University Press.

21 Miles Orvell (1989) *The Real Thing: Imitation and Authenticity in American Culture, 1800–1940*. Chapel Hill, NC: University of North Carolina Press: 295.

22 George Marcus (1995) "The Power of Contemporary Work in an American Art Tradition to Illuminate its Own Power Relations." In Marcus and Myers, *The Traffic in Culture* : 219.

Chapter 2   Authenticity and Music

1 For this distinction see Nelson Goodman (1983) "The Perfect Fake." In Dennis Dutton (ed.), *The Forger's Art*. Berkeley, CA: University of California Press.

2 Leonard Slatkin (2004) "Inauthentic Beethoven, But Authentically So." *New York Times Sunday Edition*, arts section, February 15: 16.

3 Wanda Landowska (1964) *Landowska on Music*. New York: Stein and Day: 355–6.

4 Nicholas Kenyon (1988) "Introduction: Authenticity and Early Music: Some Issues and Questions." In Nicholas Kenyon (ed.), *Authenticity and Early Music: A Symposium*. Oxford: Oxford University Press: 6.

5 Quoted in Robert P. Morgan (1988) "Tradition, Anxiety, and the Current Musical Scene." In Kenyon, *Authenticity and Early Music*: 68.

6 Richard Taruskin, Daniel Leech-Wilkinson, Nicholas Temperley, and Robert Winter (1984) "The Limits of Authenticity: A Discussion." *Early Music* 12: 3–25.

7 Christopher Small (1987) "Performance as Ritual: Sketch for an Enquiry into the True Nature of a Symphony Concert." In Avron Levine White (ed.), *Lost in Music: Culture, Style and the Musical Event*. London: Routledge and Kegan Paul: 19.

8 Joli Jensen (1998) *The Nashville Sound: Authenticity, Commercialization, and Country Music*. Nashville, TN: Vanderbilt University Press: 28–9.

9 This phrase and the notion of uptown and down-home are taken from ibid.:34.

10 The parodic 'down-home' use of Opry instead of Opera is another indication of the symbolic opposition between country and classical music genres.

11 Richard A. Peterson (1997) *Creating Country Music: Fabricating Authenticity*. Chicago, IL: University of Chicago Press: 178.

12 Jensen, *The Nashville Sound*: 134.

13 Quoted in Peterson, *Creating Country Music*: 217.

14 David Grazian (2003) *Blue Chicago: The Search for Authenticity in Urban Blues Clubs*. Chicago, IL: University of Chicago Press: 21. The concept of a more authentic nocturnal self is an extension of the notion of the 'real self' originally developed by Ralph Turner (1976) "The Real Self: From Institution to Impulse." *American Journal of Sociology* 81: 989–1016.

15 Kembrew McLeod (1999) "Authenticity within Hip-Hop and Other Cultures Threatened with Assimilation." *Journal of Communication* 49: 134–50.

16 Erving Goffman (1959) *The Presentation of Self in Everyday Life*. New York: Doubleday.

Chapter 3   Seeking Authenticity in Travel and Adventure

1 Nicholas Thomas (1994) *Colonialism's Culture: Anthropology, Travel and Government*. Princeton, NJ: Princeton University Press: 28.

2 Lawrence Osborne (2005) "Strangers in the Forest". *The New Yorker*, April 18: 124–40: 125–6.

3 Ibid.: 130, 131, 139, 136.

4 Ibid.: 131, 139, 139, 140, 140.

5 This information is contained in a special advertising section paid for by the World Travel and Tourism Council in *The New Yorker*, June 27, 2005.

6 The exotic is a matter of specific strangeness, which can be premodern or contemporary. The primitive, in contrast, is a general category marked by simplicity and a lack of material possessions. It is always remote, timeless, and exemplary. For this distinction, see Thomas, *Colonialism's Culture*.

7 Dean MacCannell (1999) *The Tourist: A New Theory of the Leisure Class*. Berkeley, CA: University of California Press: 15. (Original publication 1976.)

8 Michael Harkin (1995) "Modernist Anthropology and Tourism of the Authentic." *Annals of Tourism Research* 22: 650–70: 653.

9 Thomas de Zengotita (2005) *Mediated: How the Media Shapes Your World and the Way You Live in It*. New York: Bloomsbury: 214.

10 Graham Dann (1996) *The Language of Tourism: A Sociolinguistic Perspective*. Oxford: Cab International.

11 Lesley Stevenson (2003) "Developing Cultural Tourism through Music: Authenticity and the Folk Music Session." Paper presented at the Conference on Developing Cultural Tourism, Nottingham, England.

12 Jean Baudrillard (2001) "Simulacra and Simulations." In Mark Poster (ed.), *Jean Baudrillard: Selected Writings*. Cambridge: Polity Press.

13 Umberto Eco (1986) *Faith in Fakes: Essays 1967*. London: Secker and Warburg: 8.

14 Edward Bruner (2001) "The Maasai and the Lion King: Authenticity, Nationalism, and Globalization in African Tourism." *American Ethnologist* 28: 881–908: 894.

15 Tim Oakes (1997) "Ethnic Tourism in Rural Guizhou: Sense of Place and the Commerce of Authenticity." In Michel Picard and Robert Wood (eds.), *Tourism,*

Ethnicity, and the State in Asian and Pacific Societies. Honolulu, HI: University of Hawaii Press.

16 Bruner, "The Maasai and the Lion King": 897.

17 Orvar Lofgren (1993) "Naturalizing the Nation in Sweden and America." *Ethnos* 3–4: 162–96.

18 Ann Anagnost (1993) "The Nationscape: Movement in the Field of Vision." *Positions; East Asia Cultures Critique* 1: 585–606: 590.

19 Edward Bruner (1994) "Abraham Lincoln as Authentic Reproduction: A Critique of Postmodernism." *American Anthropologist* 96: 397–415.

20 The term 'credibility armor' is taken from Eric Gable and Richard Handler (1996) "After Authenticity at an American Heritage Site." *American Anthropologist* 98: 568–578.

21 Anna Louise Huxtable, quoted in ibid.: 570.

22 MacCannell, *The Tourist*: 155.

23 Stephen Lyng (2005) "Sociology at the Edge: Social Theory and Voluntary Risk-Taking." In Stephen Lyng (ed.), *Edgework: The Sociology of Risk-Taking*. London: Routledge: 22.

24 De Zengotita, *Mediated*: 214.

25 Quoted in Nicole Hayes (2001) "Insiders and Outsiders: Boundary Maintenance and the Construction of Identity Among Youth Travellers in Whistler, British Columbia." Master's thesis, Dept of Anthropology, McMaster University: 117, 124.

26 Jennifer Lois (2005) "Gender and Emotion Management in the Stages of Edgework." In Lyng, *Edgework*: 121.

27 David le Breton (2000) "Playing Symbolically with Death in Extreme Sports." *Body and Society* 6: 1–11: 3.

28 Lyng, *Edgework*: 34.

29 Ibid: 24, 47.

30 Jeff Ferrell (2005) "The Only Possible Adventure: Edgework and Anarchy." In Lyng, *Edgework*: 85.

31 Jack Katz (1988) *The Seductions of Crime: Moral and Sensual Attractions to Doing Evil*. New York: Basic Books.

Chapter 4   The Commodification of Authenticity

1 Miles Orvell (1989) *The Real Thing: Imitation and Authenticity in American Culture, 1800–1940*. Chapel Hill, NC: University of North Carolina Press: 55.

2 Ibid.: 42.

3 Jonathan Friedman (1994) *Cultural Identity and Global Process*. London: Sage Publications: 103.

4 Daniel Miller (1994) *Modernity an Ethnographic Approach: Dualism and Mass Consumption in Trinidad*. Oxford: Berg: 54.

5 Jean Baudrillard (2001) "Simulacra and Simulations." In Mark Poster (ed.), *Jean Baudrillard: Selected Writings*. Cambridge: Polity Press: 174.

6 Daniel Boorstin (1995) "Consumer's Palaces." In Ruth Boorstin (ed.), *The Daniel J. Boorstin Reader*. New York: Modern Library: 251–3.

7 Quoted in Orvell, *The Real Thing*: 172–3.

8 Ibid.: 144.

9 Quoted in ibid.: 173.

10 Quoted in ibid.: 163.

11 Ibid.: 290.

12 This is far from a universal belief. A great many indigenous ethnopsychologies posit that individuals can and should change their inner feelings to be more in line with what is culturally favored. See Charles Lindholm (2005) "An Anthropology of Emotion." In Conerly Casey and Robert Edgerton (eds.), *A Companion to Psychological Anthropology: Modernity and Psychocultural Change*. Oxford: Blackwell Publishing.

13 Alasdair MacIntyre (1981) *After Virtue: A Study in Moral Theory*. London: Duckworth: 11.

14 Orvell, *The Real Thing*: 299.

15 David Brooks (2000) *Bobos in Paradise: The New Upper Class and How They Got There*. New York: Simon and Schuster.

16 Edward Digby Baltzell (1964) *The Protestant Establishment: Aristocracy and Caste in America*. New York: Random House.

17 Brooks, *Bobos in Paradise*: 41.

18 Ibid.: 111.

19 Ibid.: 83.

20 David Lewis and Darren Bridges (2001) *The Soul of the New Consumer: Authenticity – What We Buy and Why in the New Economy*. London: Nicholas Brealey.

21 Brooks, *Bobos in Paradise*: 85.

22 See chapter 5 of Lewis and Bridges, *The Soul of the New Consumer*.

23 Francis Fukuyama (2000) *The Great Disruption*. New York: Touchstone Press: 90–1.

24 Quoted in Lewis and Bridges, *The Soul of the New Consumer*: 22.

25 Thomas Frank (2004) *What's the Matter with Kansas: How Conservatives Won the Heart of America*. New York: Harry Holt and Company: 113. (Emphasis in the original.)

26 Lewis and Bridges, *The Soul of the New Consumer*: xiii, 206. (Emphasis in the original.)

Chapter 5   Authenticity and the Self

1 Charles Lindholm (1982) *Generosity and Jealousy: The Swat Pukhtun of Northern Pakistan*. New York: Columbia University Press.

2 Napoleon Chagnon (1977) *Yanomamo: The Fierce People*. New York: Holt, Rinehart, and Winston.

3 Unni Wikan (1990) *Managing Turbulent Hearts: A Balinese Formula for Living*. Chicago, IL: University of Chicago Press.

4   Quoted in Norbert Elias (1982) *Power and Civility*. New York: Urizen: 272. For an analysis of the relationship between emotional expressivity and social structure, see Charles Lindholm (1988) "The Social Structure of Emotional Constraint." *Ethos* 16: 227–46.

5   Ralph Turner (1976) "The Real Self: From Institution to Impulse." *American Journal of Sociology* 81: 989–1016.

6   The phrase is from Christopher Lasch (1977) *Haven in a Heartless World*. New York: Basic Books.

7   Arlie Hochschild (1983) *The Managed Heart: Commercialization of Human Feeling*. Berkeley, CA: University of California Press: 19.

8   Ibid.: 198. For another account of the complexities of a commodified relationship, see Katherine Frank (2002) *G-Strings and Sympathy: Strip Club Regulars and Male Desire*. Durham, NC: Duke University Press.

9   The term 'world affirming' is taken from Roy Wallis (1984) *The Elementary Forms of the New Religious Life*. London: Routledge and Kegan Paul.

10 See Christal Whelan (2006) "Religious Responses to Globalization in Japan: The Case of the God Light Association." Doctoral dissertation, Dept of Anthropology, Boston University; C. Julia Huang (2003) "Weeping in a Taiwanese Buddhist Charismatic Movement." *Ethnology* 42: 73–86; Tulasi Srinivas (forthcoming) *Frontiers of Faith: Rethinking Religion and Globalization*.

11 William James (1982) *Varieties of Religious Experience*. New York: Viking Press. (Original publication 1902.)

12 Richard Marsh (1975) "I'm the Cause of My World." *Psychology Today* 9: 38.

13 Quoted in Paul Heelas (1996) *The New Age Movement: The Celebration of Self and the Sacralization of Modernity*. Oxford: Blackwell Publishing: 58.

14 William Butler Yeats (1920) "Prayer for my Daughter." In William Butler Yeats, *Michael Robartes And The Dancer*. Churchtown, Dundrum: The Cuala Press: 20.

15 Robert Bellah (ed.) (1973) *Émile Durkheim on Morality and Society*. Chicago, IL: University of Chicago Press: 51–2. (Emphasis in the original.)

16 Edmund Burke (1986) *Reflections on the Revolution in France*. London: Penguin: 170–1. (Original publication 1790.)

17 Charles Lindholm (1993) *Charisma*. Oxford: Blackwell Publishing.

18 Eric Hoffer (1951) *The True Believer*. New York: Harper and Row.

19 Daniel Miller (1994) *Modernity an Ethnographic Approach: Dualism and Mass Consumption in Trinidad*. Oxford: Berg: 12.

20 Ibid.: 286.

21 Roland Littlewood (1985) "An Indigenous Conceptualization of Reactive Depression in Trinidad." *Psychological Medicine* 15: 275–81.

22 Abner Cohen (1993) *Masquerade Politics: Explorations in the Structure of Urban Cultural Movements*. Berkeley, CA: University of California Press.

23 Miller, *Modernity an Ethnographic Approach*: 322.

24 Thomas De Zengotita (2005) *Mediated: How the Media Shapes Your World and the Way You Live in It*. New York: Bloomsbury: 98.

25 Jeff Ferrell (2005) "The Only Possible Adventure: Edgework and Anarchy." In Stephen Lyng (ed.), *Edgework: the Sociology of Risk-Taking*. London: Routledge: 85.
26 Carlo Petrini (2001) *Slow Food: The Case for Taste*. New York: Columbia University Press: xxiii.
27 Ibid.: 69, 110.
28 Ibid.: 18.
29 Ibid.: 18–19, 39.
30 Ibid.: 73.

Chapter 6 Authentic Cuisine and National Identity

1   Advertisement from the first self-proclaimed Belizean restaurant to be opened in Belize, quoted in Richard Wilk (1999) "'Real Belizean Food': Building Local Identity in the Transnational Caribbean." *American Anthropologist* 101: 244–55: 246.
2   Richard Wilk (2006) *Home Cooking in the Global Village: Caribbean Food from Buccaneers to Ecotourists*. Oxford: Berg:166.
3   Wilk, "Real Belizean Food": 249.
4   Wilk, *Home Cooking in the Global Village*: 167.
5   Wilk, "Real Belizean Food": 249.
6   Erick Castellanos and Sara M. Bergstresser (2006) "Food Fights at the EU Table: The Gastronomic Assertion of Italian Distinctiveness." In Thomas M. Wilson (ed.), *Food, Drink, and Identity in Europe*. Amsterdam: Rodopi Publishers.
7   Cited in ibid.: 190.
8   Ibid.: 190.
9   Arjun Appadurai (1988) "How to Make a National Cuisine: Cookbooks in Contemporary India." *Comparative Study of Society and History* 30: 3–24.
10 Tulasi Srinivas (2007) "Everyday Exotic: Transnational Spaces, Identity and Contemporary Foodways in Bangalore City." *Food, Culture and Society* 10: 85–107.
11 Quoted in ibid.: 101.
12 Appadurai, "How to Make a National Cuisine": 18.
13 Eugen Weber (1979) *Peasants into Frenchmen: The Modernization of Rural France, 1870–1914*. Stanford, CA: Stanford University Press.
14 Quoted in Kolleen M. Guy (2003) *When Champagne Became French: Wine and the Making of a National Identity*. Baltimore, MD: Johns Hopkins University Press: 137.
15 Carlo Petrini (2001) *Slow Food: The Case for Taste*. New York: Columbia University Press: 8.
16 Guy, *When Champagne Became French*: 44, 4, 1.
17 Pierre Nora (1997) *The Realms of Memory: The Construction of the French Past*. Vol. 2, *Traditions*. New York: Columbia University Press.
18 Guy, *When Champagne Became French*.
19 Ulin, Robert C. (1995) "Invention and Representation as Cultural Capital: Southwest French Winegrowing History." *American Anthropologist* 97: 519–27: 521.

20 Ibid.: 520.
21 Pierre Boisard (2005) *Camembert: A National Myth*, Berkeley, CA: University of California Press.
22 Susan J. Terrio (1996) "Crafting *Grand Cru* Chocolates in Contemporary France." *American Anthropologist* 98: 67–79.

Chapter 7 Authentic Dance and National Identity

1 Helen Thomas (1995) *Dance, Modernity and Culture: Explorations in the Sociology of Dance*. London: Routledge: 64.
2 Quoted in Marta E. Savigliano (1995) *Tango and the Political Economy of Passion*. Boulder, CO: Westview Press: 97.
3 Quoted in Roderyk Lange (1975) *The Nature of Dance: An Anthropological Perspective*. London: MacDonald & Evans: 11.
4 Émile Durkheim (1965) *The Elementary Forms of Religious Life*. New York: Free Press: 246–7. (Original publication 1912.)
5 Ibid.: 249–50.
6 Martha Ellen Davis (2002) "Dominican Folk Dance and the Shaping of National Identity." In Susanna Sloat (ed.), *Caribbean Dance from Abakuá to Zouk: How Movement Shapes Identity*. Gainesville, FL: University Press of Florida.
7 Yvonne Daniel (1995) *Rumba: Dance and Social Change in Contemporary Cuba*. Bloomington, IN: Indiana University Press: 7.
8 Quoted in ibid.: 88.
9 Ibid.: 62.
10 Ibid.: 100.
11 Julie Taylor (1998) *Paper Tangos*. Durham NC: Duke University Press: 36.
12 Quoted in Savigliano, *Tango and the Political Economy of Passion*: 48. Tangos with words are generally not danced to but the lyrics express the tango mood and are well known to dancers.
13 Sigmund Freud (1962) *Civilization and its Discontents*. New York: Norton. (Original publication 1930.)
14 Savigliano, *Tango and the Political Economy of Passion*: 144.
15 Taylor, *Paper Tangos*: 75.
16 Ibid.: 117.

Chapter 8 Modes of Authenticity in the Nation-State

1 For some contrasting theories of the origin of the modern nation-state, see Ernest Gellner (1983) *Nations and Nationalism*. Oxford: Blackwell Publishers; Liah Greenfeld (1992) *Nationalism: Five Roads to Modernity*. Cambridge, MA: Harvard University Press; Benedict Anderson (1991) (rev. edn.) *Imagined Communities: Reflections on the Origin and Spread of Nationalism*. London: Verso.

2   For reasons of space, I am leaving aside discussion of sacred kingdoms in which the state was envisioned as a cosmos, with the ruler the symbolic center and source of all life.

3   Émile Durkheim (1965) *The Elementary Forms of Religious Life*. New York: Free Press: 62. (Original publication 1912.)

4   Émile Durkheim (1984) *The Division of Labor in Society*. New York: Free Press: 306–7. (Original publication 1893.)

5   Michael Herzfeld (1995) "It Takes One to Know One: Collective Resentment and Mutual Recognition Among Greeks in Local and Global Contexts." In Richard Fardon (ed.), *Counterworks: Managing the Diversity of Knowledge*. New York: Routledge: 138.

6   Johann Gottfried von Herder (1968) *Reflections on the Philosophy of the History of Mankind*. Chicago, IL: University of Chicago Press: 58. (Original publication 1791.)

7   Quoted in Olivia Harris (1995) "Plural Identities and the Antimonies of Loss in Highland Bolivia." In Fardon, *Counterworks*: 107.

8   Isaiah Berlin, quoted in Ian Buruma and Avishai Margalit (2004) *Occidentalism: The West in the Eyes of Its Enemies*. New York: Penguin: 77, 78.

9   For a history of this process, see Robert J. C. Young (1995) *Colonial Desire: Hybridity in Theory, Culture and Race*. London: Routledge.

10 Andrew Buckser (1996) *Communities of Faith: Sectarianism, Identity, and Social Change on a Danish Island*. Providence, RI: Berghahn.

11 Robert Waite (1977) *The Psychopathic God: Adolf Hitler*. New York: Basic Books: 343.

12 Quoted in Theodore Abel (1938) *Why Hitler Came to Power: An Answer Based on the Original Life Stories of Six Hundred of his Followers*. New York: Prentice Hall: 244.

13 Quoted in Joachim Fest (1974) *Hitler*. New York: Harcourt Brace Jovanovich: 445, 159.

14 Even so, Hitler's hatred of the Jews was not shared by many of his devoted followers, at least according to a 1938 survey in Abel, *Why Hitler Came to Power*.

15 Quoted in Hermann Rauschning (1940) *The Voice of Destruction*. New York: Putnam: 241, 238.

16 Fred Weinstein (1980) *The Dynamics of Nazism: Leadership, Ideology and the Holocaust*. New York: Academic Press: 93. For my own reading of the Hitler movement, see Charles Lindholm (1993) *Charisma*. Oxford: Blackwell Publishing.

17 A version of this opposition goes back at least to the Roman Empire. See Patrick Geary (2003) *The Myth of Nations: The Medieval Origins of Europe*. Princeton, NJ: Princeton University Press.

18 The history of French citizenship is complex. For example, in 1804 the previous rule that every child born on French soil was automatically French was rejected, and blood relationships introduced. Naturalization laws now take account of marriage and length of stay in France, while also granting citizenship to its colonial subjects.

19 Eleonore Kofman, Annie Phizacklea, Parvati Raghuram, and Rosemary Sales (2000) *Gender and International Migration in Europe: Employment, Welfare and Politics*. New York: Routledge: 99.

20 Riva Kastoryano (2002) *Negotiating Identities: States and Immigrants in France and Germany*. Princeton, NJ: Princeton University Press.

21 Alec G. Hargreaves (1995) *Immigration, 'Race' and Ethnicity in Contemporary France.* New York: Routledge: 2.
22 Quoted in Kastoryano, *Negotiating Identities*: 34.
23 Veiling of girls in college does not elicit government intervention, since the students are then over 18 and as independent citizens are free to wear whatever they like.
24 Kofman et al., *Gender and International Migration*: 101.
25 Quoted in Michael Dietler (1994) "'Our Ancestors the Gauls': Archeology, Ethnic Nationalism, and the Manipulation of Celtic Identity in Modern Europe." *American Anthropologist* 96: 584–605: 587.
26 Ibid.: 586.
27 Joseph de Maistre, quoted in Kastoryano, *Negotiating Identities*: 44.
28 The term missionary politics is taken from José Pedro Zúquete (2004) "Missionary Politics in Contemporary Europe: Jean Marie Le Pen's National Front and Umberto Bossi's Northern League." Doctoral dissertation, Dept of European Studies and Modern Languages, University of Bath. Forthcoming as *Missionary Politics in Contemporary Europe*. Syracuse, NY: Syracuse University Press.
29 Jean-Marie Le Pen, quoted in ibid.: 50.
30 Le Pen, quoted in ibid.: 53.
31 Le Pen, quoted in ibid.: 108–9.
32 Umberto Bossi and Daniele Vimercati, quoted in ibid.: 124.
33 Umberto Bossi, quoted in ibid.: 116.

Chapter 9   Israel and Authentic Jewish Identity

1 Daniel Elazar, quoted in Sara Bershtel and Allen Graubard (1992) *Saving Remnants: Feeling Jewish in America.* Berkeley, CA: University of California Press: 124.
2 Quoted in Alanna Cooper (2000) "Negotiating Identity in the Context of Diaspora, Dispersion and Reunion: The Bukharan Jews and Jewish Peoplehood." Doctoral dissertation, Dept of Anthropology, Boston University: 299.
3 Conversion to Judaism has become more common. Orthodox rabbis do not presently recognize converts who have been accepted into Reform or Conservative synagogues. Since the Orthodox define Jewish identity in Israel, this can make a difference when a convert is seeking citizenship.
4 Some messianic splinter groups, such the Shabbatean movement, argued that halakha was no longer binding. But even they saw halakha as a common grounding, and continued to view themselves as Jews. Gershom Sholem (1973) *Sabbatai Sevi: The Mystical Messiah, 1626–1676.* Princeton, NJ: Princeton University Press.
5 At the beginning of the twentieth century innovators were divided between more liberal and more traditional wings. These now make up the Reform and the Conservative segments of Judaism.
6 Emil Fackenheim (1970) "Jewish Existence and the Living God: The Religious Duty of Survival." In Arthur D. Cohen (ed.), *Arguments and Doctrines: A Reader of Jewish Thinking in the Aftermath of the Holocaust.* New York: Harper and Row: 262.

7   Peter Loewenberg (1971) "Theodore Herzl: A Psychoanalytic Study in Charismatic Political Leadership." In Benjamin Wolman (ed.), *The Psychoanalytic Interpretation of History*. New York: Basic Books: 171.

8   For a summary, see Ian Buruma and Avishai Margalit (2004) *Occidentalism: The West in the Eyes of Its Enemies*. New York: Penguin Press: 137–142.

9   Charles Liebman and Eliezer Don Yehiye (1983) *Civil Religion in Israel: Traditional Judaism and Political Culture in the Jewish State*. Berkeley, CA: University of California Press.

10   Though some variations did exist. See chapter 1 in Tamar Katriel (2005) *Dialogic Moments: From Soul Talk to Talk Radio in Israeli Culture*. Detroit, MI: Wayne State University Press.

11   The term Sabra was used mainly by the parents' generation. The Sabra called themselves '*yelidei ha'aretz*' – those born in the land of Israel/Palestine.

12   The tzabar (the original Arabic term) is also claimed by Palestinian Arabs as a symbol of their local roots and resistance to occupation. In this chapter, I focus on the internal construction of Jewish/Israeli identity, but with awareness that this identity is contested by and constructed in relationship to the indigenous Arabic culture.

13   Oz Almog (2000) *The Sabra: Creation of the New Jew*. Berkeley, CA: University of California Press: 4.

14   Almog (ibid.) estimates that Israelis who actually corresponded to the ideal definition of the Sabra never were more than 10 percent of the total population.

15   Quoted in ibid.: 177.

16   Katriel (*Dialogic Moments*: 223–6) contrasts confrontational, self-oriented, practical dugri speech with *musayra*, a valued Arabic speech style that is indirect, effusive, deferential and soothing.

17   Ibid.: 162.

18   Shabeai Teveth, quoted in Almog, *The Sabra*: 218.

19   The strongly masculine character of the Sabra ideology is evident everywhere, but investigation of the cultural reasons for this attitude lie outside this analytical frame.

20   This phrase is taken from Moshe Shokeid (1998) "My Poly-Ethnic Theme Park: Some Thoughts on Israeli-Jewish Ethnicity." *Diaspora* 7: 225–48.

21   This distinction of the Ashkenazim from the Sephardim derives from the fourteenth century when France expelled its Jewish population. The Mizrachim (those from the East) designation is a recent attempt to provide a more egalitarian nomenclature.

22   Eliezer Ben-Rafael and Stephen Sharot (1991) *Ethnicity, Religion and Class in Israeli Society*. Cambridge: Cambridge University Press.

23   Ibid.: 83.

24   Virginia R. Dominguez (1989) *People as Subject, People as Object: Selfhood and Peoplehood in Contemporary Israel*. Madison, WI: University of Wisconsin Press: 152.

25   Ibid.: 151–2. Since Dominguez wrote there has been increased Mizrachi resistance to Ashkenazi domination.

26 Shokeid, "My Poly-Ethnic Theme Park": 238.

27 For the Bukharan example, see Cooper, "Negotiating Identity".

28 Quoted in S. Zalman Abramov (1976) *Perpetual Dilemma: Jewish Religion in the Jewish State*. Rutherford, NJ: Fairleigh Dickinson University Press: 287, 288.

29 Yoram Hazony (2000) *The Jewish State: Struggle for Israel's Soul*. New York: Basic Books.

30 Ben-Rafael and Sharot, *Ethnicity, Religion and Class*: 236.

Chapter 10 Authenticity On the Margins

1 Erving Goffman (1963, *Stigma: Notes on the Management of Spoiled Identity*. New York: Simon and Schuster) distinguishes between discredited identities which are visible and cannot be denied (such as race) and discreditable identities which are not obvious and so can be hidden (such as sexual orientation or a criminal record). Each implies different strategies for self construction.

2 E. A. Foster, M. A. Jobling, P. G. Taylor, et al. (1998) "Jefferson Fathered Slave's Last Child." *Nature* 396: 27–8.

3 Paul Brodwin (2002) "Genetics, Identity, and the Anthropology of Essentialism." *Anthropological Quarterly* 75: 323–30.

4 Referred to in Carl Elliott and Paul Brodwin (2003) "Identity and Genetic Ancestry Tracing." *British Medical Journal* 325: 1469–71: 1469.

5 For more see William Harlen Gilbert (1946) "Memorandum Concerning the Characteristics of the Larger Mixed-Blood Racial Islands of the Eastern United States." *Social Forces* 24: 438–47.

6 N. Brent Kennedy (1997) *The Melungeons: The Untold Story of a Proud People: An Untold Story of Ethnic Cleansing in America*. Macon, GA: Mercer University Press: 7.

7 For this concept, see Simon Harrison (1999) "Identity as a Scarce Resource." *Social Anthropology* 7: 239–51.

8 Kevin Jones, quoted in Paul Brodwin (2005) "'Bioethics in Action' and Human Population Genetics Research." *Culture Medicine and Society* 29: 145–78: 167.

9 Ibid.: 168.

10 Mary Waters (1990) *Ethnic Options: Choosing Identities in America*. Berkeley, CA: University of California Press.

11 Ronald Niezen (2003) *The Origins of Indigenism: Human Rights and the Politics of Identity*. Berkeley, CA: University of California Press: 4.

12 For the history of the Western perception of 'savages' see Nicholas Thomas (1994) *Colonialism's Culture: Anthropology, Travel and Government*. Princeton, NJ: Princeton University Press.

13 Ronald Niezen (2004) *A World Beyond Difference: Cultural Identity in the Age of Globalization*. Oxford: Blackwell Publishing: 3.

14 See Morton Fried (1967, *The Evolution of Political Society*. New York: Random House) on 'tribes' as creations of confrontation between unorganized peoples and centralized state systems.

15 For this argument, see Charles Taylor (1994) *Multiculturalism*. Princeton, NJ: Princeton University Press.

16 Renée Sylvain (2002) "'Land, Water, and Truth': San Identity and Global Indigenism." *American Anthropologist* 104: 1074–84: 1080.

17 Allan Hanson (1989) "The Making of the Maori: Culture Invention and its Logic." *American Anthropologist* 91: 890–902; Roger Sandall (2001) *The Culture Cult: Designer Tribalism and Other Essays*. Boulder, CO: Westview Press.

18 Ranginui Walker (2004) *Ka Whawhai Tohu Matou: Struggle Without End*. Auckland: Penguin. I take no position on the objective truth of either argument.

19 Jocelyn Linnekin (1983) "Defining Tradition: Variations on Hawaiian Identity." *American Ethnologist* 10: 241–52: 244, 247. See also Jocelyn Linnekin (1992) "Cultural Invention and the Dilemma of Authenticity." *American Anthropologist* 93: 446–9.

20 Linnekin, "Defining Tradition": 70.

21 Jonathan Friedman (1994) *Cultural Identity and Global Process*. London: Sage Publications: 112, 132.

22 Theresa DeLeane O'Nell (1996) *Disciplined Hearts: History, Identity, and Depression in an American Indian Community*. Berkeley, CA: University of California Press: 55.

23 Niezen, *The Origins of Indigenism*: 14–15.

24 O'Nell, *Disciplined Hearts*: 177.

An Anthropology of Authenticity

1 Émile Durkheim (1965) *The Elementary Forms of Religious Life*. New York: Free Press: 88. (Original publication 1912.)

2 For some other recent anthropological efforts in this direction, which I only became aware of after I had completed this manuscript, see the essays in the Dutch journal *Etnofoor* 17 (1/2) (2004). (Special issue, *Authenticity*.)

3 Jonathan Friedman (1994) *Cultural Identity and Global Process*. London: Sage Publications: 140.

4 Oliver Roy (2004) *Globalized Islam: The Search for a New Ummah*. New York: Columbia University Press.

Bibliography

Abel, Theodore (1938) *Why Hitler Came to Power: An Answer Based on the Original Life Stories of Six Hundred of his Followers.* New York: Prentice Hall.

Abramov, S. Zalman (1976) *Perpetual Dilemma: Jewish Religion in the Jewish State.* Rutherford, NJ: Fairleigh Dickinson University Press.

Almog, Oz (2000) *The Sabra: Creation of the New Jew.* Berkeley, CA: University of California Press.

Anagnost, Ann (1993) "The Nationscape: Movement in the Field of Vision." *Positions: East Asia Cultures Critique* 1: 585–606.

Anderson, Benedict (1991) (rev. edn.) *Imagined Communities: Reflections on the Origin and Spread of Nationalism.* London: Verso.

Appadurai, Arjun (1988) "How to Make a National Cuisine: Cookbooks in Contemporary India." *Comparative Study of Society and History* 30: 3–24.

Baltzell, Edward Digby (1964) *The Protestant Establishment: Aristocracy and Caste in America.* New York: Random House.

Baudrillard, Jean (2001) "Simulacra and Simulations." In Mark Poster (ed.), *Jean Baudrillard: Selected Writings.* Cambridge: Polity Press.

Bellah, Robert (ed.) (1973) *Émile Durkheim on Morality and Society.* Chicago, IL: University of Chicago Press.

Ben-Rafael, Eliezer, and Stephen Sharot (1991) *Ethnicity, Religion and Class in Israeli Society.* Cambridge: Cambridge University Press.

Benjamin, Walter (1969) "The Work of Art in the Age of Mechanical Reproduction." In Walter Benjamin, *Illuminations.* New York: Schocken Books.

Berman, Marshall (1970) *The Politics of Authenticity: Radical Individualism and the Emergence of Modern Society.* New York: Atheneum.

Bershtel, Sara, and Allen Graubard (1992) *Saving Remnants: Feeling Jewish in America.* Berkeley, CA: University of California Press.

Binski, Paul (1996) *Medieval Death: Ritual and Representation*. London: British Museum Press.

Boisard, Pierre (2005) *Camembert: A National Myth*. Berkeley, CA: University of California Press.

Boorstin, Daniel (1995) "Consumer's Palaces." In Ruth Boorstin (ed.), *The Daniel J. Boorstin Reader*. New York: Modern Library.

Brodwin, Paul (2002) "Genetics, Identity, and the Anthropology of Essentialism." *Anthropological Quarterly* 75: 323–30.

—— (2005) "'Bioethics in Action' and Human Population Genetics Research." In *Culture Medicine and Psychiatry* 29: 145–78.

Brooks, David (2000) *Bobos in Paradise: The New Upper Class and How They Got There*. New York: Simon and Schuster.

Bruner, Edward (1994) "Abraham Lincoln as Authentic Reproduction: A Critique of Postmodernism." *American Anthropologist* 96: 397–415.

—— (2001) "The Maasai and the Lion King: Authenticity, Nationalism, and Globalization in African Tourism." *American Ethnologist* 28: 881–908.

Buckser, Andrew (1996) *Communities of Faith: Sectarianism, Identity, and Social Change on a Danish Island*. Providence, RI: Berghahn.

Burke, Edmund (1986) *Reflections on the Revolution in France*. London: Penguin. (Original publication 1790.)

Buruma, Ian, and Avishai Margalit (2004) *Occidentalism: The West in the Eyes of Its Enemies*. New York: Penguin.

Castellanos, Erick, and Sara M. Bergstresser (*2006*) "Food Fights at the EU Table: The Gastronomic Assertion of Italian Distinctiveness." In Thomas M. Wilson (ed.), *Food, Drink, and Identity in Europe*. Amsterdam: Rodopi Publishers.

Chagnon, Napoleon (1977) *Yanomamo: The Fierce People*. New York: Holt, Rinehart, and Winston.

Cohen, Abner (1993) *Masquerade Politics: Explorations in the Structure of Urban Cultural Movements*. Berkeley, CA: University of California Press.

Cooper, Alanna (2000) "Negotiating Identity in the Context of Diaspora, Dispersion and Reunion: The Bukharan Jews and Jewish Peoplehood." Doctoral dissertation, Dept of Anthropology, Boston University.

Daniel, Yvonne (1995) *Rumba: Dance and Social Change in Contemporary Cuba*. Bloomington, IN: Indiana University Press.

Dann, Graham (1996) *The Language of Tourism: A Sociolinguistic Perspective*. Oxford: Cab International.

Davis, Martha Ellen (2002) "Dominican Folk Dance and the Shaping of National Identity." In Susanna Sloat (ed.), *Caribbean Dance from Abakuá to Zouk: How Movement Shapes Identity*. Gainesville, FL: University Press of Florida.

De Zengotita, Thomas (2005) *Mediated: How the Media Shapes Your World and the Way You Live in It*. New York: Bloomsbury.

Descartes, René (1996) "Third Meditation." In René Descartes, *Meditations on First Philosophy with Selections from the Objections and Replies*. Cambridge: Cambridge University Press. (Original publication 1641.)

161

Dietler, Michael (1994) " 'Our Ancestors the Gauls': Archeology, Ethnic Nationalism, and the Manipulation of Celtic Identity in Modern Europe." *American Anthropologist* 96: 584–605.

Dominguez, Virginia R. (1989) *People as Subject, People as Object: Selfhood and Peoplehood in Contemporary Israel*. Madison, WI: University of Wisconsin Press.

Durkheim, Émile (1965) *The Elementary Forms of Religious Life*. New York: Free Press. (Original publication 1912.)

—— (1984) *The Division of Labor in Society*. New York: Free Press. (Original publication 1893.)

Eco, Umberto (1986) *Faith in Fakes: Essays 1967*. London: Secker and Warburg.

Elias, Norbert (1982) *Power and Civility*. New York: Urizen.

Elliott, Carl, and Paul Brodwin (2003) "Identity and Genetic Ancestry Tracing." *British Medical Journal* 325: 1469–71.

Errington, Shelly (1998) *The Death of Authentic Primitive Art and Other Tales of Progress*. Berkeley, CA: University of California Press.

Etnofoor 17 (1/2) (2004). (Special issue, *Authenticity*.)

Fabian, Johannes (1983) *Time and the Other: How Anthropology Makes its Object*. New York: Columbia University Press.

Fackenheim, Emil (1970) "Jewish Existence and the Living God: The Religious Duty of Survival." In Arthur D. Cohen (ed.), *Arguments and Doctrines: A Reader of Jewish Thinking in the Aftermath of the Holocaust*. New York: Harper and Row.

Ferrell, Jeff (2005) "The Only Possible Adventure: Edgework and Anarchy." In Stephen Lyng (ed.), *Edgework: The Sociology of Risk-Taking*. London: Routledge.

Fest, Joachim (1974) *Hitler*. New York: Harcourt Brace Jovanovich.

Foster, E. A., M. A. Jobling, P. G. Taylor, et al. (1998) "Jefferson Fathered Slave's Last Child." *Nature* 396: 27–8.

Frank, Katherine (2002) *G-Strings and Sympathy: Strip Club Regulars and Male Desire*. Durham, NC: Duke University Press.

Frank, Thomas (2004) *What's the Matter with Kansas: How Conservatives Won the Heart of America*. New York: Harry Holt and Company.

Freud, Sigmund (1962) *Civilization and its Discontents*. New York: Norton. (Original publication 1930.)

Fried, Morton (1967) *The Evolution of Political Society*. New York: Random House.

Friedman, Jonathan (1994) *Cultural Identity and Global Process*. London: Sage Publications.

Fukuyama, Francis (2000) *The Great Disruption*. New York: Touchstone Press.

Gable, Eric, and Richard Handler (1996) "After Authenticity at an American Heritage Site." *American Anthropologist* 98: 568–78.

Geary, Patrick (1986) "Sacred Commodities: The Circulation of Medieval Relics." In Arjun Appadurai (ed.), *The Social Life of Things: Commodities in Cultural Perspective*. Cambridge: Cambridge University Press.

—— (2003) *The Myth of Nations: The Medieval Origins of Europe*. Princeton, NJ: Princeton University Press.

Gellner, Ernest (1983) *Nations and Nationalism*. Oxford: Blackwell Publishing.

Gilbert, William Harlen (1946) "Memorandum Concerning the Characteristics of the Larger Mixed-Blood Racial Islands of the Eastern United States." *Social Forces* 24: 438–47.

Goffman, Erving (1959) *The Presentation of Self in Everyday Life*. New York: Doubleday.

—— (1963) *Stigma: Notes on the Management of Spoiled Identity*. New York: Simon and Schuster.

Goodman, Nelson (1983) "The Perfect Fake." In Dennis Dutton (ed.), *The Forger's Art*. Berkeley, CA: University of California Press.

Graburn, Nelson (ed.) (1976) *Ethnic and Tourist Arts: Cultural Expressions from the Fourth World*. Berkeley, CA: University of California Press.

Grazian, David (2003) *Blue Chicago: The Search for Authenticity in Urban Blues Clubs*. Chicago, IL: University of Chicago Press.

Greenfeld, Liah (1992) *Nationalism: Five Roads to Modernity*. Cambridge, MA: Harvard University Press.

Guy, Kolleen M. (2003) *When Champagne Became French: Wine and the Making of a National Identity*. Baltimore, MD: Johns Hopkins University Press.

Hanson, Allan (1989) "The Making of the Maori: Culture Invention and its Logic." *American Anthropologist* 91: 890–902.

Hargreaves, Alec G. (1995) *Immigration, 'Race' and Ethnicity in Contemporary France*. New York: Routledge.

Harkin, Michael (1995) "Modernist Anthropology and Tourism of the Authentic." *Annals of Tourism Research* 22: 650–70.

Harris, Olivia (1995) "Plural Identities and the Antimonies of Loss in Highland Bolivia." In Richard Fardon (ed.), *Counterworks: Managing the Diversity of Knowledge*. New York: Routledge.

Harrison, Simon (1999) "Identity as a Scarce Resource." *Social Anthropology* 7: 239–51.

Hayes, Nicole (2001) "Insiders and Outsiders: Boundary Maintenance and the Construction of Identity Among Youth Travellers in Whistler, British Columbia." Master's thesis, Dept of Anthropology, McMaster University.

Hazony, Yoram (2000) *The Jewish State: Struggle for Israel's Soul*. New York: Basic Books.

Heelas, Paul (1996) *The New Age Movement: The Celebration of Self and the Sacralization of Modernity*. Oxford: Blackwell Publishing.

Hegel, G. W. F. (1967) *The Phenomenology of Mind*. New York: Harper and Row. (Original publication 1807.)

Herder, Johann Gottfried von (1968) *Reflections on the Philosophy of the History of Mankind*. Chicago, IL: University of Chicago Press. (Original publication 1791.)

Herzfeld, Michael (1995) "It Takes One to Know One: Collective Resentment and Mutual Recognition Among Greeks in Local and Global Contexts." In Richard Fardon (ed.), *Counterworks: Managing the Diversity of Knowledge*. New York: Routledge.

Hochschild, Arlie (1983) *The Managed Heart: Commercialization of Human Feeling*. Berkeley, CA: University of California Press.

Hoffer, Eric (1951) *The True Believer*. New York: Harper and Row.

Bibliography

Huang, C. Julia (2003) "Weeping in a Taiwanese Buddhist Charismatic Movement." *Ethnology* 42: 73–86.

Hughes, Richard (1961) *The Fox in the Attic.* New York: Harper and Row.

Hunt, Lynn (1984) *Politics, Culture, and Class in the French Revolution.* Berkeley, CA: University of California Press.

James, William (1982) *Varieties of Religious Experience.* New York: Viking Press. (Original publication 1902.)

Jensen, Joli (1998) *The Nashville Sound: Authenticity, Commercialization, and Country Music.* Nashville, TN: Vanderbilt University Press.

Kastoryano, Riva (2002) *Negotiating Identities: States and Immigrants in France and Germany.* Princeton, NJ: Princeton University Press.

Katriel, Tamar (2005) *Dialogic Moments: From Soul Talk to Talk Radio in Israeli Culture.* Detroit, MI: Wayne State University Press.

Katz, Jack (1988) *The Seductions of Crime: Moral and Sensual Attractions to Doing Evil.* New York: Basic Books.

Kennedy, N. Brent (1997) *The Melungeons: The Resurrection of a Proud People: An Untold Story of Ethnic Cleansing in America.* Macon, GA: Mercer University Press.

Kenyon, Nicholas (1988) "Introduction: Authenticity and Early Music: Some Issues and Questions." In Nicholas Kenyon (ed.), *Authenticity and Early Music: A Symposium.* Oxford: Oxford University Press.

Kofman, Eleonore, Annie Phizacklea, Parvati Raghuram, and Rosemary Sales (2000) *Gender and International Migration in Europe: Employment, Welfare and Politics.* New York: Routledge.

Kopytoff, Igor (1986) "The Cultural Biography of Things: Commoditization as Process." In Arjun Appadurai (ed.), *The Social Life of Things: Commodities in Cultural Perspective.* Cambridge: Cambridge University Press.

Landowska, Wanda (1964) *Landowska on Music.* New York: Stein and Day.

Lange, Roderyk (1975) *The Nature of Dance: An Anthropological Perspective.* London: MacDonald & Evans.

Lasch, Christopher (1977) *Haven in a Heartless World.* New York: Basic Books.

Le Breton, David (2000) "Playing Symbolically with Death in Extreme Sports." *Body and Society* 6: 1–11.

Lewis, David, and Darren Bridges (2001) *The Soul of the New Consumer: Authenticity – What We Buy and Why in the New Economy.* London: Nicholas Brealey.

Liebman, Charles, and Eliezer Don Yehiye (1983) *Civil Religion in Israel: Traditional Judaism and Political Culture in the Jewish State.* Berkeley, CA: University of California Press.

Lindholm, Charles (1982) *Generosity and Jealousy: The Swat Pukhtun of Northern Pakistan.* New York: Columbia University Press.

—— (1988) "The Social Structure of Emotional Constraint." *Ethos* 16: 227–46.

—— (1993) *Charisma.* Oxford: Blackwell Publishing.

—— (2005) "An Anthropology of Emotion." In Conerly Casey and Robert Edgerton (eds.), *A Companion to Psychological Anthropology: Modernity and Psychocultural Change.* Oxford: Blackwell Publishing.

Linnekin, Jocelyn (1983) "Defining Tradition: Variations on Hawaiian Identity." *American Ethnologist*: 241–52.

—— (1992) "Cultural Invention and the Dilemma of Authenticity." *American Anthropologist* 93: 446–9.

Littlewood, Roland (1985) "An Indigenous Conceptualization of Reactive Depression in Trinidad." *Psychological Medicine* 15: 275–81.

Lofgren, Orvar (1993) "Naturalizing the Nation in Sweden and America." *Ethnos* 3–4: 162–96.

Loewenberg, Peter (1971) "Theodore Herzl: A Psychoanalytic Study in Charismatic Political Leadership." In Benjamin Wolman (ed.), *The Psychoanalytic Interpretation of History*. New York: Basic Books.

Lois, Jennifer (2005) "Gender and Emotion Management in the Stages of Edgework." In Stephen Lyng (ed.), *Edgework: The Sociology of Risk-Taking*. London: Routledge.

Lyng, Stephen (2005) "Sociology at the Edge: Social Theory and Voluntary Risk-Taking." In Stephen Lyng (ed.), *Edgework: The Sociology of Risk-Taking*. London: Routledge.

MacCannell, Dean (1999) *The Tourist: A New Theory of the Leisure Class*. Berkeley, CA: University of California Press. (Original publication 1976.)

MacIntyre, Alasdair (1981) *After Virtue: A Study in Moral Theory*. London: Duckworth.

McLeod, Kembrew (1999) "Authenticity within Hip-Hop and Other Cultures Threatened with Assimilation." *Journal of Communication* 49: 134–50.

Marcus, George (1995) "The Power of Contemporary Work in an American Art Tradition to Illuminate Its Own Power Relations." In George Marcus and Fred Myers (eds.), *The Traffic in Culture: Refiguring Art and Anthropology*. Berkeley, CA: University of California Press.

Marsh, Richard (1975) "I'm the Cause of My World." *Psychology Today* 9: 38.

Michelet, Jules (1967) *History of the French Revolution*. Chicago, IL: University of Chicago Press. (Original publication 1853.)

Miller, Daniel (1994) *Modernity an Ethnographic Approach: Dualism and Mass Consumption in Trinidad*. Oxford: Berg.

Morgan, Robert P. (1988) "Tradition, Anxiety, and the Current Musical Scene." In Nicholas Kenyon (ed.), *Authenticity and Early Music: A Symposium*. Oxford: Oxford University Press.

Morphy, Howard (1995) "Aboriginal Art in a Global Context." In Daniel Miller (ed.), *World's Apart: Modernity Through the Prism of the Local*. London: Routledge.

Mullin, Molly (1995) "The Patronage of Difference: Making Indian Art 'Art, Not Ethnology'." In George Marcus and Fred Myers (eds.), *The Traffic in Culture: Refiguring Art and Anthropology*. Berkeley, CA: University of California Press.

Nietzsche, Friedrich (1969) *On the Genealogy of Morals and Ecce Homo*. New York: Vintage. (Original publication of *On the Genealogy of Morals* 1886.)

Niezen, Ronald (2003) *The Origins of Indigenism: Human Rights and the Politics of Identity*. Berkeley, CA: University of California Press.

—— (2004) *A World Beyond Difference: Cultural Identity in the Age of Globalization*. Oxford: Blackwell Publishing.

165

Bibliography

Nora, Pierre (1997) *The Realms of Memory: The Construction of the French Past*. Vol. 2, *Traditions*. New York: Columbia University Press.

Oakes, Tim (1997) "Ethnic Tourism in Rural Guizhou: Sense of Place and the Commerce of Authenticity." In Michel Picard and Robert Wood (eds.), *Tourism, Ethnicity, and the State in Asian and Pacific Societies*. Honolulu, HI: University of Hawaii Press.

O'Nell, Theresa DeLeane (1996) *Disciplined Hearts: History, Identity, and Depression in an American Indian Community*. Berkeley, CA: University of California Press.

Orvell, Miles (1989) *The Real Thing: Imitation and Authenticity in American Culture, 1800–1940*. Chapel Hill, NC: University of North Carolina Press.

Osborne, Lawrence (2005) "Strangers in the Forest." *The New Yorker*, April 18: 124–40.

Peterson, Richard A. (1997) *Creating Country Music: Fabricating Authenticity*. Chicago, IL: University of Chicago Press.

Petrini, Carlo (2001) *Slow Food: The Case for Taste*. New York: Columbia University Press.

Phillips, David (1997) *Exhibiting Authenticity*. Manchester: Manchester University Press.

Rauschning, Hermann (1940) *The Voice of Destruction*. New York: Putnam.

Rousseau, Jean Jacques (1954) *The Confessions of J. J. Rousseau*. Harmondsworth: Penguin. (Original publication 1781.)

—— (1974a) "The Social Contract." In Jean Jacques Rousseau, *The Social Contract and the Discourse on the Origin and Foundations of Inequality Among Mankind*. New York: Washington Square Press. (Original publication 1762.)

—— (1974b) "Discourse on the Origin and Foundations of Inequality Among Mankind." In *The Social Contract and the Discourse on the Origin and Foundations of Inequality Among Mankind*. New York: Washington Square Press. (Original publication 1754.)

—— (1979) *Reveries of the Solitary Walker*. London: Penguin. (Original publication 1782.)

Roy, Oliver (2004) *Globalized Islam: The Search for a New Ummah*. New York: Columbia University Press.

Sandall, Roger (2001) *The Culture Cult: Designer Tribalism and Other Essays*. Boulder, CO: Westview Press.

Savigliano, Marta E. (1995) *Tango and the Political Economy of Passion*. Boulder, CO: Westview Press.

Shokeid, Moshe (1998) "My Poly-Ethnic Theme Park: Some Thoughts on Israeli-Jewish Ethnicity." *Diaspora* 7: 225–48.

Sholem, Gershom (1973) *Sabbatai Sevi: The Mystical Messiah, 1626–1676*. Princeton, NJ: Princeton University Press.

Shklar, Judith (1984) *Ordinary Vices*. Cambridge, MA: Harvard University Press.

Slatkin, Leonard (2004) "Inauthentic Beethoven, But Authentically So." *New York Times Sunday Edition*, arts section, February 15.

Small, Christopher (1987) "Performance as Ritual: Sketch for an Enquiry into the True Nature of a Symphony Concert." In Avron Levine White (ed.), *Lost in Music: Culture, Style and the Musical Event*. London: Routledge and Kegan Paul.

Srinivas, Tulasi (2007) "Everyday Exotic: Transnational Spaces, Identity and Contemporary Foodways in Bangalore City." *Food, Culture and Society* 10: 85–107.

—— (forthcoming) *Frontiers of Faith: Rethinking Religion and Globalization.*

—— (forthcoming) *Sacred Webs: Globalization, Religion and the Transnational Sathya Sai Movement.*

Stevenson, Lesley (2003) "Developing Cultural Tourism through Music: Authenticity and the Folk Music Session." Paper presented at the Conference on Developing Cultural Tourism, Nottingham, England.

Sylvain, Renée (2002) "'Land, Water, and Truth': San Identity and Global Indigenism." *American Anthropologist* 104: 1074–84.

Taruskin, Richard, Daniel Leech-Wilkinson, Nicholas Temperley, and Robert Winter (1984) "The Limits of Authenticity: A Discussion." *Early Music* 12: 3–25.

Taylor, Charles (1989) *Sources of the Self: The Making of the Modern Identity.* Cambridge, MA: Harvard University Press.

—— (1991) *The Ethics of Authenticity.* Cambridge, MA: Harvard University Press.

—— (1994) *Multiculturalism.* Princeton, NJ: Princeton University Press.

Taylor, Julie (1998) *Paper Tangos.* Durham, NC: Duke University Press.

Terrio, Susan J. (1996) "Crafting *Grand Cru* Chocolates in Contemporary France." *American Anthropologist* 98: 67–79.

Thomas, Helen (1995) *Dance, Modernity and Culture: Explorations in the Sociology of Dance.* London: Routledge.

Thomas, Nicholas (1994) *Colonialism's Culture: Anthropology, Travel and Government.* Princeton, NJ: Princeton University Press.

Thompson, Michael (1979) *Rubbish Theory: The Creation and Destruction of Value.* Oxford: Oxford University Press.

Tipton, Steven (1982) *Getting Saved From the Sixties.* Berkeley, CA: University of California Press.

Trilling, Lionel (1972) *Sincerity and Authenticity.* Cambridge, MA: Harvard University Press.

Turner, Ralph (1976) "The Real Self: From Institution to Impulse." *American Journal of Sociology* 81: 989–1016.

Ulin, Robert C. (1995) "Invention and Representation as Cultural Capital: Southwest French Winegrowing History." *American Anthropologist* 97: 519–27.

Waite, Robert (1977): *The Psychopathic God: Adolf Hitler.* New York: Basic Books.

Walker, Ranginui (2004) *Ka Whawhai Tohu Matou: Struggle Without End.* Auckland: Penguin.

Wallis, Roy (1984) *The Elementary Forms of the New Religious Life.* London: Routledge and Kegan Paul.

Waters, Mary (1990) *Ethnic Options: Choosing Identities in America.* Berkeley, CA: University of California Press.

Weber, Eugen (1979) *Peasants into Frenchmen: The Modernization of Rural France, 1870–1914.* Stanford, CA: Stanford University Press.

Weinstein, Fred (1980) *The Dynamics of Nazism: Leadership, Ideology and the Holocaust.* New York: Academic Press.

Bibliography

Whelan, Christal (2006) "Religious Responses to Globalization in Japan: The Case of the God Light Association." Doctoral dissertation, Dept of Anthropology, Boston University.

Wikan, Unni (1990) *Managing Turbulent Hearts: A Balinese Formula for Living*. Chicago, IL: University of Chicago Press.

Wilk, Richard (1999) "'Real Belizean Food': Building Local Identity in the Transnational Caribbean." *American Anthropologist* 101: 244–55.

—— (2006) *Home Cooking in the Global Village: Caribbean Food from Buccaneers to Ecotourists*. Oxford: Berg.

Yeats, William Butler (1920) "Prayer for my Daughter." In William Butler Yeats, *Michael Robartes And The Dancer*. Churchtown, Dundrum: The Cuala Press.

Young, Robert J. C. (1995) *Colonial Desire: Hybridity in Theory, Culture and Race*. London: Routledge.

Zúquete, José Pedro (2004) "Missionary Politics in Contemporary Europe: Jean Marie Le Pen's National Front and Umberto Bossi's Northern League." Doctoral dissertation, Dept of European Studies and Modern Languages, University of Bath. Forthcoming as *Missionary Politics in Contemporary Europe*. Syracuse, NY: Syracuse University Press.

Index

Abbanus, St 15
aborigines
    Australian 16–17, 88–9, 147
    connection with place 132–3
    global self-determination
        movements 128–33
    see also American Indians; primitive
        cultures
Acuff, Roy 30
advertising 54, 55–6, 61
Africa 44, 126, 130–1
airline stewardesses 67
Almog, Oz 157
alpha consumers 61–2, 69–70
American Indians
    art 20–1
    display of emotions 65
    Flatheads' search for identity 133–7
ancestry studies see family history studies
anthropology: and authenticity 141–2
anti-Semitism see Jews and Judaism
architecture 56
Arcigola 72–4
Argentina 94–7
art 13–24
    and commodification 18, 20
    establishing correspondence
        15–16, 18
    mechanical imitation 18–19, 53
    postmodern 21–4, 56–7

primitive 13–14, 16–17, 19–21
    and ritual 13–14, 16–17
    and search for personal identity 58–9
    and singularity 17
    tourist art 21
    tracing genealogy 15, 18
artists, cult of the 16–17, 22–3, 24
Australian aborigines see aborigines
authenticity
    of content 2
    definition 1–3
    distinction from sincerity 4
    forms of 2
    historical development of
        concept 3–10
    importance to humans 144–5
    of origin 2
    web search on 52
autoexoticism 96–7

Bach, Johann Sebastian 26–7
Bangalore 82
Baudrillard, Jean 43–4, 50, 53
Beethoven, Ludwig 26
Belize 77–80, 82–3
Ben-Gurion, David 112
Ben-Rafael, Eliezer 118–19
Benjamin, Walter 13
Bergstresser, Sara 81
Berra, Yogi 35

Index

blues   34–5
Boas, Franz   141
bobos (bohemian bourgeoisie)   59–63
Boorstin, Daniel   54
Bossi, Umberto   109–10
Bra, Italy   72
brands: and price premiums   84–6
Bridges, Darren   64
Brodwin, Paul   126
Brooks, David   59
Bruner, Edward   44, 45, 46
La Bruyère (French courtier)   65
Burger King   63
Burke, Edmund   69
Bushmen   130–1
buzz   61

Camembert   86
capitalism
   and consumption   52–6, 60–4
   and development of authenticity
      concept   5–6
carnival   70–1
Carson, fiddlin' John   30, 32
Cash, Johnny   34
Castellanos, Erick   81
celebrity culture
   alpha consumers   61–2, 69–70
   artists   16–17, 22–3, 24
   sports figures   51
champagne   84–5
cheeses   86
children: perceived authenticity   9, 66
China   45
Chirac, Jacques   105
chocolate   86
Chromolithographs   52
cinema: effect on experience of
   reality   53
citizenship authentication   100–1,
   103–11, 112–24
civilization: effect on individualism
   9, 95–6

class, social
   and authenticity   63–4, 70
   and taste in food   78–9, 80
Cline, Patsy   32
clothes see dress
clubs
   bobos   59–63
   music   34–5
coffee shops   63, 67
collectables   58–9
collectives see identity, collective
colonialism and postcolonialism
   aboriginal global self-determination
      movements   128–33
   and national cuisine   78–80
   and national dance   90, 92, 96–7
commodification
   and art   18, 20
   of authenticity   52–64
   and music   35–8
   and travel   48
concerts
   and historical authenticity   28
   see also performance, musical
Confessions (Rousseau)   8
consumption
   and bobos   60–3
   growth of conspicuous   52–3
   historical development   52–9
   and the internet   53–4
   modern merchandising
      techniques   62–3
   and personal identity   53–64, 69–70
content, authenticity of   2
crafts   56, 58–9
criminals: motives   51
Cuba   91–4
cultural theme parks   45–7
culture: challenges of studying   143–4
culture shock   142

dance   88–97, 115
danger: power of   47–51

Daniel, Brother (Carmelite monk)   122
Daniel, Yvonne   94
Dayan, Moishe   117
democracy: and development of
    authenticity concept   6
Denmark   101
Les Demoiselles d'Avignon (painting;
    Picasso)   19
department stores   54
Descartes, René   4–5
Dietler, Michael   106, 107
Dolmetsch, Arnold   26
Dominican Republic   89–91
dress
    country musicians   30–1
    historical theme parks   46
    style and fashion   60–2, 69–70
Duchamp, Marcel   22
Duncan, Isadora   88
Durkheim, Émile   13–14, 68–9,
    88–9, 98–9

Eco, Umberto   44
edgework   47–51
Elizabeth II, Queen of Great Britain and
    Northern Ireland   79
Emerson, Ralph Waldo   57
emotions
    and charismatic religions   67–9
    displaying   65–6
    ensuring genuineness   66
    and gender   66
    workplace expectations   66–7
emotivism   57–8, 65
equality: and development of
    authenticity concept   6
Errington, Shelley   20
Eskimos   141
Estée Lauder   62
Ethiopia: Jews   120–1
European Union   110–11
exotic
    autoexoticism   96–7

distinction from primitive   149
exploration
    and development of authenticity
        concept   5
    see also tourism

family history studies   125–8
fascism   101–3
fashion mavens *see* alpha consumers
feudal system   3
first nations   128–33
Flathead Indians   133–7
food
    and national identity   77–87
    Slow Food movement   71–4
Ford automobiles   55
Foucault, Michel   50
France
    Breton nationalism   110
    citizenship, immigration, and
        integration   104–9
    development of national identity and
        cuisine   83–7
    under Louis XIV   65
    National Front   108–9
    see also French Revolution
Frank, Thomas   64
freedom *see* individualism
French Revolution
    attitude to citizenship   106
    rebels' motives   7
Freud, Sigmund   7, 95
Fried, Morton   158
Friedman, Jonathan   133, 143–4

Gajdusek, Carleton   40
gender
    and emotions   66
    and Sabra ideology   117, 157
genetic testing   125–8
Germany   100–3
gibnuts   77, 78, 79
globalization   108–10

Index

Goethe, Johann Wolfgang von 101
Goffman, Erving 37, 158
Graham, Martha 88
Grand Old Opry 30, 31, 33, 35, 36, 148
Grazian, David 35, 37
Greece: Greek attitude to the nation 99
Grundtvigian movement 101
Guizhou 45

Haiti 90
halakha 113
Hamlet (Shakespeare) 4
Harel, Marie 86
Hawaiian people 132–3
Hayes, Nicole 48–9
hedonism 70–4
Hemings, Sally 125
Herder, J. G. 100–1
Herzfeld, Michael 99
Herzl, Theodor 114
Hess, Rudolf 102
historical theme parks 45–7
Hitler, Adolf 102, 103
Hobsbawm, Eric 101
Hochschild, Arlie 67
Holocaust 102–3
Hugh, Bishop of Lincoln 14
Hunt, Lynn 7
hype 61

identity, collective
   culture as 143
   and dance 88–9
   emotional power of collectives 7, 9
   and fashion 61–2, 69–70
   first nations 128–33
   and Flathead Indians 133–7
   by genes 125–8
   and music clubs 34–5
   by nation *see* nationalism and
      nation-states
identity, national *see* nationalism and
   nation-states

identity, personal
   and charismatic religions 67
   and collectives 7
   and consumption 53–64, 69–70
   and emotional expressivity 67
   and extreme tourism 47–51
   historical development of 3–10
   and introspection 57
   and transience 70–4
   see also individualism
imitation
   and art 18–19
   and consumption 52–3
   of trendsetters 61–2, 69–70
immigration 100, 104–9, 110
India 81–3
individualism
   bobos 59–63
   carnival as expression of 70–1
   civilization's effect on 9, 95–6
   clubs and the nocturnal self 34–5
   dance as expression of 95–6
   among musicians 37–8
   and travel 42–3, 49
integration
   aboriginal resistance to 128–33
   and immigration 100,
      104–9, 110
internet: and consumption 53–4
introspection 57
Inuit 141
Ireland: American Catholic attitude
   to 128
Islam: Muslims in France 104–6
Israel 112–24
   defining who belongs 120–4
   ethnic composition and
      integration 118–24
   origins and foundation 112–25
   relations with Palestinian Arabs
      123–4
   Sabra form of national identity
      115–18

Italy
    development of national cuisine
        80–1, 82–3
    Northern League   109–10

James, Henry   55, 56
James, William   68
Jefferson, Thomas   125
Jews and Judaism
    Ashkenazim   115, 118, 119, 157
    Bene Israel   121
    Beta Israel (Falasha)   120–1
    conversion from and to   113,
        122, 156
    definition   113–15, 120–4
    different ethnic types   118–24
    final religious authority   121
    Lemba people   126
    Mizrachim   118, 119, 123–4, 157
    Nazi attitude   102–3
    Reform and Conservative
        segments   156
    Sephardim   118, 157
    see also Israel
Joan of Arc   108

Kant, Immanuel   101
Katriel, Tamar   117, 157
Kichwa Tembo Tented Camp   44
Kombai people   39–40

labor
    conditions in the new industries
        59–60, 63, 66–7
    see also capitalism
Landowska, Wanda   26
Le Pen, Jean Marie   108–9
Lemba people   126
Lewis, David   64
Lincoln, Abraham   46
Linnekin, Jocelyn   132
Louis XIV, King of France   65
Lyng, Stephen   48, 50, 51

Maasai people   44–5
MacCannell, Dean   41–2, 48
McDonald's   63, 72
MacIntyre, Alasdair   57–8
Mahler, Gustav   26
management techniques, modern
    59–60
Maori people   131–2, 132–3
Marcus, George   22
marketing techniques   54, 55–6, 61–4
mazurka   90
media: effect on experience of reality   53
Meir, Golda   122–3
Melungeon people   126–8
Mendelssohn, Moses   113
meringue   89–91
Miao people   45
Michelet, Jules   7
Miller, Daniel   53, 70, 71
modernity
    and authenticity   3–4, 136
    manufactured goods   58
    personal style in   70, 71
multiculturalism see integration
music   25–38
    blues   34–5
    country fans' view of classical
        fans   29–30
    country music   29–36
    history vs heart in classical   25–9
    pressures on performers   35–8
    for tourists   43, 44
musical instruments
    country music   30
    manufacturing historically
        authentic   28
musicians
    pressures of authenticity   35–8
    self-destructiveness   37–8

Namibia   130–1
Napoleon I, Emperor of France   106–7
Napoleon III, Emperor of France   107

Nashville *see* Grand Old Opry
nationalism and nation-states
    aboriginal resistance to
        integration   128–33
    as cause of racism   100–3
    defining who belongs   100–1, 103–11,
        112–24
    development of national cuisines
        77–87
    development of national dances
        88–97
    French Revolutionary concept of
        nation's relationship to
        individual   7
    Israel and Jewishness   112–24
    origins and psychological force   98–9
    sacred kingdoms   155
Native Americans *see* American Indians
Nazis   101–3
New Salem Village   46
New Zealand   131–2, 132–3
Nietzsche, Friedrich   2
Niezen, Ronald   129
noble savage concept *see* primitive
    cultures
nonconformity *see* individualism

objectification   53–64
O'Nell, Theresa   134, 136
Opry *see* Grand Old Opry
origin, authenticity of   2
Orvell, Miles   52
Osborne, Lawrence   39–40
other, the
    autoexoticism   96–7
    and collectives   7
    Palestinian Arabs as   123–4
    primitives as   5, 40, 96–7
overseas aid   129–30

Pachelbel, Johann   27
Palestine: Arabs' relations with
    Jews   123–4

Papua New Guinea   39–40
Passover   115
pasta   80–1
Patrick Henry College   52
performance, musical
    atmosphere of country   36
    authentic venues   34–5
    history vs heart in classical music
        25–9
    history vs heart in national dance   94
    pressures on performers   35–8, 94
Pérignon, Dom Pierre   84–5
Peterson, Richard   31–2
Petrini, Carlo   72, 73–4
photography   56
Picasso, Pablo   19
place: aboriginal connection with
    132–3
Portrait of a Lady (James)   55, 56
postcolonialism *see* colonialism and
    postcolonialism
postmodernism: in art   21–4, 56–7
primitive cultures
    art   13–14, 16–17, 19–21
    dance   88–9
    distinction between primitive and
        exotic   149
    perceived authenticity   5, 8–9, 19–21,
        130–2
    primitives as 'the other'   5, 40, 96–7
    travel in search of   39–43, 44–5
    see also aborigines; American Indians
Protestantism
    development of nonconformism   6–7
    and sincerity   4
Pukhtun people   65

racism   100–3, 108–10
reality
    and advertising   55–6
    media's effect on experience of   53
    religion as means of heightening   69
    self-conscious mediation   53

tourism as means of heightening
39–51
relics, holy   14–15
religion
    art and ritual   13–14, 16–17
    charismatic   67–9
    consumption as substitute   64
    Hitler worship   102
    and national identity in Israel
    112–24
    nationalism as substitute   98–9
    relics   14–15
    totems   13–14, 19
    see also Jews and Judaism;
    Protestantism
ritual
    and art   13–14, 16–17
    Nazi   102
Rockefeller, Nelson   19
Rogers, Kenny   34
Roman Empire: as model for
    republicanism   106–7
Rousseau, Jean Jacques   8–10
rumba   91–4

Sabra   115–18
St Denis, Ruth   88
Salish and Pend d'Oreilles Indians
    133–7
San people   130–1
Savigliano, Marta E.   96–7
Schultz, Howard   63
scientific reason: and development of
    authenticity concept   4–5
Scotland   43
self-help books   68
Serengeti   44
sex: and tango   96–7
Shakespeare, William   4
Shalit, Benjamin   122
shamans   16
Sharot, Stephen   118–19
Shenzhen   45

Shklar, Judith   6
shopping *see* consumption
Sieyès, Abbé de   106
simulacra: Baudrillard's theory of
    ubiquity   43–4
sincerity
    distinction from authenticity   4
    evolution into authenticity   4–6
    origins   3–4
singularity: and art   17
Skansen   45
Skillet Lickers   32
social mobility: and development of
    authenticity concept   3–4
society, forms of *see* identity, collective
South Africa   126, 130–1
Splendid China Park   45
sports figures, cult of   51
Starbucks   63, 67
Stokowski, Leopold   26
Sweden   45

tango   94–7
    with words   154
taste: development of concept   54–5
Taylor, Charles   17
terroir   83–4
theme parks, historical and cultural
    45–7
Toscanini, Arturo   26
totems   13–14, 19
tourism   39–51
    authenticity vs comfort and political
    correctness   46–7
    dancing for tourists   93, 94
    extreme (edgework)   47–51
    popular destinations   41
    reasons for popularity   40–3, 47–8
    staging authenticity   43–7
    tourist art   21
    and the world economy   41
transcendentalism   57
transience   70–4

Index

travel
    and development of authenticity
        concept   5
    see also tourism
trendsetters *see* alpha consumers
Trilling, Lionel   3, 16
Trinidad: carnival   70–1
Trujillo, Rafael   90
tzabar   116, 157

Ulin, Robert   86
United States
    capitalism and consumption   52–64
    ethnic identity   128
    genetic testing   125–8
    Hawaiian nationalism   132–3
    prejudice against newcomers   104

Valentino, Rudolf   96
veiling   105

Vidal de la Blache, Paul   83–4

Walker, Ranganui   132
Waters, Mary   128
Weber, Eugen   83
Weber, Max   16, 50, 101
Weinstein, Fred   103
Weston, Edward   56
Whistler, Canada   48–9
Wilk, Richard   80
Williams, Hank   31, 33
Williamsburg, colonial   46
wine   84–6
work *see* labor
Wright, Frank Lloyd   56

Yanomamo Indians   65
Yeats, W. B.   68

Zionism   114–15